ARCHITECTURE
THE INDISPENSABLE ART

Gloucester Cathedral from the South-East. Central tower 225 feet high, built about 1454–57. A masterpiece of the Severn Valley masons

ARCHITECTURE
THE INDISPENSABLE ART

illiam onald

W. R. Dalzell ARCA

London
MICHAEL JOSEPH

First published by
MICHAEL JOSEPH LTD
26 *Bloomsbury Street*
*London, W.C.*1
1962

Set and printed in Great Britain by Tonbridge Printers Ltd,
Peach Hall Works, Tonbridge, Kent, in Times ten on
eleven point, on paper made by Henry Bruce at Currie,
Midlothian, and bound by James Burn at Esher, Surrey

CONTENTS

ILLUSTRATIONS

Frontispiece
Gloucester Cathedral

Between pages 80 *and* 81
The Parthenon
The Pantheon
Greensted-juxta-Ongar
Earl's Barton
Castle Hedingham
The Tower of London: Chapel of St John
Lincoln Cathedral: exterior and interior of Chapter House
Spandrels of St Mary's, Stone
Beverley Minster: The Percy Tomb
Ss Peter and Paul, Lavenham
Model of Hammerbeam Roof
Plymtree: Rood Screen
King's College Chapel: The Ante-Chapel
Oxburgh Castle
Holy Trinity, Stratford-upon-Avon

Between pages 144 *and* 145
Hardwick Hall: The Long Gallery
Aston Hall: Fireplace in the Long Gallery
Parham Park: The Great Hall
Knole Park: The Great Staircase
Wilton House: The Double Cube Room
The Banqueting House, Whitehall
The Queen's House, Greenwich
The Royal Naval Hospital, Greenwich

To my wife

ACKNOWLEDGEMENTS

I have received such generous encouragement and help throughout the production of this book, that it is quite impossible to disentangle 'official' and personal acknowledgements. My publishers have been more than generous in the personal interest they have taken in the progress of the book, and I am indebted particularly to the enthusiasm and encouragement of the Hon. Mrs Michael Joseph and Mr Peter Hebdon who did so much to pilot me through the difficult initial stages of its production.

Special mention however, must be made of the assistance and advice I have had at every stage of the book from Alderman Richard Turner, Chairman of the Bedford Corporation Town Planning Committee, with whom I have spent so many happy hours of discussion and who is largely responsible for the compilation of the Index. I am also deeply indebted to Mr G. Glazier, the Librarian of the Bedfordshire County Library, and Mr C. Hargreaves of Bedford Borough Library and their most efficient and courteous staffs who have helped me with research, and to my architect friends, Robert Hart, Alexander Chrystal and Bernard West, A/A.R.I.B.A. who have always been willing to help me in so many ways. I should also like to acknowledge the assistance of Mr John Lander of the Photographic Library of the Royal Institute of British Architects for tracing the sources of some of the more obscure photographs, and to thank the staff of the National Buildings Record for their generous help.

For the photographs reproduced I am indebted to the following:

The National Buildings Record: Church of St Andrew, Greensted-juxta-Ongar; Chapel of St John, Tower of London; The Chapter House, Lincoln; St Mary, Stone; Parham Park, Sussex; St John the Baptist, Plymtree; Oxburgh Castle, Norfolk; Holy Trinity, Stratford-upon-Avon; Banqueting House, Whitehall; St Stephen, Walbrook; Holkham Hall, Norfolk; Pagoda, Kew Gardens; Chester Terrace, London; The Red House, Bexley Heath.

Country Life Ltd: Blenheim Palace, Woodstock; Syon House, Isleworth; Strawberry Hill, Twickenham; Harleston Park.

The Ministry of Works: Westminster Hall; Queen's House, Greenwich; Royal Naval Hospital, Greenwich; Chiswick House; Palm House, Kew Gardens.

Mr A. F. Kersting: Beverley Minster, Yorks; Hardwick Hall, Derbyshire; Aston Hall, Birmingham; Wilton House, Wiltshire; St Bride's Church, London.

The Royal Commission on Historical Monuments: Castle Hedingham, Norfolk; King's College Chapel, Cambridge.

The British Travel and Holidays Association: Gloucester Cathedral; Ss Peter and Paul, Lavenham.

London Transport Executive: Arnos Grove Underground Station.

Harlow Development Corporation: Mark Hall County Secondary School, Harlow; The Market Square, Harlow.

Fox Photos Ltd: The Parthenon, Athens; Back-to-back houses.

Photo Precision Ltd: Knole Park, Sevenoaks.

Air Ministry: St Pancras Hotel and Railway Station.

The Architects' Journal: I.C.I. Research Laboratories, Welwyn.

Alexander Chrystal, A.R.I.B.A.: Earls Barton Church, Northants.

Reverend E. Rumens: Coventry Cathedral.

Commonwealth Institute: Model of Institute.

Italian Cultural Institute: The Pantheon, Rome.

Denis Martineau, M.A., A.R.I.B.A.: Mompesson House, Salisbury.

Edwin Smith and Gordon Fraser Gallery Ltd: University Museum, Oxford.

Letchworth Garden City Museum: Early Garden City architecture.

Jeremy Baker: Brutalised Adam Façade.

British Broadcasting Corporation: Television Centre.

The Athlone Press: diagrams of the Baths of Caracalla and The Orders of Architecture from *A History of Architecture on the Comparative Method* by Banister Fletcher.

Chapter One

CLASSICAL PRELUDE

*'The longer you can look back, the
farther you can look forward.'*
WINSTON S. CHURCHILL.

THE civilisations of Ancient Greece and of Ancient Rome have
had such a profound effect on our own that no book on
architecture, however slight, can ignore the impact of Greek
and Roman architectural thought on our own way of thinking about
architecture.

Basically, the Greek method of building was extremely simple. A
child can place a cylinder of wood or stone upright on its end, fix
another a short distance away, and then balance a beam of wood or
stone across the two. It is no more difficult to add a third, and a
fourth and a fifth, at regular distances, and with beams of equal
length to bridge the gaps between them. This is the basis of *trabeated*
or *post and beam* construction used with variations by the Greeks
throughout their glorious history. With this simple means they
produced buildings so perfect that they have been the inspiration of
architects all over the Western world.

The Greek genius expressed itself not in any ingenuity of construction but in the subtle and beautiful relationships of the parts
of the building to each other and to the whole. The post and beam
construction is not suitable for making very large buildings, nor for
bridging wide gaps, but since the majority of the Greek buildings
were temples, which were treated more as precious caskets in which
the Gods dwelt than as places in which worshippers assembled, this
limitation was of little importance. It did, in fact, leave the Greeks
free to concentrate on finding by trial and error the most beautiful
and most satisfying arrangement of the parts of the building.
During their experiments they evolved a unit, called a *module*. This
unit, which measured half the width of the base of the column to be
used throughout the building, was sub-divided into thirty equal parts.
The module, or a sub-division of the module, determined the exact

proportion of the height of the column to its base, of the height of the capital which topped the column, and the proportion of the superstructure or entablature as it is called which bridged the gaps between the columns. Having established the main relationships of the order of architecture, as this series of standardised measurements is called, the Greeks then evolved even more subtle adjustments – many to rectify defects they had observed in earlier buildings, which were not due, however, to faulty craftsmanship, but to optical illusion. Some of these carefully planned modifications are to be seen in the Parthenon – the Greek temple built in 447–432 in Athens and acknowledged to be one of the loveliest buildings in the world. It is constructed by using a series of proportions known as the *Doric Order*. As you will see in the diagram, this order has a severe sturdy quality all its own, and could not be confused with the other two Orders most commonly used, the *Ionic Order*, with its more slender column, and the slightly more florid *Corinthian Order*.

Three of the modifications to be found on the Parthenon are sufficiently important to warrant our attention here. In the earlier Greek buildings, the shaft of the column tapered gently, but the sides were straight. Nevertheless, with columns as tall as 30 feet, the Greeks found that absolutely straight-sided shafts looked as though they curved inwards very slightly. To counteract this concave appearance, they contrived a most carefully calculated bulge on the sides of the column called an *entasis* – a swelling so subtle (it was only three quarters of an inch on a 34 foot column) that it is not apparent to the casual observer who is only aware that the columns appear to have straight sides.

A second optical illusion which had to be corrected concerns the overall appearance of the building. The Parthenon is about 101 feet wide and 228 feet long and stands on a shallow flight of three steps, called a *stylobate*. Earlier buildings had shown that if the stylobate on so large a building was built absolutely level, it appeared to sag in the centre as though bent by the mass of the building above. This illusion was corrected by building the stylobate with a most gentle curve which only rose to a height of about $2\frac{1}{2}''$ over a distance of 101 feet, and a height of less than $4\frac{1}{2}''$ on the 228 feet sides of the building.

The Greeks also found that the columns at the corners of the building, silhouetted against the deep blue sky, looked slenderer than columns of exactly the same dimensions with a wall behind them. Corner columns were therefore made slightly more robust than those surrounding the building. (*Plate 1.*)

Similar refinements may be found in buildings constructed from other orders of architecture – in the Erechtheion, one of the loveliest temples of the Ionic Order, which stands a little to the North of the

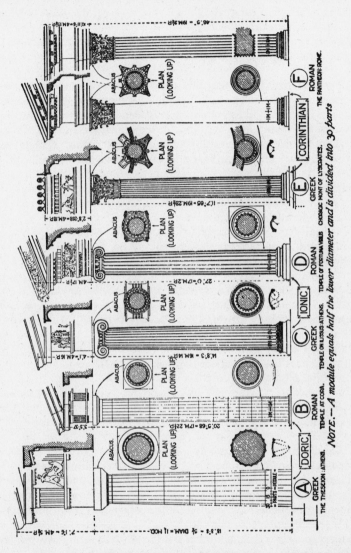

Fig. 1. The Orders of Classical architecture. This diagram shows the series of proportions finally evolved for the design of columns and entablatures by the Greek architects, together with those adapted and invented by their Roman successors

Parthenon, and in the Corinthian Order of the charming little Tower
of the Winds, erected *c.* 100–35 B.C. as a sort of Athenian 'Big-Ben,'
to house a water-clock within, and sundials outside. It is typical of
the Greek devotion to the beauty of mathematics that so much care
should be lavished on what was only an instrument for measuring
time.

We have seen that, having decided upon the exact code of measurements to be used, the Greeks, unimpressed by mere size (unlike their
contemporaries, the Egyptians), proceeded to erect small buildings
of exquisite beauty incorporating all the refinements which they had
acquired during centuries of studying the problems of scale, proportion, space and mass. This pre-occupation with such refinements
does not, of course, exclude the functional aspect of architecture,
but rather, in the deepest sense, renders the building more fitted for
its purpose. As we have said the Greek temple was only intended to
enclose the sacred image and to emphasize the presence of the God.
When the Athenian ploughman was at work in the fields, when the
labourer pruned his vines clustered round the base of the Acropolis,
when the merchant was scrutinising the shining black olives for sale
in the market, they were all conscious of the presence of Athena,
high up in the Parthenon, blessing their labours, or checking their
faults. They had no need to file with solemn faces into a large building once a week to worship – they had only to lift their eyes to the
shining temple above them (and how the newly hewn stone must have
shone in the clear Athenian light) to know that their Goddess was at
hand, to hear their prayers or to punish their offences.

For the Greeks, therefore, the beauty of the building was an integral part of its function – it was an extension of the act of worship
itself, not something added after the practical use of the building had
been settled.

The Romans, an essentially military people, took over the forms
of Greek architecture, added methods of construction unused by the
Greeks, and produced something very different. The difference is,
perhaps, well summed up by the expressions commonly used to
distinguish one civilisation from the other 'the Glory that was
Greece, the Grandeur that was Rome'. To use another simile, if we
can compare the architecture of the Greeks to a string quartet, then
we can imagine the Romans bringing in whole new sections of
instruments, scoring for the full orchestra, with wood winds, brass,
percussion all playing their part – with perhaps a little too much
brass in certain passages. They retained the post and beam method
used by the Greeks, but to this they added the *arch*, the *vault*, and
the *dome*, three forms of construction particularly suitable for the

size and variety of their buildings, far greater than those of the Greeks.

A military and colonising nation, the Romans found the post and beam construction too dependent on stones of sufficient size and strength and on a supply of highly skilled craftsmen. As the boundaries of the great Roman Empire extended, they had need of a method of construction which could be used in districts where little stone was to be found and only the crudest of labour available.

They therefore adopted the arch – a construction principle already in use by the Etruscan neighbours who had been absorbed into the Roman State. From the arch, which could be erected from quite small pieces of stone, or from brick where no stone was available, they developed the vault. This in turn enabled them to roof areas of much greater size uninterrupted by the supporting columns demanded by post and beam and which led quite naturally to the use of the dome, which, after all, is a succession of arches crossing at the centre, like the ribs of an umbrella. None of these constructive principles, however, could have been so effective if the Romans had not developed a new material – concrete.

The invention of concrete was a revolutionary step in the evolution of architectural form. Limitations previously imposed by the need for supplies of local stone suitable for building, and of a pool of craftsmen to work it, were no longer important. A military commander, with a handful of serving technicians, a 'blue print' from headquarters in Rome and a wealth of unskilled labour, could erect in almost any part of the Roman Empire, buildings indistinguishable from those in Rome itself. His technicians could supervise the erection of the wooden centering for the arches, and the moulds of wood in which the concrete would be poured for the walls. They would determine the depth of the boxes or *coffers* forming the wooden moulds for the vaulted roof or dome, set the unskilled labourers to work mixing concrete, in Spain, in Britain, in North Africa or in the Middle East. When the concrete had set and the moulds were eased away, the building would be a truly Roman building – a bath, amphitheatre, palace or temple, no matter how alien the country.

Thus Roman architecture became part of the landscape all over the known world, as the Roman military camp hardened into a pattern of permanent buildings, and as the Roman law replaced the tribal law with an international code of justice and order which was valid from Tarragona in Spain to Baalbek in Syria, from Londinium in England to Leptis Magna, on the North African coast.

The Romans took the Greek Orders of Architecture, adapted them to a wider variety of uses, and added another two of their own.

The Roman commander had a need of some standardisation of building methods and proportions, and it was to his superiors in Rome that he looked for direction.

Important sources of information on Roman architecture and architects are the writings of Vitruvius, or to give him his full name, Marcus Vitruvius Pollio, who was a successful architect under the Emperor Augustus. The ten books of Vitruvius, written in the year A.D. 27, show that there was widespread interest in architecture at every level of Roman society, from the Emperor to freed slaves, who could eventually train and become architects themselves. The architect was held in high esteem. One became a Consul, another a member of the Senate, and Vitruvius gives a remarkable list of accomplishments which an architect was expected to possess, and the range of knowledge demanded of him by the complicated and sophisticated society in which he lived. That he should be skilled at mathematics and geometry, drawing and history, and have a sound technical knowledge seems obvious, but he was also expected to understand philosophy, music and even to have knowledge of astronomy and the stars.

The Roman architects had to solve architectural problems unknown to the Greeks, and to solve these problems with different materials from those previously in use. The range of buildings erected by the Roman architect was much greater, and the Roman genius expressed itself most clearly in those very buildings for which there was no Greek model to follow.

In building bridges, aqueducts, and amphitheatres, and for vaulting over the vast Roman baths and Halls of Justice, the Roman relied on his remarkable flair for engineering and for his mastery over the new architectural forms – the arch, the vault and the dome. It is in such buildings and with such architectural forms that the Roman architect is seen at his best. Their beauty is the beauty of efficiency, and the shapes evolved are those which are dictated by the jobs they have to do and the right use of the materials with which they carry it out. To see such buildings as the magnificent aqueduct at Nîmes known as the Pont du Gard, even in ruins, is to marvel at the Roman genius not only for efficient construction but for the creation of beautiful form.

It is regrettable therefore that, having erected a splendid aqueduct or the complex series of buildings which constitute a Roman bath, the architect was not able to let well alone, but must then smother them with lavishly applied ornament, copied from the Greek constructional forms but playing no part in the structure of the building. The result is a form of architectural dishonesty – the columns and entablature which are actually superficial decoration appear to be the structural principles, whilst the arches which do in fact form the construction appear to be mere in-filling of the areas between the columns.

This architectural dishonesty is not, of course, confined to Roman architecture. We are equally guilty today. It is possible to see in practically every English town buildings in which the real structure has been carefully disguised by the application of mock-Roman or Renaissance ornament, by columns which support nothing, or creosoted plywood beams which mimic the Elizabethan timber-framed house with no hint of the actual construction buried beneath the spurious exterior.

Much of the superficial ornament on the Roman buildings, however, has long since crumbled away, leaving the splendid structural forms stark against the sky. It seems likely, therefore, that shorn of this ornament Roman architecture is even more impressive now than when it was first built, for the grandeur of the proportions is no longer masked by a layer of trivial and ostentatious decoration.

Some of the most remarkable ruins still to be seen in many parts of the former Roman Empire are those of the aqueducts. Their great arches are to be seen in France, in Spain, in North Africa, and of course, converging on Rome itself.

Nearly a score of aqueducts supplied the population of Rome with water. Vast quantities of water were needed if the huge Roman baths were to function, and if the fountains were to throw their cooling spray into the bright August sky. Remnants of these aqueducts still dominate the flat land surrounding Rome. Their concrete masses, on more than one occasion, defied the most modern demolition equipment of the last war. Engineers of modern armies trying to make room for airfields and for gun emplacements found their drills helpless against remnants left by the engineers of a mighty military power long since dead.

Of the Roman baths, one of the most impressive must have been the Thermae of Caracalla, built between A.D. 211 and 217. To the Roman a bath was at once a social centre, an athletic stadium, a debating club, and finally, a bath. The complicated series of rooms, the heating arrangements, the water storage, corridors and shops occupied a vast area. The main building alone occupied over 285,000 square feet and offered accommodation to about 1,600 people.

The vast arches, deeply coffered, were enriched with marble inlay and encrusted with gleaming mosaic. Subject races, labouring in remote parts of the great empire contributed sheets of alabaster, slabs of porphyry, jasper and other semi-precious stone. Craftsmen beat out gold to tissue paper thinness trapping it within glass cubes to make the gleaming mosaics, or cut the many-coloured marbles into dice and pressed them into wet plaster to cover the walls with mosaic patterns. Others spread layers of fine plaster over the coarse concrete before painting their gay frescoes on the huge areas of wall. Of all this splendour, nothing but the vast shell remains. This has been converted into an open air opera house, and is once again a social centre, of a different kind, for the citizens of Rome and for the foreigners who now come voluntarily to pay their tribute to this great city.

The Roman architects' mastery over dome construction can still be remarkably well seen by studying the Pantheon in Rome. Despite alteration, plunder and restoration, despoiled of its gold and bronze decoration, the vast circular temple is still roofed by one of the finest domes in the world. (*Plate 2.*)

This dome, largely of brick and thick mortar, is about 142 feet across, resting its rigid semicircular cup on walls of concrete 20 feet thick. Deeply coffered to reduce the weight and to relieve the monotony of a smooth unbroken surface, it was originally decorated with bronze ornaments. Later generations, not only the barbarians who sacked Rome, but Christians who felt peculiar satisfaction in despoiling a pagan shrine to enrich a Christian church, tore off the metal fittings, melted them down and left this magnificent shell behind. The building is lit by one circular hole, 27 feet in diameter, in the centre of the dome, through which the sun and rain pour in impartially, and from the open doors. Now it is no longer a Roman temple dedicated to a collection of pagan gods; it was consecrated in the seventh century by Pope Boniface IV to St Maria ad Martyres, and contained the bones of martyred Christians, brought from the Catacombs. Today it is known simply as S. Maria Rotunda.

Of the many other temples still to be seen in Rome, in various states of preservation, mention must be made of the smaller temple of Fortuna Virilis, a simple cell or room surrounded by Ionic columns and occupying a space about 30 feet wide by 79 feet long, which, oddly enough, was to be the inspiration, many hundreds of years later, for Birmingham Town Hall.

More important architecturally, however, is the building which, to most people, represents Imperial Rome and all it stood for. This is the Colosseum, a huge oval building which was started in the reign of the Emperor Vespasian in A.D. 70, completed some 12 years later in the reign of Domitian, and had a final upper storey added to it considerably later in the third century.

In plan, it is an ellipse 620 feet by 513 feet, capable of seating 50,000 spectators. The actual arena is 287 feet by 180 feet. It is a most remarkable tribute to the engineering and architectural skill of the Romans. The Greek architect would have utilised a hillside, scoop-

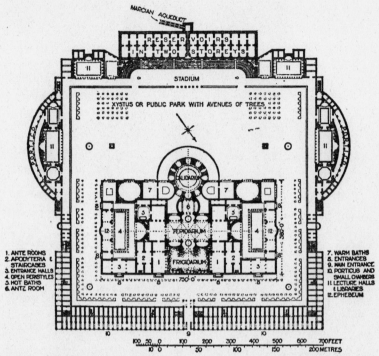

Fig. 2. The Baths of Caracalla, Rome, A.D. 211–217. The plan of a vast structure, over 750 feet across, which was a bath, social centre, etc. Its ruins have now been converted into an open-air opera house

ing out the bowl shape to form the seating for the spectators. The Roman architect, however, has started with the level ground and erected on foundations of solid lava rock a series of concrete and pumice vaults to support the rising tiers of seats, with supporting walls of brick and tufa. The porous tufa and pumice make a light superstructure without loss of strength, and the wedge-shaped piers radiating inwards supporting the concrete vaults give an impression of immense power, even today. Although successive generations plundered it, the barbarians wrenching out the bronze clamps to make tips for their spears or blades for their swords, while later inhabitants of Rome, no less ruthless, used it as a quarry for stone, the Colosseum is still sufficiently intact to enable us to see how skilfully the architect made use of the old orders of architecture for a decorative façade.

The external face of the building, which is 157 feet high, is divided into four beautifully proportioned storeys. The three lower storeys are pierced with innumerable arches, flanked by attached columns. Those on the lowest storey are in a Roman version of the Doric Order, those on the second are in the Ionic. The third storey, and the top unpierced storey (added in A.D. 222–224) both have Corinthian columns.

The rich interplay of light and shade against the brilliant Italian sky still make the Colosseum one of the most splendid buildings in Rome. When the surfaces were intact with their multi-coloured marbles, when the statues of gleaming stone stood relieved against the deep pools of shadow in the arches, and when the great tent-like *velarium* shaded the packed audience from the noonday glare, the Colosseum or the Flavian Amphitheatre as it should be called, must have been one of the wonders of the civilised world. It was, of course, used for the most savage displays – gladiatorial combats of sensational brutality, in which neither men nor beasts were spared. In a television broadcast, Sir Mortimer Wheeler drew a most apt comparison between the sports attended by the bloodthirsty Roman mob and the bullfights enjoyed by the inhabitants of modern Spain, which often take place in arenas erected many years ago by the Roman colonists. The word 'arena' means 'sand' or 'beach' and refers directly to the sand strewn on the ground to absorb the blood.

Similar displays, together with chariot races and horse racing, took place in the Circus. The most extensive Circus, the Circus Maximus, has long since disappeared, but it must have been a vast building. Pliny the Elder, writing about the middle of the 1st century, claims that a quarter of a million people gathered there to watch elephants fighting tigers and lions and a host of other wild animals imported from distant parts of the Roman Empire.

The wild beast fights and chariot races would be only part of the rejoicings of the population at the triumphant return of their generals. More permanent marks of respect would follow: a Triumphal Arch, and perhaps a Pillar of Victory. The Arch of Titus in Rome, erected to celebrate the capture of Jerusalem in A.D. 70, shows the Emperor and his victorious troops returning, laden with the spoils of war. The low reliefs record the looting of the Temple at Jerusalem and the sacred seven-branched candlesticks being borne off in triumph. The Emperor Trajan had similar arches erected in Beneventum and at Ancona, and his Pillar of Victory, in Rome, erected to commemorate his success over the Dacians in A.D. 114, is one of the most famous columns in the world. The Arc de Triomphe in Paris, built for Napoleon, and our own Nelson's Column in Trafalgar Square are two modern imitations of the Roman Arch and Pillar of Victory.

The Roman Basilica was both a Hall of Justice and an Exchange for commercial transactions. The early Christians, once Christianity was officially accepted, were unwilling to convert existing Roman Temples into buildings for Christian worship. They therefore adapted the Basilica to their religious needs, and thus provided a link between Classical architecture and Christian churches. The Basilica was particularly suitable for the new forms of worship, as we shall see.

In its original form, the basilica seems to have been a rectangular building about twice as long as it was broad, rows of columns supporting the whole length of the building dividing it into three or five aisles. The building was entered normally at a single door at the end or in the middle of one side. At the far end was a semi-circular extension, called an apse, housing a low dais. The seat for the judge occupied the centre of the dais behind a low altar at which certain sacrifices would be made before proceeding with the main business of the court. It was, in fact, very like a small church.

But it is with the Roman town as a whole, and with the domestic architecture of the Romans, that we should now concern ourselves. The Roman was essentially a town dweller, for a barracks is a form of town after all, and wherever the Roman Eagle standards were planted grew a Roman town.

Three types of Roman dwelling were commonly used, for we are not here concerned with the mighty palaces of the Emperors.

The ordinary house was called a *domus*, the country house the *villa*, and for the Roman city dweller there were blocks of flats or tenements called *insulae*. Perhaps the best preserved examples of the domus are to be seen at Pompeii near Naples in Italy, but remnants of the *villa* are found in many parts of this country. Remarkably well preserved or restored examples of the apartment type house or tenement which was the usual home of the city people are still to be seen in Ostia, the great port of ancient Rome, now some distance from the sea.

At Pompeii, thanks to the preservation by volcanic ash from Vesuvius which overwhelmed the city in the catastrophic eruption of A.D. 79, we are able to examine the construction and the interior decoration of a number of houses in remarkable detail.

Some of the houses appear to be bungalows, although the light superstructure and stairs may well have been of wood and therefore burnt during the eruption. As with the typical Moorish house in Tunis or Algiers today, you would have deduced little about the inside of the Roman house from the street. With the modern European house it is fairly easy to guess the nature of the rooms and the layout of the plan by walking round the outside of it. Not so the Roman house. The few windows to be seen in the large areas of blank brick wall are fitted with grilles as a precaution against intruders. In some of the Pompeian houses shop fronts act as a further insulation from noise and intrusion from the narrow streets.

The typical house is a long rectangle entirely enclosed by a high wall, with one entrance in the centre of one of the short sides. Entering through the small door, the visitor would find himself in a vestibule leading to a court, open to the sky in the centre, but roofed on all sides. The rainwater from the inward sloping roofs feeds the small pool or *implurium* in the centre of the court. The only lighting to the small rooms surrounding the court is from the doors which open into it. (In Italy, many months of the year, sunlight is something to be kept out of the room. People are grateful for any relief from the blinding glare.) The rooms are surprisingly small and sparsely furnished, but richly decorated with paintings. Rooms little bigger than the spare bedroom of a modern council house are made to look bigger by the painting on the walls of columns supporting dummy recesses and alcoves, containing in some examples a mimic window opening on to an imaginary landscape. The illusion of space, where there is only a blank wall, is quite astonishingly successful, and the frescoes decorating the rooms are often in a remarkable state of preservation.

Immediately in front of the small pool which the visitor would walk round is a central room, open to form a passage, called the *tablinum*, which could, however, be curtained off to form a reasonably sized salon. Beyond this the visitor would reach an open courtyard surrounded by columns and known as the *peristyle*, the core, as it were, of the private part of the house. It was in fact, part garden, part room, giving light to the surrounding rooms and permitting a circulation of air during the torrid Italian summer.

During the winter the rooms must have been heated with charcoal braziers – as they are indeed in some parts of Italy today – and no doubt the Pompeian girls suffered the same mottled disfigurement to their legs through sitting too near to the fire as their Italian counterparts in our own time!

Dining rooms and bedrooms, reception rooms and quiet private apartments surround the peristyle. Through the central salon the visitor would see the garden, gay with flowers, and decorated with little spurting fountains held in the hands of greenish bronze figures, or falling in a glistening shower on the marble flesh of gods and goddesses. The floors are often decorated with mosaic pictures of scenes from classical mythology, and in dining rooms the artist has derived his patterns from foodstuffs – fish of many kinds, shells, and the writhing shapes of the succulent octopus.

The Roman *villa* would of course not be subject to the gridiron street pattern of the town, and since only the wealthy could afford

to leave the appalling heat and noise of the town during the hot
summer days and go to their country retreats, the *villas* themselves
exhibit a richness of decoration and a refinement of life even more
pronounced than the average house in Pompeii. The Roman *villa* was
in fact a country house, and in England at least there is a wide range
of buildings which might reasonably be called *villas*. Remains of at
least 500 have been found, many of them in Kent, West Sussex,
Hampshire, Somerset, and Gloucestershire. One of the most remarkable examples is to be seen at Chedworth some nine miles north of
Cirencester.

Most *villas* were built in a sheltered position, facing south to take
advantage of the fickle English sunshine, and usually within easy
reach of a Roman road. Many of them were farmsteads with well
organised series of farm buildings associated with the *villa* itself. The
living quarters were heated by a furnace which supplied hot air
through a most ingenious series of hollow earthenware pipes called
a *hypocaust*. Similar arrangements are found in the bath-houses
with which a number of the *villas* were provided. It should be stressed
that the Roman bath was much more like a modern Turkish bath or
a Finnish steam bath. The bather was subjected to a sweating process
in a hot room to cleanse him and a plunge bath was used to revive
him afterwards.

Most *villas* appear to have had at least one important room with a
floor richly inlaid with mosaic, and examples of these mosaic floors
and of tessellated pavements have been uncovered at Low Ham
near Langport in Somerset, at Lullingstone Park in Kent, and of
course at such important town sites as Verulamium near St Albans.

Many of the *villas* were timber-framed houses, with stone or brick
lower storeys and with a light plaster in-filling for the upper rooms.
Others seem to have been bungalows and the timbers have long since
rotted away or been destroyed by fire.

Fire was indeed a constant danger to the Roman household. The
insula in the city was particularly prone to outbreaks of fire, for there
was always a temptation for the speculator to build the tenement far
too high for safety, and as stone was too heavy and too expensive for
the upper rooms, timber construction was used instead. Sooner or
later, with ominous rumblings portions of the *insula* would collapse,
bringing with them the fiery shower of hot coals from the braziers.
The naked flame of the torches lighting the rooms would lick round
the dry timbers and the whole tenement and perhaps half the street
would soon be ablaze.

This was by no means an uncommon occurrence, and indeed in
Rome a cheerful scoundrel named Crassus made a fortune by buying
up houses which were on fire and then erecting tenements of his own

with a team of architects and builders whom he had acquired as slaves.

Sufficient evidence, however, of the architecture of the *insulae* survives at Ostia to enable archaeologists to make extremely fine reconstructions of the appearance of the street in the first century of the Christian era. They look astonishingly modern. The shops were set back under an arcade whose arches shield the pedestrian from sun or rain. Over the arcade were living quarters with balconies and with roof gardens. The windows were for the most part unglazed, and the ones in the rear overlooked neat courtyards with little fountains of bronze and with flowering trees.

Apart from Imperial Rome – and there is considerable doubt still about the size of its population – the cities were by no means as large or as populous as our own today. The estimated size of even so important a centre as Cirencester is only 240 acres, and Silchester, with four temples and one Christian Church, a forum and baths, covered only 100 acres. The amphitheatre at Silchester was outside the city walls, near the East Gate.

Nevertheless, to the Romanized Briton or to the demobilised Roman soldier living at Gloucester, Colchester, Lincoln or York, his city must have seemed a solid permanent thing. He lived in a house with advantages and refinements undreamed of by the native Briton blinking miserably in the reek of his wretched turf hut or wattle-and-daub hovel. The Roman law protected him as he moved on the solid roads, and brought civilisation even to the foothills of the Welsh mountains where, from time to time, the disgruntled and dispossessed tribes made occasional raids and returned discomfited to their cold and insanitary caves.

But the sense of security and of permanence were but an illusion. Roman cities were wholly dependent on the Roman army for their protection. They had been built on sites with few natural defences – it was all part of the Roman plan for the subjection of the Britons. Once the strong British hill forts were overrun, they were destroyed so that they should threaten the Romans no more, and a new Roman town, with the familiar chess-board pattern was built in the plain – a pattern very like that of the temporary Roman camp. The most obvious example of this process may be seen in the substitution of Dorchester, in the valley, for the strong, defensive earthworks of Maiden Castle.

The defence of the ordinary civilian was then the affair of the Roman army. Under its protective shield, the businessman and farmer, the lawyer and the landowner, paid their taxes and were free to concentrate on their own affairs. Life, for over 300 years was peaceful and comparatively settled. There were occasional campaigns against such rebels as the Iceni of East Anglia, led by their queen Boudicca (Boadicea) and incessant guerrilla warfare with the Welsh and with the Scots. Coastal defences too were necessary against the piratical attacks of Saxon ships, and from Brancaster in Norfolk and Bradwell in Essex to Reculver, Lympne and Richborough in Kent, special fortifications had to be erected to deal with this threat.

The threat of the Saxon pirates, however, was but an indication of more extensive troubles besetting the Roman Empire. The situation in the heart of the Empire became so menacing that in A.D. 407 the legions were recalled to defend Rome itself, leaving Britain disarmed and defenceless.

We are not concerned here with the historical consequences of the withdrawal of the Roman armies, but architecturally it was a catastrophe. In less than 150 years Britain lapsed from a civilised country into a barbarian jungle.

Chapter Two

THE DARK AGES

IT must not be imagined that the inhabitants of Roman Britain were swiftly or easily overwhelmed by a concerted and organised invasion. A number of probing attacks would be made by isolated groups of the invading forces, ripe for quick loot and ready to retreat to the sandy marshlands of Friesia or the rocky fjords from which they had set out. Emboldened by their success they came in larger numbers and penetrated still further into the country, their advance helped by the straight firm roads of Imperial Rome. As the invaders probed deeper and deeper they would gradually have realised that here in this rich land were cattle to be taken, crops which could be harvested and land to be colonised, slaves to be kept.

At first the Romanized Britons resisted well. There were enough retired ex-legionaries and young recruits to contain the invaders within an area near to the coast. Prudent men, dismayed at the disturbing turn of events, buried their choicest silver plate against less troubled times, but were put to the sword before they could recover it. Such a hoard was found on a windswept hillside in Suffolk during the early years of the Second World War and, known as the Mildenhall Treasure, is now in the British Museum.

However, the invaders came in ever-increasing numbers and fought with savage exultation. They poured in from the flat lands at the mouth of the Rhine and the Ems, from the valley of the Elbe. Their shallow-draught boats driven across the open sea by thirty or forty oars grounded on the Norfolk and Suffolk coasts, forced a passage up the Thames and its tributaries, and discharged their wild cargoes at the very gates of London. A last desperate stand made by Romano-British forces in A.D. 582 represented the final phase of a struggle which had lasted over 150 years. The flood gates were down, the alien torrent swept in – and stayed.

The effect on architectural evolution was disastrous. The invaders were a seafaring people, with some skill in boat building, workers in metal and wood, but architecturally they were savages. Their buildings were those of the frontiersman: crude wooden huts, temporary

bivouacs clustered together for mutual protection but owing nothing
to the civilisation which they destroyed. No record exists of the
Saxons ever having occupied the villas from which the original
inhabitants had fled. The wooden framework succumbed to the
invading flame, the fair marble pavements and mosaics split and
crumbled under the falling debris, and the charred shell of the villa,
once so splendid, yielded up its prize of silver and bronze to the
barbarian Saxon, who had neither time nor understanding to take
advantage of the refinements or comfort offered by the empty Roman
house. The skill to maintain the hypocaust, to repair the damaged
rood and treat the ravaged marble, disappeared with the reek of
smoke and the stains of battle. Even the craft of brick making was
lost and it was nearly eight hundred years before bricks came to be
made again in Britain.

Some of us can remember how swiftly the rosebay willow herb, the
ragwort and the sycamore seedlings covered the heaps of rubble left
by bombs in London, Liverpool, Birmingham and a score of British
cities during the second World War. The process which erased the
Romano-British ruins must have been even more rapid. The forest
was never very far away, and whilst the marauding Saxons were
establishing their squalid little settlements away from the ravaged
towns, the forest was silently, surely, reclaiming the hard-won Roman
villa, and its farmlands. A few frosts to break the soft red brick or
to split the marble, a few seasons of soaking rain and hot sun to
encourage the undergrowth and inhabit the roofless rooms with
rabbit and rat, and all traces of the mighty Roman civilisation would
disappear. Here and there, at Lincoln for example, a Roman entrance
gate would stand, and Hadrian's Wall, now unmanned, still snaked
across the open fields. Little else survived but the roads by which
the Saxons had come.

Despite the onslaught of the pagan hordes, Christianity somehow
survived. In Ireland and in Wales, a Celtic version still sustained
some of the standards of civilised life, and the fact that neither the
Welsh nor the Irish had ever really surrendered their independence
to the Romans was now to be a powerful factor in the maintenance of
Christianity. But their architectural skill was no better than that of
the barbarian Saxons, and it was to the Roman missionaries therefore that we owe the revival of architecture in this country. Among
these was the wise and courageous St Augustine, who, welcomed by
Ethelbert of Kent, whose wife was a Christian, established himself
in a Romano-British Christian church. We have no record of the sort
of building in which he and his new converts worshipped but in plan
it may well have been like the Roman basilica.

Yet another brave man sent by Pope Gregory was Paulinus, who converted the Kingdom of Northumbria to Christianity and paved the way for the revival of cultural life in the far North.

The battle for supremacy between the rival religions was long and bitter. Now Christ was triumphant, now the followers of Woden overthrew the altars and reinstated the pagan shrines. The Lindisfarne Gospels and the magnificent Celtic crosses testify to the vigour and splendour of Christian culture during these troubled years. But manuscripts and isolated stone crosses are not architecture, and the wooden churches, however splendid they may have been, were so easily destroyed that nothing of the early Christian building survives. Traces of stone buildings suggest that the early missionaries, whether they came from Ireland or from Rome had little architectural skill and certainly constructed nothing comparable in scale to the Roman baths and basilicas whose ruins by this time lay several feet under a mass of wind blown soil and leaf mould.

Yet had times been more settled and had the skill been developed, buildings might have been erected on English soil to rival those arising in Northern Italy, in Ravenna, for example, where such magnificent churches as San Vitale and San Apollinare Nuovo were already being clothed in their glittering sheaths of mosaic. Some time in the seventh century, a monk named Ceolfrid had brought a copy of the works of Vitruvius to the monastery at Jarrow, and this document, which might have revolutionised English architecture, lay undetected until discovered in recent years. As it was, a thousand years were to pass before the impact of classical architecture was to be felt in this country.

Records of building in the period between the coming of the first Christian missionaries and the Norman Conquest some four hundred and fifty years later are so incomplete that we are obliged to admit that we know very little about it. One Saxon church of wood has miraculously survived in Essex, at Greensted-juxta-Ongar, and a few stone churches are to be seen in various parts of the country. Neither the Saxons, nor the Vikings who overthrew them later, were skilled in the use of stone and neither knew how to fashion bricks. Their architecture therefore was largely of wood, and wooden buildings are too vulnerable to survive for very long. Examples of the stone churches of this period are to be seen at Brixworth, and Earl's Barton in Northamptonshire, at Bradford-on-Avon near Bath, and at Sompting in Sussex. Fragments of Saxon details are to be found embedded in the fabric of later churches in many parts of the country.

The plan of the church was normally rectangular, with a slightly smaller rectangle forming the *chancel*. Immediately behind the altar, some churches have a semicircular end called an *apse*. Roofs are

generally of wood, for the builder having made shift to erect a
rudimentary arch to the door, to the narrow slit windows, and
perhaps to the chancel opening was at the limit of his architectural
resources, and rarely attempted to vault the main body of the church.
Many windows are not even properly arched, but have a semicircular stone at the head with a semi-circular hole in it. The result
is rather like a stone version of the piece of bread and butter with a
bite out of it carried by the Mad Hatter in *Alice in Wonderland*. In
more ambitious windows, as in the tower of St Benet at Cambridge,
the top of the window may have two bites, supported in the centre
by a crudely turned chair-leg of stone. The size of the windows was
not entirely due to the architectural timidity of the builders. The
church was not only a place in which to worship; it was at once a
watch tower, and if need be, a fort. A deeply recessed, narrow window
could be more readily defended than a large one, and a bowman
standing by it would present a far more difficult target to the attacker.
Small windows were often triangular, being made from three
separate pieces of stone, the lower one forming a platform on which
the wedge formed by the sides of the window could be firmly held.

A very elaborate and well preserved Saxon tower is to be seen at
Earl's Barton, on the borders of Northamptonshire and Bedfordshire.
As you will see by the illustration, although the tower is of stone the
construction is very like that of a wooden building. You have only to
imagine each long slab of stone painted black to see that the tower
would look very like the timber-framed structure of an Elizabethan
house. A very characteristic feature of Saxon building is the arrangement of the stones forming the corners of the tower. This alternation
of long stones and flat stones is a somewhat awkward attempt to
strengthen the corner of the building – always a vulnerable part.
Since the *quoins*, as these stones are called, present alternately one
long side and one short side, the whole scheme is referred to as
'long and short work.' This is probably the most easily recognisable
feature of Saxon architecture. (*Plate 4.*)

Many churches disappeared entirely during the Viking raids,
together with the monasteries and their occupants, and it seems
reasonably certain that the church at Deerhurst, near Tewkesbury,
with its ambitious vaulted roof, is now the largest Saxon church in
the country.

Another factor which is sometimes overlooked in studying the
architecture of pre-Conquest Britain, is the heavy burden imposed by
the Danegeld – a bribe extracted by the marauding Danes for peace.
A country which was subjected to the continual drain on its financial
resources amounting to thousands of pounds of silver a year, in
addition to the loot acquired during the collection of this 'protection'

"WATTLE" TO BE
FILLED IN WITH "DAUB"

SIMPLE CRUCK
CONSTRUCTION

Fig. 3. The primitive cruck structure which persisted, wherever wood was available, well into the fifteenth century in England. Still in use in certain parts of Europe

money, would have little left over for architecture except of the most simple kind. In A.D. 994 a combined force led by Sven Forkbeard, the Dane, and Olaf Tryggvason the Norwegian, extracted 16,000 pounds in weight of silver, and much loot beside, and in 1018, a tribute of 10,500 pounds in weight of silver from London and 72,000 pounds from the rest of the country must have left very little in the coffers to be devoted to church building.

Even less evidence exists of the domestic architecture of the period. The towns were enclosed in a wooden stockade, somewhat resembling those erected by the early settlers in North America as a protection against attack by Red Indians. The church at Greensted-juxta-Ongar, in Essex, its walls made of split logs standing on end, may well be characteristic of the building methods in use in pre-conquest Britain.

A house at Dalderby in Lincolnshire called 'Teapot Hall' showed a form of construction common to primitive communities in many parts of Europe where wood is available. An intelligent boy scout could erect such a house with little difficulty, so simple is the construction. It is, in fact, like a hike tent, in wood. Two timbers, fixed firmly into the ground at either end, are joined by a ridge pole. A light framework of struts, covered with turf or heather form both walls and the roof. This *cruck* construction, as it is generally called, has one great disadvantage, an inconvenience which it shares with the hike tent – there is very little head room. However, combined with a wattle and daub front and back, it could be a reasonably snug protection against the wind and rain, and if it should catch fire, its occupants could build another house in a comparatively short time.

The Vikings themselves, in Scandinavia, skilled in woodwork and well able to use timber for ships or for houses, evolved a great barn-like hall house, which with but slight modification was to become the standard pattern for our own mediaeval house. A somewhat similar type of hall-house, containing cattle, hay, store and dwelling apartments all under one vast roof may still be seen in use in some parts of Holland and Belgium (the districts from which some of the early Saxon settlers came) and in primitive English society this kind of communal hall with man and beast living in close proximity to each other became common. A slightly different type of house was evolved in the far North, and in Ireland, but it was with the coming of the Normans that English architecture made its first real advance.

Chapter Three

ENGLISH ROMANESQUE
OR NORMAN ARCHITECTURE 1066-1200

BEFORE attempting to describe the characteristic qualities of architecture in England from the middle of the eleventh century to the beginning of the thirteenth century, it would be as well, perhaps, to explain the complicated title to this chapter. 'Romanesque' architecture is a term used to describe buildings which derive their architectural inspiration, however remotely, from Roman sources. When people describe a cottage they have seen in idyllic surroundings in the country as 'picturesque' they imply that however deficient it may be in plumbing and other essential conveniences, the cottage looks 'like a picture.' In the same way, buildings erected after the fall of the Roman Empire which retained a number of features generally associated with Roman architecture – the round arch, for example – were described as Romanesque. As we have seen, the buildings in the Dark Ages were so crude and inept by comparison with those of Ancient Rome that they could hardly be called architecture at all.

In the early years of the tenth century, however, a new influence, brought about by the interchange of ideas with the Normans on the mainland of Europe, began to modify the primitive nature of Saxon buildings. This version of the Romanesque style, brought to England by the more sophisticated and competent Normans can therefore be regarded either as English Romanesque, or simply as Norman architecture. We shall continue to use the term Norman for the sake of brevity, but it must be understood that the architecture so described was in itself derived from much further afield than the province of Normandy. The Normans, and their Viking forebears, had trafficked as far south as Sicily and the other Mediterranean countries. They knew the splendour of Byzantium itself and the magnificence of the Byzantine churches in Venice and Ravenna, and they brought to this island not a provincial formula for building but the architectural inheritance of the whole of Europe.

The dates allocated to every period of architecture in this book are a rough and ready method of enabling the reader to relate the architecture to events taking place in other fields of human activity but they should not be taken too literally. Norman architecture did not appear in these islands for the first time on that savage October day in 1066, when the Normans landed in Sussex, and building in the Norman style did not cease abruptly on New Year's Eve, 1199. Architecture evolves slowly and grows like a plant. The seed germinates unnoticed in the dark earth. The roots wind about and probe deep below ground before the first green shoot appears. In some districts the plant will flourish rampant, flower, wither and die whilst in other parts of the country less favourable to growth, it may be slow to take root and reluctant to die, once established.

The seeds of Norman architecture probably took root about 1042, the year that Edward the Confessor was proclaimed king, for, trained in a Norman monastery, his mother the daughter of a Norman Duke, the new English king would be predisposed to Norman ways and to Norman ideas on architecture. With the king came many able and intelligent churchmen. They were not necessarily all priests, for the Church was the only training ground for a young professional man, whether he aspired to be a lawyer, a doctor, a writer or an architect. His only chance of advancement was through the Church, unless he was capable of distinguishing himself on the battle-field, and the accession of Edward to the English throne obviously offered fresh opportunities of promotion to any young man who found the narrower courts of Normandy cramping to his ambition.

Architectural ideas from Normandy, and therefore from the whole of the continent of Europe, began to infiltrate into these islands some time before the Conquest. Edward's newly appointed Norman bishops would naturally expect new buildings to be like those of their native Normandy, or to resemble in most respects the Italian monasteries where they had received their early training. The Abbey Church of Westminster, begun about 1050, must have seemed a revolutionary building to the Saxons who laboured on it. New standards of precision in the handling of masonry replaced the rough and ready methods which had produced the crude Saxon towers all over the country. The Norman use of arch and vault demanded a technique unequalled in the country since the departure of the Romans in the dark days of the fifth century. Traces of pre-Conquest construction are to be seen in the cloisters at Glastonbury, and at Canterbury as well. Nevertheless the most obvious additions to the architecture of England made by the Normans were the castles they erected to consolidate their position after the victory of the Battle of Senlac. The first were, of course, made of wood, for not even the well-organised Norman armies could wait for the slower growth of a stonebuilt castle to make their positions defensively secure. The country was parcelled out to the victorious Duke's followers as ample loot for the rigours of the campaign, and each lord then made himself responsible for the lands thus in his possession. The Norman cavalry rode North and West, and as the country became more and more subservient and the dispossessed Saxons were liquidated, the great wooden castles, so vulnerable to fire, were replaced by stone structures.

It was clear to the astute Norman that once the foothills of Wales were reached, his cavalry would be at an increasing disadvantage as they pushed into the difficult country ahead. If you look at a contour map you will see that for all practical purposes, the most effective area of penetration must be about the four hundred foot contour. Past that height, the Welsh could wage such a war of attrition by guerrilla tactics that the heavily armed Norman knight could never hope to win. The Conqueror therefore established strategic bases from which he could control and contain the Welsh, and mighty castles were erected at Chester, Shrewsbury, Hereford, Gloucester, Cardiff and Pembroke. The plans of these castles, broadly speaking, are much the same. They are all based on the *motte and bailey* plan, a method of fortification developed in France. Having chosen a sound defensive position, the Norman commander, pressing into service any manpower available, caused a huge mound or *motte* of earth to be erected, some sixty feet high, with a flattened top. This mound was surrounded by a deep ditch, with a wooden palisade and could only be crossed by a drawbridge. A wooden tower surmounted the motte. Yet another ditch and palisade entirely enclosing the motte and its defences was then built – a *bailey* of perhaps two or three acres, to house the remainder of the garrison, cattle and sheep for food, the horses and the camp followers.

One of the first of the motte and bailey castles would appear to have been at Berkhampsted, where Duke William finally received the submission of his new subjects and, although considerable stonework was added later, the ruins still display the great mound of earth about 45 feet in height and with a diameter of about 60 feet across its flattened top. The rectangular bailey covers an area of about 13,500 square feet and both motte and bailey were originally surrounded by moats, filled with water.

A great deal of work was necessary, of course, to convert the wooden fortresses all over the country into the more permanent stone castles. Time had to be allowed for the huge mound of loose earth to settle down before it was fit to bear the many tons of stone from which the castle would be built. Wells had to be dug, to enable

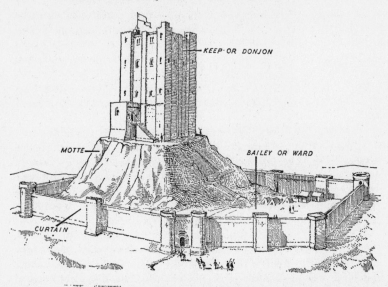

Fig. 4. A typical 'motte-and-bailey' castle. The 'motte' was usually an artificially constructed mound, and the first defences would have been timber. Later this stone castle would have replaced the early defensive position. Note that 'donjon' means the whole keep, not underground rooms

the inhabitants of the castle to withstand siege. The surrounding forest or woodland had to be razed to give the defenders ample warning of the approach of hostile natives – for so the Normans must have regarded the Saxons. Communications had to be assured, and the stone quarried and brought to the site. Supplies of stone itself might well be a problem and it was sometimes easier to import Caen stone from Normandy by boat and by ox wain than to rely on local stone in a flat countryside.

One of the first permanent stone castles built by the Normans is now known all over the world as the Tower of London, that massive castle keep which, apart from the absurd pepperpot caps on the four corner towers, is much the same now as it appeared to the overawed citizens of London in the early years after the Conquest.

Even a superficial examination of the main building and the White Tower will confirm the impression of the solidity and strength so typical of the massive Norman walls and coarse but powerful masonry. The arches to the doorways and windows are semicircular and are true arches, the individual stones being wedge-shaped, so that as the weight above them grew, each stone was driven more tightly against the other, forming a tense, firm half-ring, locking the stones together, and embedding them in the mortar. The windows are splayed – narrow slits in the outer wall, but widening inwards so that a defender might manoeuvre himself in the embrasure without exposing himself to the attacker. Entrance to such a castle, once past the drawbridge and outer defences of the bailey, was up a flight of stairs to the first floor. The ground floor, often windowless, was devoted to storage and in some cases to dungeons for difficult prisoners.

Huge circular slabs of stone topped by a simply hewn capital took the thrust of the semicircular vaults built to sustain the weight of the floors above. The Norman vault may be regarded as a series of arches joined together – not unlike the more familiar railway tunnel – and where the main thrusts of the vault reached the outer walls shallow buttresses were added, to meet those thrusts and to reinforce the massive appearance of the whole structure. (*Plate 6*.)

If no large blocks of stone were available to build solid columns, the Norman mason would often construct hollow columns of stone with the interior filled with rubble and small irregular pebbles. Since the same weight had to be borne by the rubble-filled columns as those made of solid stone, the former had to be made far larger in circumference, and even then, despite their impressive size, stone and rubble pillars have often failed in their duty, and Norman towers have crashed in ruins.

Life within the castle was dominated by defensive needs. Stair-cases built within the thickness of the walls are narrow and wind from left to right, an arrangement which might well have presented difficulties to a right handed swordsman trying to force an entry. Small rooms, again within the thickness of the walls, afforded a little more privacy than that obtainable in the main hall which was the core of the communal life of the garrison. In Hedingham Castle, one of the best preserved of the castle interiors of this period, wall fire-places show that some degree of comfort could be achieved even as early as 1140, and together with the vellum stretched over the narrow windows, the worst rigours of the winter could be kept out. Shafts leading down to the moat dealt with the problem of sewage. These *garderobe* shafts are sometimes described as *oubliettes* to tourists, who are left with the impression that hapless prisoners were dropped down them and expired in agony at the bottom. Perhaps *oubliette* is meant to indicate that the uses of the shaft were best forgotten. (*Plate 5*.)

Within the bailey, wooden structures with thatched roofs or possibly roofs covered with tiles of oak called *shingles*, were in-habited by the more humble followers, and slowly the Saxon cruck construction was improved by the introduction of low walls, giving much needed headroom, and later enlarged by an upper storey reached by an outside ladder and used for sleeping quarters.

In some of the better established cities, effectively protected by the city walls and a powerful and ruthless overlord, more permanent houses were built. Two of these have somehow survived, the so-called Jew's House at Lincoln, a two-storied house built of stone, and, in a poor state of preservation, the large house of a merchant at Southampton. Both these houses were built about the middle of the twelfth century.

A second and equally important development in Britain due to the Norman Conquest was the construction of a large number of monasteries and abbeys, and the establishment of a great many parish churches to replace and to augment the poor wooden structures of the early Christian Church.

The first monasteries had been little more than a group of hermits, in rude huts, usually as inaccessible as possible. The establishment of a monastery at Tintagel on the wild Cornish coast, and at Whitby facing the North Sea, are early examples of men consecrating themselves to a life of contemplation and prayer in as remote a district as possible.

The Norman monastery, however, was a vastly more complex structure in every way, and whilst the core of the Norman castle was the great central hall, that of the monastic design was the great Abbey Church, with all other buildings subservient to it. We are accustomed to regard man as a composite creature, body, mind and spirit, and in these days, in that order. The plan of a monastery makes it evident that the Church was well aware of the three aspects of man, but regarded them in exactly the reverse order of precedence. Monks devoted the greater part of their waking hours to the service of God, and it was fitting that the greatest care and enrichment possible should be lavished on the church in which they worshipped. Provision had to be made for all the complicated aspects of the monastic life. Room had to be found in the design for cloisters, offering privacy for personal contemplation and reflection, and a covered way from the Church to the other parts of the monastery. *Scriptoria* where sacred books and scientific works as well might be written and translated, were needed, and libraries, where they might be consulted.

There would certainly be workshops and studios for the making of essential furniture and for the production of the lovely carving in wood and stone, painting, stained glass and embroidery, metalwork and enamels with which to adorn the abbey church, or to send to other foundations perhaps less fortunate in their membership.

A refectory for eating and drinking, a dormitory for sleep, an infirmary for the sick, both within the monastery or for those to whom the monks ministered, kitchens, a butchery, a bakery, a dairy, a brewhouse – all had to be welded into a satisfactory and functional unity.

We have been considering the design of a monastery but it will be appreciated that much the same analysis could be made of a nunnery or a priory.

There was no standard plan for any monastery – no blueprint which would serve for the erection of one in any part of the country. The plan is, in every case, a flexible and intelligent method of providing accommodation for all aspects of monastic life, on the site available, and with the materials at hand. You could apply the principles governing the design of a monastery just as easily to the design of a barracks, an aerodrome, a football stadium, or a town hall. Siting, function, materials, access and communications, and the limitations or demands peculiar to the building have to be considered in each case, and although, for the sake of convenience, they have been presented in that order, it is clear that they are actually incapable of being disentangled.

An outstanding feature of all Norman architecture is its complete sense of unity. The various parts of the building are beautifully fitted together, forming an integrated whole. This should be stressed, for as we examine the different parts of the building in detail, admiring the way in which the weight of the massive tower is held by the great piers at the crossing of the transepts, or revelling in the intricacy of the carving on capital and column, it is all too easy to become absorbed in these details and to miss the pervading sense of fitness and unity which is so typical of Norman architecture.

The dominant building was, naturally enough, the church, cruciform in plan and with the altar to the east. The Cistercian Order forbade the erection of large towers, but no such rule was in operation at Tewkesbury or at St Albans, where each mighty central tower symbolises the splendour and permanence of the Christian Church, or at Durham where the rocklike structure is emphasised by an additional pair of towers, scarcely less imposing, at the western end of the nave.

The church formed one side of the courtyard round which the cloister unit was built and the position of the other three sides to the north or to the south, varied according to the nature of the site. Since the cloisters normally contained the dormitory (built on the second floor) and the latrines and lavatories for washing, their position was to some extent governed by the slope of the land to permit efficient drainage.

The Chapter House, second only in importance to the church itself, was conveniently sited to permit easy assembly of the members of the community each day. In the Chapter House, what would correspond to the Daily Routine Orders of a Royal Air Force Station of today, would be issued. Lists of monks with special duties to perform were read out, faults admitted and punishments allotted. This was, in fact, the administrative centre of the monastery, and it was in the Chapter House that a visiting bishop would conduct any enquiry into the running of the community, if it lay within his jurisdiction.

The frater range, or dining hall, was on the side of the cloister opposite to that occupied by the church, and generally took up the whole of that wing. It resembled the great hall of the castle, but normally had a pulpit high up at the eastern end and reached by a staircase built into the thickness of the wall, from which one of the brethren would read aloud during meals.

Near to the frater range, but not necessarily connected to it physically, was the kitchen, and the adjacent pantry and buttery formed a link with the dining hall itself.

The western wing of the cloister was usually devoted to bulk storage of food and other essentials for the monastery, and for convenience had direct communication with the courtyard connected with the outside world.

The Infirmary would be sited at the extreme end of the eastern side of the cloister well away from any noise from the street, from the clangour of the bells, and from such workshops liable to disturb the patients. This area, too, housed the prior or the abbot and his more distinguished guests, and looked out upon the orchards, vineyards and gardens which would supply the monastery, and perhaps the fishponds where fish could be reared and kept for meatless fast days.

It may be said here that monastic life did not resemble versions shown on Christmas cards and popular calendars, where fat monks are seen gormandising on huge sides of beef or emptying foaming tankards at loaded tables. The discipline and frugality of a monastery would send most people of today back to a forty-hour week and to their comfortable armchairs by the television, within a couple of days. It is worth noting that the most common complaint from which the monks of Westminster Abbey suffered, according to documents still held in the Muniment Room there, was 'Housemaid's Knee,' contracted through prolonged kneeling on hard cold stones, and not indigestion or blood pressure brought on by over indulgence.

There are, of course, plenty of local variations of the plan we have described. At Ely, for example, a cathedral monastery, the plan differs from that of Tynemouth Priory, which is built in a castle precinct, but all of them have that commonsense unified planning, and complete integration of the various buildings.

We have dealt at some length with this question of planning because although the monastery and its life was destined to be modified and reshaped during the next four hundred years, the plan remained basically the same and later differences are only those of detail and not of principle.

In the same way, the abbey church and its plan underwent certain changes as the years passed, but its early pattern laid the foundations quite literally for many cathedrals and to a large extent dominated the planning of many hundreds of parish churches all over the British Isles.

It should be emphasised that during the Norman period and indeed right through the Middle Ages, the differences between sacred buildings and any others are almost entirely those of planning. The functions and materials of a building determined its plan, but the details were basically the same in each building. A door was a door whether it opened into a church or into a barn, and a window was a window, whether it gave light to a kitchen or to a chapel. The enrichment of the door or window opening would be more pronounced in sacred buildings, for it would not be seemly to lavish elaborate ornament on a barn door, but the form of the door itself would be identical.

None of the great Norman cathedrals has survived in its original form. All have undergone some addition or modification by later architects of the Middle Ages, many with reverence and understanding, before impious hands desecrated the sculpture, hewing off the heads of the saints, wrenching the statues from their niches, and reducing the splendour of their glass to a ruin of brittle fragments. Others, perhaps more fortunate, survived the Reformation, only to fall into the hands of the Cromwellian soldiery, or to be 'restored' with more ingenuity than understanding by Victorian clergy with a taste for the picturesque.

Few of these great cathedrals are more than pallid ghosts of their robust and vigorous originals. The visitor with imagination can glimpse something of the inspired and sensitive minds which could plan such a perfect relationship of form and space, and such a satisfying balance of structure and decoration. But the raw colourless stone, stripped of its glowing colour and splendid mural painting, and the tame glass which now replaces the glory of the mediaeval windows leave an impression of drab cold which must be entirely unlike the passionate vitality of the original building.

We must emphasise that this book must never be read as a substitute for a visit to the buildings described in it. Nothing can replace the experience of actually moving within the walls and under the mighty vaults of these cathedrals or even of standing in the shadow of a noble ruin. The scale of the building is often so impressive and the distances spanned by the stone arches so vast that it is quite impossible to convey their impact on the visitor by looking at a diagram or photograph. Physical exploration of any architecture is absolutely essential, no matter whether you are trying to understand a complex structure such as a cathedral or to assess the proportions of a single room.

The plan of a Norman cathedral (a Latin cross), is divided into three main parts. The first two, the nave and the presbytery (or chancel) lie on the main east-west axis, the *nave* to the west, the *presbytery* to the east. They are crossed at right angles by the third, consisting of two *transepts* which project on either side of the main body of the cathedral to the north and south, and which form the arms of the cross.

Ordinary people were allowed to worship in the nave and the aisles running parallel on either side of it. The presbytery was reserved for the use of the clergy, and was isolated from the nave by a high stone screen known as the *pulpitum*. The *pulpitum*, which is pierced by a central door forms the western wall of the choir, the most westerly part of the presbytery.

The great central tower bestrides the open space formed by the crossing of the nave and the transepts, although occasionally the presbytery may intrude into this area, as at St Albans, and the *pulpitum* is then built across the last arch of the nave. The *sanctuary*, containing the High Altar, is at the most easterly end of the presbytery, and the *screen* or *reredos* behind the altar would, in a parish church, be part of the inner wall of the church. In many abbey churches and cathedrals, however, the side aisles of the presbytery continue round behind the reredos and are called an *ambulatory*.

Many continental cathedrals favoured an elaborate series of chapels radiating fanwise from the eastern end of the ambulatory, but this system seems to have been less popular in Norman England, and the builders here seem to have been content either with a plain square end, or a simple arrangement of rounded ends, called apses, each apse containing a separate altar. At the Abbey Church of St Albans, now St Albans Cathedral, Abbot Paul of Caen placed the shrine and altar of St Alban in the presbytery, but yet another shrine and altar of St Amphibalus (who had converted Alban to Christianity) was in the apse to the rear. The aisles on either side of the presbytery also ended in an apse.

You can perhaps get some idea of the size and scale of these great Norman buildings more readily, by comparing them with something familiar to everyone today – a tennis court. The dimensions of a tennis court are 78 feet long and 36 feet wide. At St Albans, therefore, even before later additions to the nave, it would have been possible to insert two full-sized tennis courts from the west end of the nave to the *pulpitum*, yet another two from the *pulpitum* to the altar, and still leave a generous space over in the apse, without encroaching on the aisles, or on the transepts.

Later additions to our cathedrals have increased the length of many of them – the simple apsidal end of the Norman builders being pulled down and replaced by a splendid Lady Chapel, for example so that the dimensions of St Albans are not those of an exceptionally large cathedral. Winchester now measures 556 feet in length (or seven times the length of a tennis court) and Ely 537 feet.

Such a large ground plan does, of course, imply an equally large and impressive superstructure, and the Norman cathedrals, like the Norman castles with which they have so much in common, are indeed remarkable for their rugged and massive strength, with clifflike towers, thick walls and deeply inset doors and windows.

It is this rocklike quality which impresses the visitor entering the nave from the west end, confronted for the first time by the powerful columns which are spanned by rugged semi-circular arches scarcely wider than the columns themselves.

The sides of the nave are divided into three stories. At ground level, a series of bays is formed by a succession of columns and the arches which span the space between them. The columns are so thick, and the arches between so narrow that the nave is virtually divided from the side aisles by a wall, with spaces cut through it. The simple, almost brutal decorations of some of the Norman work emphasise the massive quality of the construction. It is not until some fifty years after the Norman Conquest that certain cathedrals, such as Durham, begin to show some modification of this almost primitive quality. The columns themselves, rounded or somewhat slimmer, admit more space between them, and the voids thus created begin to play an increasingly important part in architectural composition.

The second storey to be seen from the nave is the *triforium*. This is virtually a corridor some 15 feet high built on the roof of the aisles, about 30 feet above the floor of the nave. Its arches are carefully designed to be an integral part of the nave wall, with its own system of arch, column and capital echoing that in use in the nave. The *triforium* was often used as a *scriptorium* where books were written and translations and copies made, and a library where books were kept. It was sometimes lit by small windows cut in its outer wall, but its main source of lighting was from the nave itself, which received its light from the third and topmost storey, the *clear-storey*. This is a succession of windows immediately under the roof, and is the main source of illumination to the nave and indirectly to the *triforium*. The proportions of the clear-storey windows are carefully designed to harmonise with those of the arches of the *triforium* beneath them, and also with the great arches of the nave, and by their arrangement and diminished size, are calculated to emphasise the height and the dignity of the whole conception.

The Norman nave was usually covered by a low-pitched timbered roof, and few of these have survived destruction by fire or the more ambitious vaulting schemes of later architects. Of the cathedrals, Durham alone has a stone vaulted roof over the nave built during the Norman period. The builders of most cathedrals and churches were content to vault the narrower and more easily spanned aisles, and to make a timber roof for the nave.

Unlike their Saxon predecessors, Norman architects tackled and overcame the problems of vaulting aisles of different widths and height. In doing this, they carried out research without which the mighty engineering feats of the later Gothic architecture could never have been achieved. Although the semi-circular arch and barrel vault is characteristic of practically all Norman work, the pointed Gothic arch is anticipated at Durham cathedral by several years, and although there have been examples of poor workmanship in this period, many more examples standing to this day testify to the ingenuity and skill of the builders of the Norman vaults.

At this point it must be stressed that these mighty buildings were not the product of a sort of human hive, either in this period or in the later Gothic periods. No committee, however well-meaning and talented its members, ever produced a work of art. The design of a cathedral, an abbey or a parish church could only be the product of a single mind – that of an architect. No doubt he was able to delegate various tasks to the craftsmen – but it was this architect who or-dained the proportions and scale of the building, once the site had been chosen. It was he, who, with the materials to hand, designed the complex structure to fulfil its many needs, both spiritual and physical, and welded it into a beautiful and harmonious unity.

It is often impossible to ascertain who was actually the architect responsible for the early buildings. Records may state quite clearly, for example, that 'Abbot Paul of Caen built the Abbey Church of St Alban' but there are quite a number of ways of interpreting this statement. It could, of course, mean that the new Norman abbot, just arrived from Caen, did in fact design and supervise the erection of a splendid new abbey, to replace the more humble Saxon one he found there. It is very likely that Abbot Paul had architectural training, for he spoke somewhat contemptuously of the builders of the earlier abbey as 'rudes et idiotas.' Nevertheless, it had been anticipated for some time that a new Abbey of St Albans would be needed, for building materials – the Roman bricks from which most of the Abbey Church is built had been systematically collected from the ruins of Verulamium for years. It is therefore possible that all that Abbot Paul did was to make it possible for the work to go forward, and that the real architect who designed the Abbey was 'Robert the Mason' who was so richly rewarded on the completion of the building some ten years after the Abbot's arrival from Caen.

Early records, where they exist, are somewhat confused but it seems unlikely that a master mason, as we understand that term today, however good a craftsman, would have the intellectual equipment to plan and conceive the design of so modern a building. Good craftsmen tend, by their very training, to be rather conservative (this has no political significance, of course) and are usually reluctant to accept, and even less likely to initiate, new ideas and revolutionary techniques. Even today, the building trade is dogged by this conservative and limited outlook, and when the architect has convinced his client of the need for erecting his building with modern technical devices, he still has to educate his craftsmen to accept them. It was perhaps this very difficulty which induced William of Sens, the architect called in to rebuild Canterbury Cathedral after the disastrous fire of 1174, to bring his own team of French workmen with him, and to use his own ingenious contrivances for handling the large quantities of stone imported from the quarries of Caen or from the Isle of Purbeck in Dorset. It is true that he was himself 'a man active and ready as a workman, most skilful both in wood and stone,' but he had an architect's vision as well, and his splendid and original design for the eastern end of the cathedral, the 'Corona', as it is called, stands today as a magnificent tribute to his architectural skill. In the final stages of the building, a severe fall from the fifty-foot scaffolding necessitated his return to Normandy, but his successor, 'William the Englishman,' faithfully followed his master's plan and the Corona was completed as William of Sens had designed it.

It is worth noting that the carving of the capitals carried out by French stonemasons is much more clearly influenced by the Roman Corinthian capitals – is in fact more truly Romanesque than the chunky, scalloped capitals more usually found in Norman buildings. You can readily trace the evolution of the Norman style from its sturdy beginnings until it merges almost imperceptibly into the more slender first Gothic or Early English style, without leaving Canterbury Cathedral. A brief description of the vaulting and its development to be found in Canterbury might well suffice to explain a similar, if slower, development all over the country, in abbey churches, in cathedrals, and in the many humble parish churches which sprang up during the years which saw the establishment of Norman rule.

The earliest vaulting, which William of Sens found intact after the fire of 1174, is still to be seen in Ernulf's Crypt, named after the prior who was largely responsible for its erection, during his tenure of office from 1096-1107. The weight of the great *quire* above (which perished in the fire) was sustained by simple but powerfully constructed groined vaults, resting upon strong round pillars with plain scalloped capitals, and on the massive walls of the undercroft. The main area of the crypt is divided into three aisles, and each bay consists of four arches, which when extended become cross vaults, and by intersecting, form yet two more arches – but this time diagonal ones. The *groin* which gives the name to this type of vault is the sharp edge produced by the intersecting surfaces. The effect is strong and extremely simple, but rather heavy.

The next development in the building of the vault is the substitution of a rib for the sharp edge of the groin. This can be studied readily at Canterbury by moving a little farther to the east, from Ernulf's crypt, to that of William the Englishman, built some eighty years later. Here the ribs have now assumed a constructive role and transfer the weight above as a thrust to be met by the columns and the walls, rather than as a dead weight to be held almost entirely by the vault. The ribs were seen to be a skeleton – a tense framework along which the thrust of roof and superstructure could be transferred to the pillar or wall and thence to the ground. The vault itself tended to become a mere in-filling (although a substantial one) between the stone ribs. A shallow buttress strengthened the wall where the thrust of the vault exerted most pressure.

One more difficulty had yet to be overcome, however, the awkward junction between two semicircular vaults of two different sizes. To ensure that the roof covering the junction between the nave and a narrower transept, for example, should be the same level, the arches of the transept had to be raised on *stilts* above their normal springing line – an ungainly device, but one which was inevitable all the while architects were obliged to use a semicircular vault. The semicircular vault was the accepted shape all over the country, with round-headed doors and windows harmonising with the general pattern, but, because the arches and vaults were semicircular, it made it extremely difficult to build high vaults and to give that feeling of elevation so desired by the Norman architect. A semicircular arch of ten feet from the springing line needed an aisle of twenty feet, one of twenty feet high needed an aisle forty feet wide, and so on. From Durham came the revolutionary solution to this problem and to

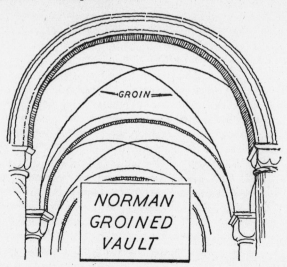

Fig. 5. Early Norman groined vault. Note the sharp edge of 'groin'

many others – the semicircular arch was replaced by a pointed arch, and the whole aspect of architecture was to change entirely.

The introduction of the pointed arch resulted in a much more flexible plan. If a builder wished to bring a narrow aisle to meet a wide nave, he could now ensure their having the same roof level and the same springing line merely by making the vault of the aisle more acutely pointed than that of the nave. He could also design high soaring vaults without having to conform to the rigid relationship of height and width so necessary when building with semicircular vaulting. The development of the ribbed vault from the groined vault had been a remarkable achievement – but the discovery of the pointed arch construction was to revolutionise European architecture.

The growth of architectural ideas is slow and uncertain. Because an unknown genius at Durham had evolved a new form to satisfy the spiritual need for height and grace, and incidentally, to provide a solution of many constructional problems, in the first quarter of the twelfth century, there was not an immediate substitution of pointed vaults for semicircular vaults all over the country. Communications were difficult, books virtually out of reach of all but a few literate men, and, as we have said, the craftsmen who built the churches were conservative. We can imagine the dubious shaking of the head and reluctance with which the news of a pointed arch was accepted. 'Whoever heard of a pointed arch? A lot of nonsense – my

Fig. 6.   Later Norman ribbed vault. Compare with groined vault

old Dad built round arches and good thick walls, and what was good enough for him is good enough for me! Pointed arches and pointed vaults – you mark my words, they'll never stand like a good old barrel vault.' And, of course, in some cases, no doubt, the dismal forebodings were justified – vaults did fall in, or inadequately buttressed, thrust the walls outward as the towers rose ever higher. Long after the pointed vault at Durham showed the way, churches such as Iffley in Oxfordshire, continued to be built with the familiar semicircular arches and thick walls with shallow buttresses.

The parish churches of each period reflect a great deal of the splendour of the cathedrals and great abbey churches, and their smaller size often made it possible for them to be completed in one style. As many of the cathedrals took well over one hundred years to build, it is not surprising that they so often show the evolution from one style of architecture to another, and that their plans reveal second thoughts, adaptations of the original scheme, unnecessary in the smaller parish churches. It should be remembered, however, that many of the parish churches of today were formerly those of abbeys and priories dispossessed during the Reformation, and that the richness of their decoration and the ambitious quality of their planning would not be encountered in an ordinary parish church.

The Norman church exhibits the same massive quality and sturdy semicircular vaulting as the Norman castle or cathedral, but its plan is far less complicated. It was more dependent on local materials and on local craftsmen for its construction, and one of the most fascinating aspects of the parish church is the richness of variation from one part of the country to another. There may be little change in the basic plan, but the granite of Cornwall, the flint of Sussex, the rust coloured Northampton stone and the compact limestones of mid-Somerset, together with local schools of masons exert a surprisingly strong influence on the appearance of the church.

Some Norman church plans are clearly a natural development of the simple aisleless box of the earlier Saxon church on the site. Usually the Norman church was cruciform, sometimes with aisles and with a squat tower sitting foursquare at the crossing of the nave and transepts. Occasionally these large Norman towers have indications that they were used to provide accommodation for the priests – one example which still survives is to be seen in Devon at Branscombe. In Norman churches there appears to have been no rule as to the position of this main tower which, besides being found at the crossing of the transepts and the aisle, is also frequently seen over the West porch, or occasionally is replaced by twin towers at the West end of the nave.

The chancel which formed the eastern end of the church may be square-ended or may end in a semicircular apse. A flat timber roof spanned the nave and if either chancel or aisles were vaulted, the construction had that same massive quality which is characteristic of all Norman work, the heavy ribs of the semicircular vaults being enriched with hewn zig-zag ornament. This is particularly well seen at Melbourne, in Dorset, and at Elkstone, in Gloucestershire. This robust quality, so apparent in the thickset pillars and ribbed vaults was echoed in the narrow splayed windows and even in such fittings as the Norman font. Nevertheless, in later Norman work a number of details point to an awareness of the need to give a lighter effect to this solid and somewhat forbidding quality. One device was the introduction of *blind arcading*, not only along the side walls of the aisles, as at Durham, but on the exterior of the heavy Norman towers as well. These were semi-circular arches, interlinked, each with its own column, but attached to the wall. (Hence the expression 'blind arcading' since the blank wall surface is encountered where normally a window opening would be seen). This blind arcading gave a lighter appearance to the wall, for the shallow depressions produced a rhythm of light and shade on its broad expanses, but they did in fact, add thickness to it. The enrichment round doors and windows, the use of the *bull's eye* window punctuating the upper part of tower and wall – all these were clearly the work of men who felt an artistic need to endow the heavy building with a lighter grace, without, however, endangering its structure, or impairing its function.

As workmen became more skilled in the use of stone, the decoration became lighter and more sophisticated. Zig-zag ornament, hewn with an axe, was replaced by a wide variety of decoration, carved with chisels. The delightful grotesques surrounding the doorway at Kilpeck, in Herefordshire, or the Romanesque designs enriching the cushion capitals in St Peter's, Northampton, show clearly that, as the twelfth century developed, a growing competence with chisel and drill had reached the parish church, even in districts fairly remote from the more up-to-date Norman cathedrals.

A period of transition between the Norman style and the Early English style to come was inevitable, but its development varied in different parts of the country. Nevertheless, the general tendency towards a lighter pillar, the increasing confidence in the use of the ribbed vault, and the more daring use of window space all point to a growing architectural awareness. Men were becoming more conscious of the possibility of diverting the downward thrust of the heavy tower and roof through selected ribs of the vault, rather than by supporting it as an inert mass with equally inert pillars and massive walls.

Once the use of a ribbed vault became an accepted technique, the way was open for an architectural revolution which was to determine the direction of architectural development for more than five hundred years. The Romanesque phase was ended, and the Gothic age had begun.

Chapter Four

EARLY ENGLISH ARCHITECTURE 1190-1280

I N studying one aspect of architecture after another, it is very easy to form the impression that at first castles were built, then cathedrals and abbeys, then parish churches, and so on. Obviously, in a country lately conquered, castles had priority, but by the middle of the thirteenth century building of all kinds was going on continuously.

If we take the year 1245 to be about the middle of the Early English period, we shall find that a great variety of buildings were under construction.

At Winchester, by orders of Henry III, the old Norman hall in the castle had been replaced by a more modern one, built in a lighter and more airy style, with slender pillars supporting a fine new timber roof.

At Lincoln work was still in progress on the splendid Angel Choir, under the direction of the famous Bishop Grosseteste, who in 1238 had gone to Peterborough to rededicate the church after the addition of the huge modern West front to the older Norman nave.

The walls of Salisbury Cathedral were beginning to rise high above the flat Wiltshire landscape, and in the vast windy north transept of York Minster, superb *lancet* windows, now known as the Five Sisters were already more than half complete.

Work was not confined to large buildings in large cities. In a remote district in Shropshire, improvements and additions had just been completed to a fortified manor house, known today as Stokesay Castle, and away in Kent, in the tiny village of Stone, near Gravesend, finishing touches were being put to some of the most exquisite carving of the period, in the little church of St Mary. There was hardly a district throughout the length and breadth of the land that was not sharing in this architectural ferment, and the buildings of this period are among some of the most daring and certainly some of the most elegant in England. There was, however, a marked difference between architectural forms developing in cathedrals and churches, and those evolving in castles. In the former, the massive Norman vaults and heavy columns were being replaced by lighter structures, but such alterations could not take place in the design of castles without seriously impairing their efficiency.

Many castles now assumed the proportions of a fortified city, for people naturally tended to congregate under the protective shadow of a powerful nobleman. It was clear that there could be no relaxation of vigilance by the defenders of the Welsh and Scottish borders, but other fortresses, some in open defiance of the King, were enlarged and strengthened in districts remote from the central government. Secure in his castle, a nobleman could rule almost like an absolute monarch until another baron, stronger and more skilled in the art of war, could penetrate his defences and overthrow him, either to take the lands for himself, or on orders from the king. By the end of the reign of Henry II, the *adulterine* castles, that is, castles built in defiance of the king, had been suppressed and many of them replaced by the large rectangular stone keeps of the Royal castles.

The changing methods of warfare naturally had a direct effect on the architecture of the castle as surely as, today, space travel is changing the appearance of the aeroplane. The First Crusade in 1096 showed how inadequate were the normal fighting methods, and such large engines of war as the battering ram, and the mangonel which hurled huge stones at the walls, caused the returning Crusaders to re-design their own castles in the light of what they had learned abroad. One of the obvious improvements was the raising of the height of the surrounding curtain wall, to defeat the attacker who tried to gain entrance by means of a high movable belfry from which his men could scale the wall, or pour a withering fire of arrows on the defenders.

Yet another dangerous mode of attack and one very difficult to counter was that of mining under the curtain wall, forming a tunnel or gallery supported by wooden props. When the attackers withdrew along the gallery they would set fire to the props, the roof of the gallery would collapse, bringing down a portion of the wall with it, and exposing the fortress to a direct assault. One method to overcome this mining operation can be seen at Kenilworth Castle, where the buttresses at the corner of the keep project so far, and are built with such solid foundations, that they are virtually small towers, making it impossible for miners to drive a sap towards the main wall of the keep. Orford Castle, Suffolk, built between 1166 and 1172, a little early for this period, perhaps, is again characteristic of the continual experiments carried out to defeat the enemy sappers. The rectangular keep here had been replaced by a polygonal one, and men in the three large rectangular turrets projecting from it were well able to direct fire across the whole face of the tower. Conisborough Castle in Yorkshire shows a further development of this plan to make it extremely costly for the attacker to approach the main defences.

The general tendency was more and more towards what we should now call defence in depth. The keep, rectangular or circular, was still the last resort of the besieged garrison. Far more attention now, however, was being paid to fortifying the curtain wall with a series of towers at regular intervals which could give covering fire to each other, and inflict heavy casualties on any attackers who managed to breach it or to break through the main gate into the courtyard.

The main gate itself became a more elaborately defended strong point with strong high semi-circular-fronted towers on either side of the entrance which could only be reached across the bridge spanning the ditch or moat. The bridge itself could be withdrawn and the doorway barred by a *portcullis*. The *portcullis*, an iron-tipped grille of stout wood, was operated from the upper chamber of the gate-house, and even if the attackers negotiated this obstacle successfully they could still be subjected to a hail of missiles dropped through holes in the ceiling above. They could be shot at through arrow-slits in the flanking guard chambers, and might still have to force an entrance through yet another *portcullis* on the inner side of the gatehouse.

Most of these hazards can still be studied, in part, at Criccieth Castle, in Caernarvonshire, or at Pevensey Castle in Sussex, by anyone sufficiently imaginative to examine the ruins of what must have been two very well organised defensive positions in the thirteenth century.

The very nature of the castle made improvement in standards of comfort difficult. Windows were usually without glass, for it seems to have been a luxury even for Henry III to have his windows glazed, and the great hall which was the centre of the life of the castle reeked with smoke from the central fire (chimneys and wall fireplaces were usually confined to the first floor rooms) and the filth accumulating among the rushes on the floor. In 1260 the Treasurer of the Exchequer was ordered to deal at once with the problem of sanitation at Westminster, even if in so doing it cost one hundred pounds – and since the equivalent sum of money today would be at least £1,500, it suggests that the monarch's patience was rapidly becoming exhausted with the primitive conditions in which he had to live. If the king himself had to endure such conditions, the living quarters of his less fortunate subjects can best be left to the imagination.

The manor houses which formed the nucleus of many village communities, apart from those grouped round a baron's castle, or attached to a monastery, were less confined by defensive considerations and therefore able to develop a more civilised kind of life. This has, oddly enough, been traced to the development, peculiar to

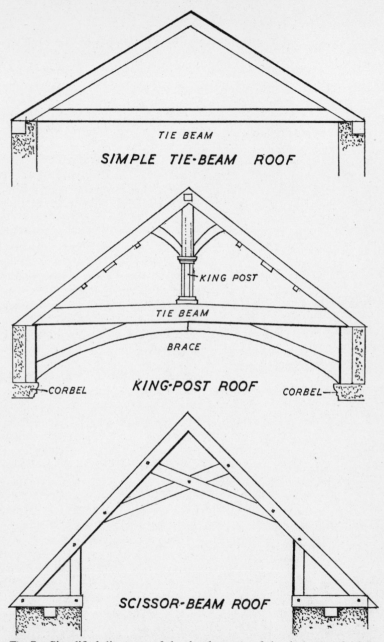

TIE BEAM

SIMPLE TIE-BEAM ROOF

KING POST

TIE BEAM

BRACE

CORBEL   **KING-POST ROOF**   CORBEL

SCISSOR-BEAM ROOF

Fig. 7. Simplified diagrams of the development of the timber roof. Note that the thrust on the King post roof is distributed down the wall and held by the corbels

England, of the country gentleman. By paying shield-money a knight could be excused from serving as a soldier in the King's army. With this money the King could hire professional soldiers – either Englishmen or foreign mercenaries – to conduct his campaigns on the Continent, and leave the English knight in peace to cultivate his lands, and to encourage the arts and crafts in the small country towns clustered near his manor. It is true that the manor house had to be reasonably secure from attack by masterless men, or an armed neighbour, but the life in a manor house was very different from that in one of the Border castles, for example, whose occupants were almost perpetually under arms. The manor house, a largely self-supporting community, not only consisted of the dwelling house, but had its own chapel, dairy, buttery, brewhouse, weaving sheds and dyeing vats, accommodation for the salting down of meat, a tannery for the hides, a smithy for iron work about the estate, and all the hundred and one requirements of a developing community. Under the protection of the king, freed from military service, the knight was able to hunt, to joust, to study and to beautify his house. Although much of the house is of a later date, Haddon Hall, in Derbyshire, is one of the loveliest of the manor houses which grew up in the kind of circumstances just described, and a study of its fabric reveals a spaciousness of life and an architectural refinement which we might well envy today.

Little Wenham Hall, in Suffolk, bridges the gap between the castle and the manor house. Built in brick, between 1260 and 1280, it is an unusually early example of the use of this material which did not become common for another two hundred years at least. Brick vaults, with stone ribs, built on the ground floor support the great hall above. The narrow windows, splayed inwards, and the generally massive quality of the construction make it much more clearly a fortified position than Haddon Hall.

The present hovel of wattle and daub, however, would show little change from the Norman Conquest until the fifteenth and sixteenth centuries, and the squalor and stench of the town houses would perhaps be comparable to the conditions in the souks of Cairo or the Casbah in Algiers today.

In the meantime, vast sums of money and almost all the craftsmen's skill available were being lavished on the magnificent abbey churches, the cathedrals and on some of the more favourably endowed parish churches.

The magnificence of the North transept at York and the splendour of the Angel Choir at Lincoln have been referred to (p. 50), but it would be difficult to find any cathedral to which some part was not added in this thriving Early English period. It can be studied at Wells,

THE MAIN DOWNWARD & OUTWARD
THRUSTS HELD BY COLUMNS OR
TRANSFERRED FROM WALLS
TO BUTTRESSES

Fig. 8.   The weight of a Gothic building is largely directed to selected points
by the vaults and then transferred by buttresses to the ground

at Salisbury, on the West Front at Peterborough, in its early stages in
the nave at St Albans, and in a score of our cathedral churches, as
the builders rejected the old solid Norman style and experimented
with this new freedom of airy ribbed vault, acutely pointed arches
and widely projecting buttresses.

As already described, the Norman architect relied on a solid wall
and column to carry the dead weight of the roof and tower upon them.
With the new ribbed construction, it was quickly realised that there
was no real necessity for the whole wall to be several feet thick. It
need only be thickened by a buttress at those points where the
thrust of the vault had to be held. The buttresses conveyed the
thrust of the vaults inside the building to the ground outside, and
between the buttresses the wall could be made much thinner and
could be pierced by larger, lighter windows than those of the old
Norman building. It is this new conception of the function of the
wall as a screen between buttresses which made it possible for such
magnificent groups of windows as the Five Sisters at York to be
evolved. Here each lancet window is 53 feet 6 inches high, and 5 feet
1 inch wide, and smaller lights above extend the area of glass almost
to the transept roof.

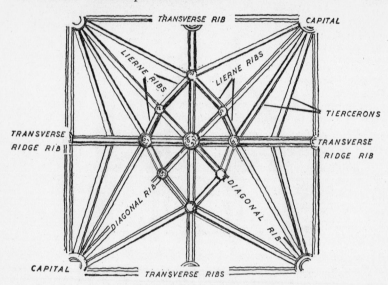

Fig. 9. The complex geometry of a later Gothic vault. The tierceron ribs appear first. Later the lierne ribs develop. This plan combines both types. They are often found together in the same roof

It was soon discovered that so long as the buttresses were strong enough to convey the thrust to the ground there was no necessity for them to be solid. Buttresses were therefore contrived which were pierced with arches, and the bridge-like struts thus formed, often spanning the roof of the *triforium*, give the impression of the stone leaping or flying across the space. These flying buttresses, as they are called, impart a remarkable sense of tension and lightness to the outside of the building, and echo the same qualities given to the interior of the building by the splendid vaulting. The vaulting itself is clearly the work of masons with confidence in their skill to manipulate the subtly curved stones locked firmly together to form the ribs and to produce the resilient but rigid framework of the vault. The introduction of a *ridge* rib which runs down the centre of the vault like the ridge pole in a hike tent, provided a key for the other ribs springing upwards from the walls and pillars, and their junction was marked by a beautifully fashioned *boss*. Intermediate ribs known as *tierceron* ribs springing from the same points as the main ones made it possible to divide the area to be vaulted into smaller compartments, and not only gave a lighter and more efficient vault, but increased its decorative quality very considerably.

With this increased skill in vaulting, it became possible to depart

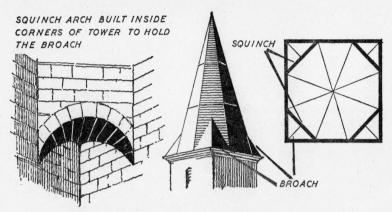

SQUINCH ARCH BUILT INSIDE CORNERS OF TOWER TO HOLD THE BROACH

SQUINCH

BROACH

Fig. 10. The broach spire and its construction

from the simple plan of the Norman church. Aisles were added to provide more accommodation for the congregation, and the humble Norman apse was pulled down to be replaced by a more elaborate square end to the sanctuary.

At the same time, the deeply inset Norman door was enclosed in a porch with a vaulted roof, and the squat Norman tower was either replaced or was raised several feet to carry a tall narrow spire.

Where the spire is octagonal in section, a device known as a *broach* was built to convey the octagonal spire on to the square tower. This is a pyramid of masonry filling the four angles of the tower, and is supported by a *squinch* – virtually a series of small arches spanning each corner of the square tower. The broach spire is characteristic of the Early English period, and may be examined in such churches as Pickworth in Lincolnshire and Warboys in Huntingdonshire.

Another thirteenth century innovation is the introduction of pillars constructed from two different types of stone, shafts of the local material – perhaps Kentish ragstone – alternating with polished shafts of darker marble from the Isle of Purbeck in Dorset, and carried considerable distances by sea and by road to enrich the cathedrals and churches.

The capitals surmounting the columns are like an inverted bell, often enriched with a remarkably beautiful leaf carving which is found only in this period. The leaf-like forms are not copied from nature – although there may be a slight resemblance to a shamrock leaf – but they grow with all the vitality of a living plant, curling downwards to form an almost spherical knot, or licking, flame-like round the deeply cut mouldings which form the upper part of the capital. Sometimes they are absent from the capital altogether, leaving the clean lines of the bell mouth to clamp the column to the heavy rolls of stone above, but they frequently appear again in the spaces between the arches of the choir, or enrich the same sort of area between the arches of an arcade. The mouldings of the arch are also deeply cut, and produce an emphatic pattern of light and shade which accentuates the curved braces of the arch, and is repeated in the vaults above. No one who has been able to examine the decorative leaves on an Early English capital can fail to be impressed with the sense of vigour and exquisite craftsmanship of the thirteenth century carver.

Not only great monastic churches such as the Priory Church at Dunstable or the Abbey Church at Selby, but also small and humble parish churches were richly decorated, and presented a very different sight when newly consecrated from the churches we see today.

The church of St Mary at Stone, near Gravesend, may be taken as typical of the loving craftsmanship lavished on the interiors of these unpretentious churches. The lancet windows at first are grouped very simply, but as you proceed from the west to the east, each succeeding window becomes more richly ornamental, rising to a kind of decorative crescendo as the chancel arch is approached. This church, as Professor E. W. Tristram has demonstrated, had its wealth of mural painting, now alas, a few fragmentary stains on the plaster. Little of its original glass has survived and the sharply cut mouldings which used to be picked out with colour are now grey channels in the monochrome stone. The chancel arch is still enriched with its ripple of *dog-tooth* moulding – an ugly term to describe so lovely a motif – but the carved *rood screen* which should separate the chancel from the nave has long since disappeared.

Perhaps the chief glory of this little church is to be seen in the chancel. On the south wall a blind arcading of cusped arches leads from the chancel to the sanctuary, a unified design with the *sedilia* and *piscina* immediately to the south of the altar. (The *sedilia* was a seat built in a recess in the wall to form a seat for the clergy, and the *piscina* was a kind of stone hand basin in which sacred vessels used in the Mass were washed.) The triangular space between each arch forming the arcading is called a *spandrel*, and it is the spandrels on the south wall of the sanctuary at St Mary's, Stone, which contain some of the most beautiful carving executed in England during this period. There is a local belief that the masons who worked on this church were qualifying to be selected to carve the decoration on the Abbey Church of Westminster which was being erected at about the same time, and certainly the carving is unsurpassed even in much more important buildings.

It must be emphasised once more that even such a small church as St Mary's was not the grey shell we see now, but once glowed with colour. If a man from the Middle Ages could see the interior of his church today, the bare walls would look as incongruous to him as it would seem to us if we saw a man walking down the street dressed only in the lining of his suit.

Some sections of the early Church declared that representational paintings and carvings disobeyed the Second Commandment, but Pope Gregory II very wisely insisted on the value of pictures in teaching an illiterate congregation the stories of the Bible and the principles of the Christian religion. The walls and windows, therefore, of the mediaeval church were the means whereby the humble worshippers were taught the glories of God and His saints, and the rewards and punishments reserved for men in the life of the world to come.

The Church exercised a rigid control on the artists: mural paintings, stained glass, illuminated manuscripts were not a riot of self-expression but a carefully organised series of symbols in accordance with a common policy. That is why, with very slight variation, a painting of St Christopher carrying the Holy Child on his back, adorning the wall of the chapel of Haddon Hall, in Derbyshire, resembles a painting of the same subject in a church in Buckinghamshire.

A man who from his childhood had been shown the Virgin Mary in a blue robe, the Mary Magdalene in a red robe, and St Peter with his great key, would have been bewildered to enter another church and to find there that the artist had decided to clothe his Virgin in a green robe, his Mary Magdalene in blue and to represent St Peter without his key.

It would need a much larger book than this to deal with the symbolism of the Church, but there are symbolic aspects in every part of the church, from the Christ in glory so often found over the church door (a man could only enter the Church through Christ) to the font near the door where baptism would make him a full member of the Church before he could take part in the service.

These considerations were no doubt what prompted the members of the Second Council of Nicea, held in A.D. 787 to declare . . . 'It is not the invention of the painter which creates pictures but an inviolable law, the tradition of the Church. It is not the painters but the Holy Fathers who have to invent and dictate. To them manifestly belongs the composition, to the painter only the execution.'

The artist of today, rejecting every kind of discipline except that imposed by himself, might have found the conditions in which his mediaeval counterpart worked intolerable, but it may be that this very discipline, far from discouraging the artist, stimulated him into producing works of art which are still among the most wonderful creations of our European civilisation.

In the northern countries, certain physical conditions were responsible for the selection of a medium – stained and painted glass – which had a profound effect upon architectural form. In Italy, the church is still a cool refuge from the blinding glare of the summer sky. The windows are kept deliberately small in order to shut out the light, and this liberates huge wall surfaces which invite artists to cover them with fine mural paintings.

In England and in Flanders, the cool, subdued light produced a demand for larger windows, and as the windows grew in size at the expense of the wall space, the attention of the artist was diverted, to some extent, from the diminishing wall surface to the larger expanses of glass now available. Stained and painted glass therefore became almost an alternative in Northern Europe to the mural painting of the South.

The development of the windows, from narrow lancets to the vast expanses of some of the later churches, is one of the most useful guides to the tracing of architectural evolution in Gothic England.

Early in the period we have been studying in this chapter, an elaboration of the simple arch form began to show itself, mainly in arcading and in the window lights. This is known as the *cusped* arch, never used as a constructional feature in the main arches of the nave, but appearing with increasing frequency in the arches of the *triforium*, the window lights and the arches spanning such features as the *sedilia*, the *piscina*, and niches for the statuary. By 1245 even St Marys' Stone, could produce a fine display of cusped arches in the sanctuary, and the Angel Choir at Lincoln Cathedral owes much of its airy grace to the leaping curves of the cusped arches in the *triforium*.

With the grouping of several window lights under one main arch, the space left above the lights became another source of decorative enjoyment. Even at Peterborough Cathedral, where the Norman *triforium* arches were grouped in pairs, some attempt was made to lighten the effect of the blank space above with a little pierced geometric ornament. This geometric ornament developed during the Early English period, the blank space being fretted out with *trefoils quatrefoils* and *cinquefoils*, later to become circular wheel windows with radiating spokes of stone and eventually to evolve into the full magnificence of the great *rose* windows which are the glory of some of our great cathedrals.

It is always difficult to detect any actual point at which one style of architecture developed into another, and this is particularly true of the emergence of the style which followed the Early English period. Some authorities would assign certain architectural features to a later development of the Early English period, others declare that they are in fact Early English no longer but regard them as an entirely new style – a transitional period between the Early English and the Decorated period to follow.

Although the Geometric style of ornament is treated here as a natural development of the Early English style, and our examination of the Decorated period begins thereafter, any such attempt to divide architectural history into rigid compartments is artificial and done for the convenience of the reader; it is not really possible to define the limits of anything so evolutionary as an architectural style.

The most obvious development of the Geometric style is to be seen in the ornamental shapes above the grouped lights in the Early English window. Early examples of *plate tracery*, as it is called, can be seen at Great Abingdon church separate from the main window tracery, but very soon the upper part of the window is seen to be pierced out in geometric patterns rather like the designs evolved for simple exercises in fretwork. Cusps make their appearance in the plate tracery, and gradually, as at Westminster Abbey, the flat simple form gives way to a more clearly contrived series of cut mouldings, firmly united, and echoing the growing control over involved sections of stone. The actual area occupied by the plate tracery, too, develops from a hole cut in a plate of stone to an economical net of mouldings with considerably more accommodation for the glass. Awkward shapes originally left blank on either side of the geometric pattern are now pierced and absorbed into a properly designed pattern which embraces the whole window.

It is at this point that the truly Decorated tracery begins to appear in more complicated forms, which will be dealt with more fully in the next chapter.

Chapter Five

THE DECORATED PERIOD 1280-1377

IN dealing with the castles which were evolved during this period, it is necessary to start some fourteen years earlier than the 'official' date with the erection of Caerphilly Castle, begun in 1266 by the 'Red Earl,' Gilbert de Clare, Earl of Gloucester. He had annexed the district of Senghenydd, a few miles north of Cardiff, and at once started to consolidate his position by building a mighty castle, the plan of which was to determine the pattern of a number of similar castles (with some local variation) built between 1283 and 1327 by Edward I, by his son, and later by his grandson.

The basic plan of these castles, of which Caerphilly was the first, is a series of defences in depth, and is known as a concentric plan. The inner curtain wall, with well-constructed towers at strategic points and a well-fortified gatehouse, is entirely surrounded by a slightly lower outer curtain wall, which in turn is strengthened by other towers and often surrounded by a wet moat. The slightly lower level of the outer wall enabled the defenders of the inner wall to fire over the heads of their friends holding the outer curtain wall without wounding them when repulsing an attack. The towers on the outer wall, however, are semicircular or D-shaped, flat and open on the inner side, so that should the attackers gain control of them, the open sided towers would afford them little protection from the fire of the defenders still holding the inner wall.

Wales was formally annexed in 1284 and Edward I had a chain of Royal castles with the concentric type of defences built, ringing in Snowdonia and denying the fertile plains of Anglesey to the rebellious Welsh chieftains. Perhaps the best known of the Edwardian castles are Conway, Beaumaris, Caernarvon and Harlech, but other existing castles such as Kidwelly Castle, Carmarthenshire, and the Tower of London were also modernised by the addition of outer curtain walls and towers to bring them into line with a general defence policy. This was only a precaution, for, with the more aggressive and potentially dangerous barons and nobility away in France conducting a highly successful campaign, the peaceably

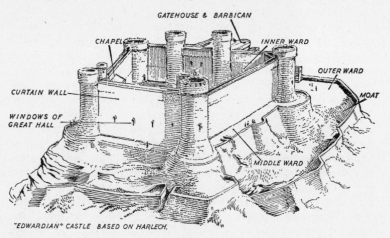

Fig. 11. The more complex system of defences of the castles erected during the reign of Edward I. Most of them are on the Welsh border

inclined members of the Court were able to develop their great estates and to cultivate a more gracious type of building. The growing prosperity of the merchants enabled them to build manor houses less concerned with defence, as well as fine town houses, their wealth secure within the thick walls of such cities as York and Southampton, Conway and Caernarvon.

Fairly typical of the country house of a wealthy merchant is the central and earliest part of Penshurst Place, on the upper reaches of the River Medway, in Kent. It was built about 1341 by Sir John de Pulteney (or Poultney), a prosperous wool merchant who helped to finance Edward III's Crecy campaign, and was Mayor of London four times.

This mediaeval house is entered from the north by a vaulted porch with a groined roof, and from the porch the visitor goes straight into the Great Hall, certainly one of the finest rooms of the period. The Hall is about 62 feet long and 40 feet wide, and spanned by a magnificent arch-braced roof, with a *louvre* in the centre to let out the smoke from the huge fire in the centre of the room which was its only means of heating. A low dais at the far end of the hall was occupied by Sir John and his privileged guests, and the remainder of the company fed at long tables in the body of the hall. At the opposite end, hiding the entrance of the porch is a wooden screen with a gallery over, which gave access to upper rooms. A pantry and a buttery were reached through the openings in the screen and a passage connects with the kitchen beyond. (The present screen replaces the older mediaeval one, but is sufficiently accurate to give a very good idea of the original.) Beside the dais, a flight of stone steps leads to the *solar*, a room to which the lord and his lady could retire for privacy when the reek and noise of the smoky hall became intolerable, and from this solar a small window enabled the lord to look down upon the hall to check the behaviour of his domestic staff.

It may seem strange that so important a person should have no better means of heating the Great Hall in the fourteenth century than his counterpart had in the eleventh century, but, as today, there seem always to have been people who thought that any concession to comfort must inevitably lead to a degenerate race. Although fireplaces with chimneys were common enough by the sixteenth century, we still have a writer named William Harrison deploring their use. Writing as late as 1577 he refers to his contemporaries as 'tender-lings' because they prefer a fireplace in the wall to the fire in the centre of the hall, and declares that just as the smoke from the fire was supposed to harden the roof timbers above, so it made tough human beings able to resist 'rheumes, catarhs and poses.'

As we have said before, the architectural details in the Middle Ages are much the same whether the window is lighting a church or a manor house, and the high windows, deeply inset in the thickness of the wall, which light the hall at Penshurst Place would look equally well in a church or an abbey of this period. The window at the end of the hall is a fine example of geometrical tracery and the buttresses supporting the vaulting of the porch and the groined vault itself are all practically indistinguishable from those to be seen in sacred buildings. The difference between the details of a wealthy church and the corresponding details in a domestic building is largely one of decoration. The Great Barn at Glastonbury in Somerset is magnificently roofed, and since it was an abbot's barn has carved decoration with symbols of the Four Evangelists on the gables, but generally halls, inns, barns and hospitals, although they are constructed on the same principles as the churches, are by no means as richly decorated.

This period did indeed see the flowering of a most delightful freedom of decoration in church architecture which, perhaps, reflects an entirely new freedom of thought sweeping through Europe. Too often, in the past, the Christian religion had been identified with the grim Hebraic conception of God as the Jehovah of the Old Testament – a terrifying Being whose main concern would appear to be the condemnation of the weak and wayward of his subjects to eternal torment. A new concept of Christian love and of Christian suffering was developing in the minds of men. The world was no longer a vale of tears, a grim ordeal with the snares of the flesh and the devil ever

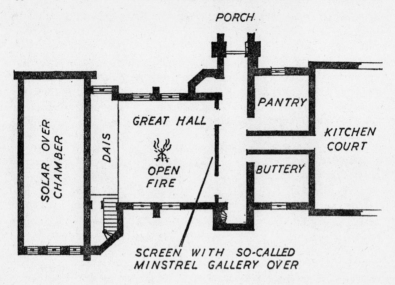

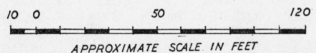

Fig. 12.   Plan of a great house, mid-fourteenth century. The open hearth
persisted in some districts until the sixteenth century

ready to trip the unwary into the bottomless pit and everlasting fire.
If God created the world and all therein, it was argued, it could not
be a wholly evil thing, and with St Francis of Assisi preaching not
only the brotherhood of man but his kinship with the other creatures,
men could look on the world in which they lived unafraid. Artists,
always more aware of the pictorial and decorative possibilities of
things around them, and now encouraged by the Church, began to
represent living things in their work. This is particularly apparent in
the capitals surmounting the columns in church architecture. The
decorative leaves of the Early English style, very beautiful in their
own way, began to be superseded in the new buildings by carvings
closely resembling the leaves, flowers and fruit of the garden and
hedgerow, the trees and the plants familiar to everyone. There is a
wave of exuberance which permeates the architecture. The windows
become yet wider, the vaults become yet more intricate, the buttresses blossom with rippling ornament. After the restrained vitality

C

of the Early English spring, the Decorated Period is luxuriant and lush high summer.

The Franciscan friars, with their mission to preach to the down-trodden and the under-privileged, reached England about 1220, and the more liberal interpretation of the Christian Faith, for which they were partly responsible, took a long time to develop, but by 1280 it is apparent from a host of details in cathedral, abbey and church that a new spirit of freedom was abroad, spreading like fire throughout England.

Little alteration could be made to the ground plans of the cathedrals, for the Norman foundations were laid down to serve a type of worship unchanged in its essential since the early days of the Christian Church. But the architects and master masons of the fourteenth century could and did elaborate and embellish the existing fabric, paring away heavy Norman columns and lightening the whole structure. They added magnificently ornamental Lady Chapels and Chapter Houses where the main fabric would have proved too difficult or costly to replace, and built towers and steeples to soar above the earlier structure.

So widespread was this architectural excitement that it would be quite impossible to examine the additions made to every cathedral in the country, from the fourteenth century nave of Worcester, the Chapter house at York, the brilliantly designed 'Bishop's Eye' – a magnificent circular window in the south transept of Lincoln – to the work at Hereford. No book of this kind could possibly ignore such landmarks in the architectural scene as the 400 foot tower and spire of Salisbury, the sculptural design of the West fronts of Wells and Exeter, the incredible ingenuity of the Octagon at Ely and the double arches at Wells inserted to remedy the settlement of the piers supporting the central tower.

The main fabric of Salisbury was erected during the thirteenth century, indeed the cathedral was consecrated in 1258 in the presence of Henry III, but the tower and spire which are its crowning glory were added in the Decorated period, and the charming little figure sculptures depicting scenes in the Old Testament, which decorate the arcading of the Chapter House anticipate, in their freedom and naturalism, the riot of carving which was to develop in the fourteenth century.

It is at Exeter, however, that we are able to study the development of the Early English style as it glides almost imperceptibly into the exuberance of the Decorated period. The work began in 1260 with the rebuilding of the presbytery, which was not, however, completed until some forty years later, to be followed by the remodelling of the Norman choir in the early years of the fourteenth century. Despite the 'Baedeker' raids – reprisal attacks carried out by the German Air Force during the last war – and other damage by vandals nearer home, the great West front, with its triple row of kings, saints and angels housed in superbly decorative niches, and its splendid central window, is still one of the most impressive monuments of the Decorated period. Its only rival in England sculpturally perhaps is the West front of Wells, for the ravaged front of Lichfield can no longer show anything comparable to the nine tiers of statues, some 8 feet in height, still intact at Wells.

The structural additions made to the interior at Wells during the Decorated period are of greater importance architecturally, however, than the sculpture of the West front. For some time, in the valley of the Severn, there had been developing a school of masons with remarkably progressive ideas of construction. At Wells, in the early years of the fourteenth century, ominous signs of weakness began to show in the main piers supporting the great central tower over the crossing of the nave and transepts. Confronted with the possibility of a disastrous collapse – the tower had only been up since 1318 – they set to work to strengthen the piers by spanning the east end of the nave and the two transepts with three inverted arches. Various authorities disagree as to the effect which this remarkable and un-orthodox construction has on the appearance of the cathedral. It is a memorable experience to stand under the airy vault, to watch the inevitable flow of the stone from the bases of the arches, past the tense ring which pierces the space between the arch and wall, and then to see the way in which the thrust of the curve crosses into the inverted arch and finally travels upward to add its strength to the original vault of the roof. But buildings must be seen, for it is impossible to get any experience of architecture merely by looking at pictures or diagrams however carefully selected. The spaces spanned by the remarkable vaults at Lincoln, at Wells and at Exeter must be crossed slowly, and the bones of their construction studied, for bones almost invariably are beautiful.

At Ely, the collapse of the Norman tower during a violent storm in 1322 had left the cathedral with a gaping hole in the roof and a sorry heap of debris on the floor from the ruin of the rubble-filled Norman piers. This accident had not been entirely unexpected, for the monks had for some time been using another part of the cathedral for their services, but they had not, unlike the occupants of Wells, been able to call in anyone to avert the disaster.

The Sacrist of the monastery at Ely, Alan de Walsingham, seems to have been a man of resource and intelligence. He dared not contemplate another tower of stone, so that some kind of wooden construction would be needed if the cathedral was to preserve the

original plan of a central tower balancing that at the western end.
There is some doubt as to the original designer of the new tower, but
Alan de Walsingham called in a master-carpenter named William
Hurley (later to become the King's Chief Carpenter), and the
remarkable structure which you can see today was perhaps devised
between them in 1334. With immense labour, the area was cleared
and an octagonal tower of wood 74 feet wide was designed. Eight
huge oak beams, 63 feet long, 3 feet 4 inches in width and nearly 3
feet in depth were needed to form the main uprights of the tower.
Eight mighty oak trees were eventually found in Bedfordshire, over
fifty miles away, felled and brought to Ely. To lift these great beams,
each weighing 10 tons, into position on the newly strengthened
vaulting ribs, about 86 feet from the floor might well tax our ingenuity today, in spite of all our mechanical contrivances. Nevertheless it was completed in five years in the fourteenth century, and
the Lantern of Ely, dominating the flat fen landscape, is one of the
most beautiful and one of the most exciting examples of mediaeval
architecture in Europe.

The Lantern was not the only contribution made at this time to the
fabric of Ely cathedral. A year before the tower fell, work had commenced on a superb Lady Chapel, notable for its extremely fine
vaulted roof, 46 feet wide. The Chapel originally contained thousands
of carved figures, mutilated and destroyed, alas, during the Reformation.

The progress of vaulting, from the simple barrel vaults of the
Norman craftsmen to the complexity of the vault of the Lady Chapel
at Ely, and in cathedrals and parish churches all over the country, is a
story of an increasing intricacy of construction and brilliance of
surface decoration which grew quite naturally from that construction.
By the middle of the Decorated Period, the vaults were constructed
from a fine mesh of stone ribs, as delicate proportionately and yet as
strong as the fibrous 'veins' you can see on any skeleton leaf in an
autumn wood. To the ridge ribs and tierceron ribs of the Early
English vault the masons of the Decorated Period added yet another
of their own – the *lierne* rib, which, acting as a bridge between the
structural ribs, added little strength to the construction, but increased
its decorative appearance considerably. The complex geometry of the
vaults is clearly the outcome of the same exuberance which enlivens
so much of the decoration in other parts of the buildings. It is
apparent in the flowing shapes of the window tracery, and in the
enlargement of the window areas as well. It is to be seen in the
undulation of the lines of crockets which flourish on the soaring
buttresses as they withstand the thrust of the intricate vaults
within.

Fig. 13. The lierne vault of the thirteenth and fourteenth centuries

The dog-tooth moulding of the Early English period is now replaced in the new buildings by another called a ball-flower. This resembles somewhat the little bells worn on a baby's reins, strung along a narrow channel. All mouldings are more shallow by comparison with the earlier ones, and this change is particularly marked in those carved on the arches of the nave.

Perhaps the finest example of the transformation which has taken place during the later thirteenth and early fourteenth centuries, however, is to be seen at Southwell Minster in Nottinghamshire. We have mentioned the obvious delight and inspiration given to the artists of this period by their study of natural forms. At Southwell, the richness and variety of natural leaf forms have provided the material for some of the loveliest mediaeval carving in England. The Minster has a Norman nave and an Early English choir, but it is the polygonal Chapter house to which we must go to see this remarkable exhibition of Decorated carving. It is certainly one of the earliest and most modern buildings of its time in this style.

A more detailed analysis of the natural forms adapted and used here as decoration is given in a charming King Penguin, *The Leaves of Southwell* by Professor N. Pevsner. It is sufficient to say that nowhere else could you more enjoyably study this wonderful new liberation of the artist from the shackles of convention than in the Chapter house at Southwell. The carved leaves which provide a ripple of pattern to each of the capitals of the arcading lining the Chapter house are derived from a variety of English plants: from the oak, with its cupped fruit, from the deeply indented leaves of buttercup and hawthorn, from the sharply flattened leaves of the maple, the fretted leaves of the hop, and from others familiar to the mason as he trudged through the English lanes to his lean-to lodge by the side of the Minster.

The conventional leaf of the Early English period also appears from time to time, as though one of the older masons was not entirely in sympathy with this new-fangled naturalism, but in other respects, the whole building, from the ripple of undulating crockets on the arcading to the daring vault, unsupported by a central pillar, which roofs the Chapter house, is alive with a new spirit of modernity – a sense of experiment and of freedom.

This rhythmic quality, this undulating movement, so apparent in the leaves and crockets is typical of the work of the Decorated period. It permeates the magnificent Percy Tomb, in Beverley Minster in Yorkshire, and the great West Window at York Minster, and gave rise to the term curvilinear and flamboyant to describe the flame-like patterning of the tracery. It is used with more restraint in England than in the corresponding period on the continent, where the very structure of the buildings could be threatened by the excessive use of rippling curves, and the stone was fretted into lacy shapes quite unsuitable for the medium. (*Plate 10.*)

This flamboyant quality was not only apparent in details such as windows and tombs. A new form of arch, with a double curve began to appear, possibly from Oriental sources. This is known as an *ogee* or *ogyval* arch, and is to be seen in the lights of the windows, as a decorative outer moulding to doorways and at the head of niches for sacred statues. It was never used structurally, but only as a powerful decorative element to enliven the surface over door and window, and in screens which mark off the tombs or chapels of the nobility from the main body of the church. It has a strangely effeminate quality which contrasts somewhat with the more masculine structural arches, but used with restraint was an invaluable addition to the grace of these huge buildings. The decorative details of this period show an extraordinary sense of fun, a love of the less serious side of life which makes Gothic art so much more human and endearing than the cold aloofness of classical sculpture. Every cathedral has examples of this aspect of the mediaeval artist. At Wells, over Bishop Button's tomb in the south aisle of the quire, a little half figure in a pointed cap grimaces with toothache, plunging a bony finger into his mouth, dragging it into a lopsided leer in an attempt to reach the source of his pain. Bosses high in the vaulted roofs, revealed for the first time by the telephoto lens of a modern camera, show a thousand similar incidents – domestic strife (a sort of mother-in-law joke of the Middle Ages), sly monks taking more than their fair share of the wine, or animals caricaturing the follies and comedies of the human race. This love of the grotesque can be seen in imps and demons who slither from carving to carving among the foliage of the spandrels, or perch precariously on the waterspouts up in the towers. The famous 'Lincoln Imp' is an example of a minor detail which commercial interests have exploited to an unwarrantable degree – most cathedrals could produce imps or demons of equal merit.

One detail, well within reach of everyone, which illustrates admirably the mediaeval sense of fun, is often to be found in the choir stalls, where the original ones have survived. The tip-up seats, known as *misereres* or *misericords*, when turned up reveal small brackets projecting at right angles from the underside. This was a device for giving some support to sick or elderly monks who were unable to endure the long hours of standing during the office. The carving which embellishes these misericord brackets is one of the most delightful sources of mediaeval fun to be seen, and some of the most comic and most charming ones are to be found tucked away in humble parish churches all over the country. They form, in miniature, a social commentary on the period in which they were carved, all too often missed by the casual visitor. Some are of topical significance, others of local interest, but taken as a whole they form a valuable addition to our knowledge of the social life of the Middle Ages. On them you may see a schoolmaster belabouring the bare buttocks of a naughty boy, a housewife chasing a fox out of the poultry yard, or haranguing a pedlar, the scholar at his books, the reaper at the harvest, or a mail-clad knight besieging a castle. There is scarcely any aspect of mediaeval life which does not appear among these carvings and it is sad to find that very often the only person to see them is the verger who gives them a dusting from time to time in the course of his duties. (*Fig. 14.*)

The new spirit which quickened the Decorative period would, of course, not reach the parish church until some time after it had worked its magic in the cathedrals and abbeys.

The rebuilding or remodelling of the parish church was neither possible nor desirable, but the addition of a fine new East window in the flamboyant style, the insertion of a richly carved tomb of the local nobility, the substitution of a new spire to replace the old

Norman tower – these may all be seen in many parts of the country. In the early years of the fourteenth century there can have been few churches free from the chaffinch-like song of the stonemason's hammer ringing out from the mason's lodge newly erected in the churchyard.

Although the earlier broach spire persisted in some districts well into the fourteenth century, it was gradually succeeded by the more ornate *parapet* spire, so called because the junction of spire and tower is hidden by a decorative parapet wall, often with pinnacles at each corner. From these pinnacles, which become increasingly enriched with decoration as the century passed, small flying buttresses leaped to sustain the outward slopes of the spire, which, in turn, were pierced with little gabled windows – perhaps two or three to each of the four faces of the spire which corresponded to the sides of the tower. The tower itself was enriched with carving and the windows embellished with the lithe *ogee* arches.

A certain amount of the new material inserted at this time was, of course, shop work, devised and executed at a central workshop, and then brought to the cathedral or church for erection. Districts with little available wood could be supplied with pre-fabricated timber roofs from others more fortunate. Roofs exist to this day with the numbers carved on them for easy assembly still visible. (We saw one quite recently in York.) Certain centres were notable in mediaeval days for specific crafts. The alabaster carvings for the reredos of many churches abroad, admired by tourists from England, may well have come originally from Nottingham, but specimens of this very lovely carving are all too rare in this country, although some excellent examples are still to be seen in the chapel at Haddon Hall, where they have been repaired and beautifully remounted.

The shafts of Purbeck marble were certainly roughed out if not actually finished near Corfe, in Dorset, before being transported by sea or road, and the masons themselves often travelled from place to place although not so widely, in general, as the French master-mason, Villard de Honnecourt. He journeyed from France to Hungary from about 1220–1235, and compiled a remarkable note-book of architectural and other matters which gradually developed into a treatise on the work of the mason. This notebook is now preserved in the National Library in Paris. The drawings show a mind quick to avail itself of any new architectural ideas he encountered on his travels, and it is clear that men like de Honnecourt were eager to incorporate any new ideas into their buildings. In some cases, the patron who was paying for the building would demand that his church or manor house should resemble another with which he was familiar, and there is plenty of documentary evidence in later

THE MISERERE IN USE

Fig. 14. The miserere or misericord – the bracket which afforded some support to aged or sick monks when the seat was normally tipped back. On the right, the seat down, on the left tipped back to expose the miserere

centuries of this likeness to another existing building being stipulated
in the contract.

The pattern of a mediaeval town was determined by a number of
factors, but the chief focal points of the town are the cathedral or
abbey, the castle, or in some, a combination of both. At Durham the
bishop was not only the spiritual ruler of a great religious community and the citizens attached to it, he was also a prince who kept
a wary eye on the wild Scots just over the border, from his strongly
fortified castle.

Because of the regularity of church services and feasts, and the
focus which the church provided to the social and administrative
activities of the town, the market place was situated near the open
square in front of it. It was on this open space that guild processions
would converge, and where the morality plays were held. It was
natural to find the market under the shadow of the church, for the
merchant knew full well that every member of the population of the
town would attend there regularly, several times in the week. The
market cross itself is not without significance when we are trying to
understand the relationship of church and town. But the market
followed the church, not the church the market.

The mediaeval streets were lined with timber-framed houses with
walls of wattle-and-daub and, more rarely, stone. (Bricks were
uncommon in the fourteenth century.) It is difficult to realise how
much open space there was available in any town in the Middle Ages,
and how very much more agricultural were even such great centres
of commerce as London. With poor communications between cities
(and a certain insularity and local hostility) the town had to depend
on its own sources of food supply, and there had to be ample land for
the grazing of cattle and the growing of crops. The pattern of buildings grouped round an open court which we see in the colleges of
Oxford and Cambridge today would be familiar to the citizen of any
town in the fourteenth century. The town tended to group itself into
trade areas, much as the Casbah at Algiers or the bazaars of Cairo
mark off certain streets for the manufacture and sale of certain goods
– the Street of the Brass workers, and so on. This pattern still persists
even in twentieth-century London. Shoreditch is still largely the
centre of the furniture-making trades, Clerkenwell still markets clocks
and watches, Houndsditch, despite bombing and replanning, is still
the main warehousing area for the clothing trade, and banking is still
carried on in Lombard Street. Bread Street, Milk Street, and a dozen
other names in London remain to remind us of the mediaeval plan.

The streets themselves were lines of communication between the
guild areas and the market place, and their narrow winding ways
intended for pedestrians rather than for wheeled traffic.

Fig. 15. The cruck construction develops. Walls have been added and provide more headroom. On the right, the upper room is supported by jetted timbers – an early form of cantilever

Trades were very much a family affair. The craftsmen and their families, their workmen, and their apprentices, worked together and lived together with little privacy for any of them. As the craftsmen and merchants prospered, the guildhalls and market halls became more imposing, and the shops, finding their sites too cramped for the expanding trade, had to make a choice of either extending to the rear, thereby absorbing essential orchard and grazing land, or growing upwards, for the narrow streets precluded any possibility of development in front.

Houses and shops now appeared with the upper storey jetted outwards. This was done by placing timbers across the lower ceiling, so that a proportion of each timber projected over the street, and then building another room on top. This is the *cantilever* principle so much in use in steel framed buildings today, and like the plank on a seesaw, so long as there was sufficient weight on the rear of the timbers which formed the floors of the new rooms, the forward ends of the rooms were in no danger of tipping into the street. (*Fig. 15.*)

Walls were normally of wattle and daub, so were of little use in bearing the weight of the floors above or of the roof, and the closely spaced timber framing, a development of the earlier cruck construction, was both functional and decorative. Windows were an expensive item, for glass was still comparatively rare, and most people would have to make do with a wickerwork lattice filled with thin sheets of vellum or of horn, and shuttered against the icy wind of winter. The shops were open to the street, so that the customer might see into the workshop beyond and satisfy himself of the standards of craftsmanship and the soundness of materials being used. Houses of two or three jetted storeys produced overhanging eaves which almost roofed the street, and provided additional protection to shopkeepers and their customers from bad weather.

The main danger to any mediaeval city at this time was, of course, fire. Naked lights everywhere, and the open hearths in the houses were a perpetual source of danger. Once out of hand, the flames could devour one house after another, leaping across the closely-knit street with appalling speed, particularly if the roofs were of thatch, or even if they were covered with small tiles of split oak, known as shingles.

Ample supplies of good water were, of course, a basic necessity to any community. It had to be easily accessible entirely within the city walls – not outside where an enemy could deny the use of it to the inhabitants in time of war. Wells in various parts of the town were obviously an advantage, not only as provision against fires, but also in providing a minor social centre. (In small provincial towns on the Continent, the town crier still makes his announcements from the village fountain). Public baths too were social centres, at this time, carrying on the traditional use of the Roman baths until they came to be regarded, with some justification, as centres of both physical and moral infection, and were closed.

Sanitation was not a difficult problem in the small communities of the fourteenth century, and certainly made no demands on the water supply, for human dung, like any other dung, went back into the land, and enriched it, and mingled with the manure of the animals was no more a source of infection or of discomfort in the open fields at the backs of the houses, than the cowyard by the farmhouse today.

But the period which began with such a promise, with this wonderful sense of architectural freedom, and increasing mastery over architectural forms was to receive a blow so heavy that it shook the whole system of government to its foundations. In 1349, a wave of disease, the bubonic plague, swept throughout England, condemning one third of the population to an obscene and dreadful death. It was like a realisation of the grim sequence of woodcuts so often made by the mediaeval artists when they portrayed the 'Dance of Death.' The Black Death slew the baron in the security of his castle, in front of his helpless men-at-arms, the bishop in his palace, the nun at her devotions. It raged through the land, sparing neither freeman nor serf, priest, noble nor commoner. The mason lay by his scattered tools, the stained-glass worker died even as he tended the molten glass, the weaver fell at his loom, his thread snapped, his shuttle stilled.

Entire villages died, and the dead rotted in the open, for there was no one to bury them. The harvest ripened, the heavy ears fell, unreaped, sprouted and grew rank again in the wilderness of weeds. Houses stood roofless, the walls crumbled for lack of the most elementary repairs. It was with the greatest difficulty that men could be found to continue with the great Abbey Church of Westminster or to finish the nave at Winchester. Work ceased entirely at Exeter, where the 'Doom' on the *pulpitum*, just completed, must have seemed to mock the few surviving craftsmen. The windows had to be filled in with wattle and daub, for there were no glass workers left to fashion the glass, and when work was eventually resumed, we are told, nets had to be hung across the chancel arch to keep the pigeons out of the choir.

Two further epidemics, one in 1361 and another in 1364 carried off more craftsmen, but as the century wore on, the numbed circulation of architecture began to stir anew. The old exuberance however, was gone. The next style was more sober and stately than the last, but it was to be more peculiarly English in character than any we have yet seen, and to bring in its train a host of buildings as fine as any in Europe. The new style is known as the Perpendicular style of architecture, and it is to its evolution that we shall devote the next chapter.

Chapter Six

THE PERPENDICULAR PERIOD 1377-1547

M ANY readers will be familiar with the splendid message spoken by the dying John of Gaunt, in Shakespeare's *King Richard II*, which begins

"This royal throne of kings, this sceptred isle,
This earth of majesty, this seat of Mars,
This other Eden, demi-paradise,
This fortress built by Nature for herself
Against infection and the hand of war . . .'

It is quoted by public speakers, for a variety of reasons, in praise of England and her greatness, but few of them ever refer to the end of the passage, and in failing to do this, omit the whole point of the speech. For John of Gaunt, as he lies dying, is contrasting the England he had known 'This happy breed of men' with the England he now saw, to his sorrow

". . . bound in with shame,
With inky blots, and rotten parchment bonds:'

The England of the last quarter of the fourteenth century was indeed but a sickly shadow of the triumphant realm we saw in the Decorated period. There were many reasons for this deterioration. The ravages caused by the Black Death, labour troubles which culminated in the Peasants' Revolt, the inroads on the nation's wealth and manhood made by the incessant and now unsuccessful French wars, the mismanagement of Richard II, and the return of disgruntled nobles with a rabble of well armed but unpaid mercenaries in their train – all these were like a fresh wave of infection attacking a weak and convalescent invalid.

The precarious state of the country is all too apparent in the architecture of the castles, and in the modifications which nobles were obliged to introduce into them. The labour troubles had given feudal lords clear indication that they could no longer rely upon the loyal obedience even of their own people. The presence of the well

78

armed mercenary garrisons, ready to fight for anyone willing to pay them, was now a threat rather than an assurance of security.

Castles were now built with a strong central fortress, not unlike the twelfth century keep, and with a well fortified gatehouse. There was restricted access to these strong points from the outer courtyards and baileys, so that should the very garrison turn mutinous, the lord with his few trusted men-at-arms could control the main entrance to his castle, and could barricade himself in his own quarters until the mutiny had been quelled.

Previously all castles had been designed to repel an attack from without the walls. Now precautions had to be taken to deal with a potential enemy within. Castles constructed during this period are known as castles of livery and maintenance, and fine examples are to be seen at Raglan, in Monmouthshire, at Ashby de la Zouche, in Leicestershire, and at Dunstanburgh in Northumberland. Clifford's Tower, at York, is actually a well designed strong point within the castle walls. More effective techniques of conducting a siege, and the increasingly successful use of gunpowder, were rendering the castle obsolete. It was apparent that the army which held the countryside surrounding the castle effectively controlled the castle and, finally, its occupants as well. Once encirclement was complete, the besieger knew that it could only be a question of time before the garrison of the castle would be obliged to capitulate.

Mere force of arms was in any case being superseded by a more subtle and a more effective weapon – that of political and of ultimately legal power. The mail clad knight with his clumsy method of getting what he wanted by naked aggression was becoming obsolete also. Lands were still annexed, heiresses carried off, rivals still 'liquidated' it is true, but subtle and far-seeing men saw that political power was more important and more lasting than the naked sword. Rival political factions might erupt violently into naked aggression and bloody conflict from time to time, as in the Wars of the Roses, but the ultimate victor in future would not be a warrior-overlord in his craggy fortress but a wise and subtle statesman in his unfortified manor, or a clever merchant-financier in his fine town house.

Buildings which were defensive strongholds for coastal areas still resembled castles, of course, and indeed a few real castles were erected to protect the coasts from piratical attacks launched from across the Channel. One of the last to be built for this purpose is at Bodiam in Sussex. Bodiam Castle, built about 1386 very much in the style of the French castles of the same period has specially designed key-hole shaped openings for cannon and, like the castles of livery and maintenance has quite separate accommodation for its noble occupant and for his retainers. Other castles designed for coastal defence are Cooling Castle in Kent, built about the same time as Bodiam, Hurstmonceux in Sussex (now almost entirely rebuilt and housing the Royal Observatory), Caister-by-Yarmouth, in Norfolk (another 'French' castle) and Dartmouth Castle.

Others wholly designed for coastal defence were to follow. Two more were in Kent at Deal and Walmer, two more in Cornwall, at St Mawes and Pendennis, and another at Hurst in Hampshire, but these are of as little architectural importance as the pill-boxes and strongpoints which dotted our coasts during the last war. As the years pass, the castle as an architectural form no longer has any significance. Certain details, such as the battlements, persisted but merely as a decorative edging to a wall – a romantic relic of the past. Far more important developments in architectural form are to be seen in the additions made to our cathedrals, in the magnificent manor houses built for the newly emerging merchant-aristocracy, and the guildhalls in which they conferred, in the parish churches they financed, the university colleges to which they sent their sons, and the schools they endowed.

We have already referred to the remarkable work of the West Country masons and the ingenious vaulting they evolved at Wells. Another unorthodox example of their work is to be seen at Bristol Cathedral, in the aisles which flank the nave. From each pier, the aisle is spanned by a great beam of stone, held in position by a pointed arch. From the centre of these beams springs a fan of stone ribs, rising to support the main central rib which runs the length of the aisle. This ability to transfer the thrust of the roof above by an ingenious system of ribs is characteristic of the Perpendicular period, although the method used here is unique.

All over the country however, masons were realising that so long as the thrust was transferred from rib to arch, and from arch to buttress, even larger areas of wall could be dispensed with, and even larger windows inserted in their place.

One of the earliest examples of this principle may be seen at Gloucester, in the choir. After the barbarous murder of Edward II at Berkeley Castle in 1327, his body was brought for burial to Gloucester and the enterprising Abbot Thokey set to work to rebuild the choir as a fitting shrine for the relics of the martyred king. Helped by Edward III and enriched by the gifts of many pilgrims, the abbot and his architect, Adam de Staunton, erected the graceful choir which we now see. The lightness and the delicacy of the white Cheltenham stone contrasts strongly with the existing Norman work. The stone is pared and fitted with an airy grace, the wide-framed windows of the clerestory leading inevitably to the vast East window

1. The Parthenon, Athens. 447–432 B.C. Architects, Ictinus and Callicrates. About 228 feet long and 100 feet wide. The refinement with which this exquisite casket was built embodies all the 'glory that was Greece'

2. The Pantheon, Rome. A.D. 120–124. Erected by the Emperor Hadrian. The dome, deeply coffered, is of brickwork and thick mortar, about 142 feet in diameter, and had a profound influence on English eighteenth century design. Now S. Maria ad Martyres

3.   Church of St Andrew, Greensted-juxta-Ongar, Essex. Saxon. The only surviving Saxon timber nave. (Foundation of brick is modern.) The architecture of a log cabin

4.   Earl's Barton Church, Northants. A.D. *c*. 1000. Stone built but suggestive of early timber buildings. Note Long and Short quoins

5. Castle Hedingham,
Essex. The Banqueting Hall.
A heavily fortified home
built at the end of twelfth
century. Note zig-zag
mouldings to doors and
fireplace

6. Chapel of St John,
the Tower of London
c. 1070–1138.
The massive simplicity of
Norman architecture.
Note the scalloped capitals
and groined vault

7 and 8. The Chapter House, Lincoln. *c.* 1235. The exterior shows the flying buttresses which contain the thrust of the interior ribs. (right) The polygonal plan with central pier from which the main ribs spring

9. The spandrels in the chancel of St Mary, Stone, near Gravesend, Kent. The lobed leaves are typical of Early English carved decoration

10. The Percy Tomb, Beverley Minster, Yorks. *c.* 1345. A magnificent
example of the vitality of the Decorated period. Notice the ogee or
ogyval arch and the enrichment of the cusps, and, in the background,
the severity of the Early English vault and mouldings

11. The Church of Ss Peter and Paul, Lavenham, Suffolk, 1485–1525. A typical 'wool' church of the Eastern counties, the walls being reduced to a minimum and the thrust of the roof held by buttresses

12. A scale model of a portion of the roof of Westminster Hall. The original roof, designed by Hugh Herland, *c.* 1395–96, covers an area of about half an acre

13. The Rood Screen of the church of St John the Baptist, Plymtree, Devon. A masterly piece of wood carving of the Perpendicular period

14. King's College Chapel, Cambridge, 1446–1515. The ante-chapel looking west. The triumphant climax of the Perpendicular Gothic period, culminating in the fan vault

15. Oxburgh Castle, Norfolk. *c.* 1482. A moated manor house of brick.
Note the retention of castle turrets, the Flemish influence in gables, the
multiplicity of chimneys, and the oriel windows

16. The church of Holy Trinity, Stratford-upon-Avon. The chancel, like a
great stone birdcage, contains Shakespeare's tomb (left-hand side by the
door). A magnificent church of the fifteenth century

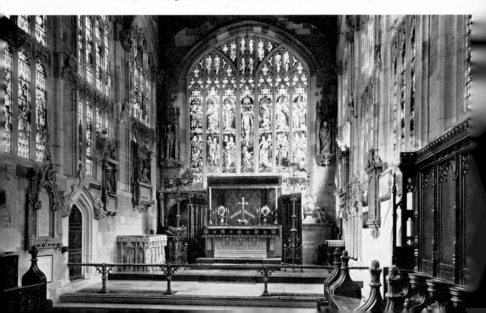

– the largest window in England. As with all Perpendicular work, the capitals which surmount the columns are simple, and much smaller in proportion than those of other periods, so that the eye is only checked momentarily before sweeping on to the splendid lierne vault soaring above. The East window itself is not flat, but has a wing on either side, set in at an angle, and the whole area of glass thus achieved is over 2,700 square feet. It is stated to be a war memorial to the men who fell in the Battle of Crecy. Few war memorials can be so impressive.

Still further to the east, behind this huge window, later abbots built the Lady Chapel, as light and as airy in construction as the choir – a great stone birdcage, with walls virtually of glass, with the most slender supports of stone – built between 1457 and 1498, when the Perpendicular period had reached full maturity. The western end of the Lady Chapel is spanned by a flattened arch bearing on its back a light framework which, whilst it bears the weight of the roof above, is so open in construction that it does not rob the light from the great East window facing it.

Fine work of the Perpendicular period is not, of course, confined to the West Country. The mastery of the new style may well have been anticipated by the mighty lantern tower at Ely, and by the designer of the Chapter House and Cloister at Old St Paul's, which was destroyed in the Great Fire of London, but it is at Gloucester that we can best study the evolution of this remarkable style, which lasted nearly two hundred years in all, and it was at Tewkesbury and at Gloucester that the earliest form of a new kind of vaulting first made its appearance.

As we have seen, the story of the English vault is one in which the system of ribs becomes increasingly complicated. The Norman groined vault became a ribbed vault. The Early English builders took the round arch and ribbed vault of the Normans, changed the shape of the arch, and developed the system of rib construction beyond anything visualised by their Norman ancestors, adding a central ridge rib, and later, the beautiful tiercerons. Yet more ribs – the liernes – were built into the vault during the Decorated period. In the Perpendicular period, we find the masons at Gloucester developing a pattern of ribs so complex that the skeleton of the vault is now concealed by a series of cone-shaped masses of enmeshed stone ribs, springing upwards fanwise from the diminished capitals, and linking with each other at the very top of the vault. This *fan-vaulting* or *fan-tracery* is the final achievement of the mediaeval vault builder, and requires such skill, that it is rarely seen in any church other than a great cathedral or abbey church, although it may appear as a decorative feature in some of the more elaborate tombs in the larger parish churches. It is here, in the cloister at Gloucester that it first made its appearance.

The windows which form the outer wall of the cloister are built with tracery not unlike that of the flamboyant or curvilinear tracery of the last period, but with one important difference. All windows of any size must have vertical members known as *mullions* to form the various window lights. In the Perpendicular period, however, a horizontal member is now seen, forming a cross bar and giving the window a somewhat gridiron appearance, particularly where the windows are large enough to warrant more than one horizontal bar. These bars are known as *transoms* and do not appear in any window until the Perpendicular period. (It is a little odd that the most certain method of identifying a window of the Perpendicular period is by its horizontal bars!)

The South wall of the cloister is divided into twenty small compartments known as *carrells*. Each carrell is, in effect, a small cell, large enough to contain a monk and his desk, for it was here that many lovely manuscripts were written, when the Benedictine monks occupied the cloisters and ran their *scriptorium* there. A *lavatorium* for the monks to wash in, and the stone cupboard for a dry towel, is still to be seen in the northern part of the cloister.

Work at Bristol and in the retrochoir at Wells demonstrate the marked emphasis on the vertical line which gave the name Perpendicular to this last and most particularly English style of Gothic architecture.

At Winchester, as early as 1346, Bishop Edington, a friend of the Black Prince, and later Chancellor of England for ten years, decided on the complete modernisation of the old Norman cathedral, and was able to see the West front redesigned before his death.

The magnificent new nave, however, was the work of his famous successor, William of Wykeham and of his master mason, William Wynford.

William of Wykeham was particularly well qualified for the huge task of reconstruction which lay before him. He had been presented to Edward III at the age of 23, we are told, 'with no other advantage than his skill in architecture.' As a layman he had been clerk of the King's works at Windsor, and a surveyor, too.

It was as Clerk of the Works that he had worked with the great Henry Yevele, the King's Mason, in the building of Queenborough Castle, on the Isle of Sheppey – a most important fortification guarding the Thames Estuary from French marauders, and he is believed to have assisted in the enlargement and strengthening of castles at Dover, at Porchester and at Winchester. His association with Henry Yevele was to be a valuable one to them both, as we shall see later. William of Wykeham had in fact been a priest only five years when he was ordained Bishop of Winchester.

His task at Winchester was a forbidding one, but with his wide experience in architectural matters, and with a fine master mason, William Wynford, to help him, he embarked on a major reconstruction of the nave.

The weight of the huge squat Norman tower had to be sustained whatever alterations took place under its massive walls. The new design necessitated the destruction of the entire Norman triforium and arches of the nave, and the grafting of high-soaring Perpendicular arches on to the old structure, channelling the mighty columns to receive the delicate shallow mouldings of the new style. The Norman work was encased within a shell of newly cut stone imported from Caen, which gave the whole of the interior of the nave an entirely modern appearance – Perpendicular in style, but Norman at the core.

The whole operation took about ten years, and the transformation resulted in one of the most impressive naves in any cathedral in this country. The shallow rectilinear carving on the piers, and the low relief carving which links bay to bay, the sweep of the wide arches unrestricted by any *triforium* and the light graceful quality of the whole structure all combine to give the visitor a sense of wonder and exultation as his eye is drawn irresistibly up the slender verticals to the lierne vault above. It is possible that the lierne vault itself was incomplete when William of Wykeham was laid in the splendid tomb which we can see today in Winchester Cathedral, but his successors carried out the superb design, and the impressive nave, one of the longest in Europe, is a completely unified whole.

Only the Norman work to be seen in the North transept betrays the presence of the earlier structure under the airy Perpendicular surface, and it is here that you can see how much spaciousness and grace William of Wykeham and his craftsmen achieved by removing the *triforium* and replacing it with the present arches.

It is significant that William of Wykeham was not only concerned with the fabric of the cathedral. He busied himself with reform in the cathedral itself, and with an enquiry into the maladministration of the Hospital of St Cross nearby. Masters had been misusing the funds of these almshouses which had been founded for the benefit of 'thirteen poor impotent men' and a number of poor scholars, and William of Wykeham secured a Papal bull ordering the use of the revenues for the benefit of the poor. Perhaps his most important contribution, however, was the foundation of Winchester College, in 1382, and, four years later, the building of New College, Oxford.

As we have said before, the main differences between mediaeval buildings of one kind and another is to be found in the plans, not in the details. Doors and windows, pillars and buttresses are much the same wherever they are found. The outer gateway at Winchester College, with its widely projecting buttresses and its flattened arch, is typical architecturally of a hundred doorways erected about the same time, for quite different kinds of buildings – a barn, a gatehouse, an almshouse, or a university college. This point is made here, since some of the most violent critics of the architecture of our own day deride it because they declare that schools resemble factories, hospitals blocks of flats, and so on. Both the resemblance and the criticism is superficial – an examination of the plan would reveal a wide difference – but too few people, of course, are willing to examine the way in which a building is planned – it is far easier to glance at external detail and then write a scathing letter to the newspapers.

No such difficulty seems to have been encountered by the mediaeval architect, and buildings were sometimes specifically ordered by the client to resemble those he had seen and admired elsewhere. The important point is that a building had to look well, and work well. If old materials had to be incorporated into the building, it had to be done with dignity and care, for good manners are as essential in architecture as anywhere else, and the tactful way in which many of our parish churches have been changed from style to style are a tribute to the good sense and good manners of the anonymous builders of the Middle Ages.

Before we deal with the remarkable developments which took place in our parish churches, we must, however, consider the work of the architect whose work at Westminster Abbey, at Canterbury Cathedral, and elsewhere, was to have a profound effect on the course of the history of the architecture of the Perpendicular period.

His name was Henry Yevele, his origin and early training obscure, but he survived the Black Death which killed the King's master mason, Master William of Ramsey, quickly came to the fore during the troublous times which followed, and, like his friend and associate Geoffrey Chaucer, eventually emerged as one of the most important figures of the day in his own particular profession.

By 1359 he was at work at Kennington Palace in Surrey for the Black Prince, and later we find him at the Tower of London and at the Palace of Westminster.

In 1361 he designed Queenborough Castle, on the Isle of Sheppey, for which important commission he collaborated with William of Wykeham who was Clerk of the Works; this association was to result in a lifelong friendship with that great and powerful man.

The following year, Yevele was back at Westminster, rebuilding the nave, restraining his own design so that it should harmonise with the existing fabric of the building and so that there should not be too obvious a difference between the old style and the new one. (A practical application of the famous motto of his friend, William of Wykeham – 'Manners makyth Man').

After several busy years during which he travelled all over the country on the King's business – sometimes impressing masons for the Royal works – we find him designing the Charterhouse, priory for the Carthusian monks in London, as a private commission; then off to deal with the problems of defence again, this time at Cowling (now Cooling) Castle in Kent. Although he had been associated with Geoffrey Chaucer at the Court of Westminster, there does not appear to have been any professional connection between the two men until Chaucer was appointed Clerk of Works in 1389. After that there is plenty of documentary evidence of their working together. Much of the architecture is attributed to Henry Yevele only because of the resemblance it bears to the style of buildings known to have been designed by him. This kind of guesswork is not nearly so doubtful as it might at first appear. Any great artist has an individual style of his own. Even the ordinary layman who would profess to know little about painting would not have much difficulty in detecting a painting by Van Gogh, for example, in an exhibition of other paintings of the same period. In exactly the same way, scholars as expert in architectural matters as Dr John Harvey are able to detect the 'architectural brushwork' as it were, of an outstanding architect, even if there is little or no documentary evidence to support their statements.

It is thought that Yevele was engaged to convert a part of the Crypt of Canterbury Cathedral into a chapel for his patron, the Black Prince, some five years after the work at Kennington Palace of which mention has already been made. The major work at this cathedral for which he was responsible was undertaken much later, in 1377 and 1381, when he redesigned the side walls of the aisles flanking the nave. Later still, he undertook the reconstruction of the nave itself, sweeping away all that remained of Lanfranc's Norman work, and substituting the lofty Perpendicular Gothic nave we see today. As with William of Wykeham's nave at Winchester, the absence of the triforium, and the added height of the nave arches which reach almost to the base of the clerestory itself, creates an inspiring upward movement which is brought to a triumphant climax in the beautifully proportioned lierne roof above.

By 1393, Henry Yevele, in the closing years of his life, undertook yet another remarkable building, even whilst Canterbury was as yet incomplete. This was the re-planning and the re-designing of Westminster Hall. The Hall was, of course, a very ancient building, having been erected originally for William Rufus some thirty years after the Norman Conquest. It was about 23 yards wide and 76 yards long but the vast area was divided into three aisles by rows of timber pillars sustaining the weight of the flat Norman roof. (If you think of it in terms of an ordinary cricket pitch, you will see that it is about three times as long as the cricket pitch, and almost exactly one pitch wide.) Such an area presented a formidable problem in vaulting. Yevele evidently decided against a lierne vault of stone, and instead, to- gether with Hugh Herland, the Royal Carpenter, devised a wooden roof without any supports from below – the vast timber construction which spans the Hall today. At the same time, the narrow Norman windows on either side were cut away and light airy Perpendicular windows inserted in the walls instead. At the south end of the Hall, a vast Perpendicular window occupies almost the whole of the wall, its mullioned and transomed surface lighting the main body of the hall. The main feature of the new design, however, is the superb roof erected by Hugh Herland, spanning the lofty hall, and making it one of the most impressive buildings in England. (*Plate 12.*)

Nowhere in Europe will you find timbered roofs to match those fashioned in England during the Perpendicular period. They are the glory of many parish churches in every part of England, and here in London is the greatest of all – this magnificent *hammerbeam* roof which was to be the inspiration of many mediaeval architects and woodworkers from then on. There is much to be admired in West- minster Hall – the carved kings in the niches, the exquisitely chiselled badges of Richard II (the White Hart), which decorate the walls, but all is subordinated to the glory of the roof.

As Dr John Harvey says in his book *Henry Yevele* 'The remarkable thing about Yevele, and it is the very kernel of his greatness, is that he did for our architecture what Chaucer did for our language, giving to it a special character which was altogether national, even though it was part of a common European heritage, like the other arts and sciences.'

It is not only the great cathedrals, however, or even palaces, with which a book of this kind should be concerned. As we have said, the glory of the English Perpendicular architecture is to be found in the many splendid parish churches in every part of the country. Fine architecture is not confined to work commissioned or encouraged by princes of the Church or of the state – it is to be found among many buildings paid for and erected by members of the solid English middle-class who were exerting an increasingly important influence on the pattern of events. It is to be seen in the growth of splendid guild halls – at Norwich and at King's Lynn, and elsewhere, in the luxurious but not ostentatious manor houses which dotted the countryside and above all in the parish churches in village and town erected during the boom of prosperity which arrived on the fleecy backs of English sheep. Wherever the flocks multiplied, wherever wool could be combed and spun, there you will find the evidence of England's architectural wealth too. The story is to be read in the exquisite pages written for us along the valley of the Stour – enriched with names such as Clare and Cavendish, Long Melford and Lavenham, Saffron Walden and Stoke-by-Nayland. It is trumpeted from the high towers which dominate the flat land of the fens – from the noble tower of Terrington St Clement to the ignobly named 'Boston Stump,' and from St Neots in Huntingdonshire to Chipping Campden in the Cotswolds. Never has there been such a spate of remarkable architecture, and never have men built more truly to the glory of God than in the few years which preceded the Reformation. And the churches were as magnificent within as they appeared from without. Despite the onslaughts of Reformer and Puritan, and the scarcely less disastrous hand of the Victorian 'restorer,' they still constitute a record of architectural vigour unrivalled in Europe. Nowhere will you find timber roofs to match those at Needham Market, Wethersden, Mildenhall, or Grundisborough, in Suffolk, at March in Cambridgeshire or at Wells in Somerset.

Examine those screens at Plymtree and Bovey Tracey in Devon which have survived the malice of the Reformer, or the relentless attack of the deathwatch beetle. It is doubtful whether such works as these could have been carried out had they not been commissioned and paid for by a general public who felt that there was no better way of laying out their wealth than by the enrichment of the church in which they worshipped. England was a nation of farmers and traders, then as now, but never has it refuted more emphatically the charge that it was that and nothing more than during the Perpendicular period.

Many parish churches, of course, were built entirely during this period, and are therefore wholly in the Perpendicular style. The plan is cruciform, as before. Smaller chapels, behind exquisite screens called *parcloses*, were reserved for the private worship, and perhaps for the tombs of particularly wealthy families.

Undoubtedly the most striking feature of the interior of a church of this period, however, is the superb timber roof. Timber roofs had been in use since the Saxon period, either as a substitute for the stone vaulting, or as a humble wooden framework to which the roofing materials could be fastened, and therefore concealed from the body of the church by the stone vaults.

A large area of tiles, slate or thatch weighs many tons, and the thrust of this weight on the walls is largely outwards, as well as downwards. A simple experiment which our readers may care to carry out using an open book for the roof and a couple of ordinary bricks as the walls will demonstrate, in miniature, the problem with which our mediaeval builder was confronted. The spine of the book represents the ridge of the roof, the covers of the book, the rafters, and the bricks, the walls on which the roof is to rest. You will find that there is a strong outward thrust exerted by the covers of the book – a thrust sufficient to push the 'walls' outwards unless they are very robust. To contain this outward thrust, the mediaeval builder tied the outer edges of the rafters together at intervals, locking the roof into a rigid frame by a series of horizontal beams spanning the whole church. This is the most simple form of *tie-beam* roof. More elaborate tie-beam roofs may have vertical members standing on these beams and giving additional support to the roof whilst other churches are roofed by a more complicated series of cross braces, forming a rigid truss. This framework, known as a *trussed rafter* roof, may be partly or wholly ceiled with planking, or may be elaborately carved and painted. In later roofs the braces are curved, and extend some distance down the wall, transmitting the thrust further down and minimizing it by distributing it over a vertical area of wall, where it could be held more readily by a buttress. (*Fig. 7.*)

By the end of the fourteenth century, the most splendid of all these timber roofs had been evolved – the hammerbeam roof – which, with elaborate variations, rivalled in wood the splendour of the lierne vaulting which was the finest achievement of the stonemason. Like its predecessor, the trussed rafter roof, the hammerbeam roof dispenses with the horizontal tie-beam, transmitting the thrust down the wall by a series of interlocked brackets, the last of each series coming to rest on a stone projection known as a *corbel*. This projection is the end of a beam of stone embedded in the main fabric of the wall. (*Plate 12.*)

We have already referred to Hugh Herland, the Royal Carpenter and his hammerbeam roof which spans Westminster Hall. In many parish churches you will find other roofs of this kind, smaller in scale but in no way inferior in design and construction. Double hammerbeam roofs are to be seen in churches at Wethersden, in Suffolk, at Knapton, in Norfolk, and in many other Perpendicular churches, intricately and beautifully carved, drawing the eye irresistibly upwards. The hammerbeam roof is the final achievement of the craftsmen of this richly endowed period, and, we may add, like the timber from which it was fashioned, it is a native product owing nothing to foreign examples or alien influences.

We have referred to the screens which still adorn some parish churches. These are known as *rood screens*, for upon the main beam which spanned the chancel arch was erected a *rood* or cross. The rood screen often had a kind of balcony transforming it into a rood loft, and reached by a small door and a flight of steps cut in the thickness of the piers from which the chancel arch sprang. (*Plate 13.*)

Even when the rood screen has long since been destroyed you may still see, some 10 feet from the ground, the shape of the door, now filled in, but still visible to those who know where to look for it. The richness of carving of the screen is echoed not only in the choirstalls, but in the end panels of the benches in which some of the congregation sat (as at Higher Bickerton, in Devon), and in other pieces of church furniture in many parish churches.

Fonts are covered with high steepling canopies, ornately carved and raised by a counterpoise, and carving decorates the few pulpits of the period which have survived. Most of the subjects chosen are, of course, religious incidents in the lives of the saints, or simple Bible stories, but a surprisingly large number of Gothic carvers portrayed incidents in everyday life. We have the seed time, the harvest, and the bagpiper at the harvest home which followed. The shepherd tends his sheep, the wool is sheared, and marketed, the good wife haggles with the pedlar and the weaknesses and follies of one's betters are exposed and derided. The wayward priest, or the worldly churchman, may appear as a fox or a swine preaching to a congregation of geese, and for every character portrayed so beautifully and with such a sense of fun in the *Canterbury Tales* you may find a dozen such in parish churches in every corner of England.

It is to the windows and to the walls, however, that we should have turned, had we been visiting a parish church in the fifteenth century, for it is there that we should have found our main source of pictorial enjoyment. In the few precious fragments which are now left to us, we can glimpse something of the treasure so wantonly destroyed during the Reformation.

In Italy, architects found it necessary to limit the size of windows in order to keep their churches cool in the blinding heat of a Mediterranean summer. The result is a concentration on the wide wall surfaces for picture-making, and a diminished use of stained glass. We, in England, in colder and more cloudy regions, as in Northern France, in Flanders found it more necessary to enlarge the window spaces at the expense of the wall – to let the light in, not to keep it out. Although we also indulged in mural painting to a degree not normally appreciated these days, it was to the window with its stained and painted glass that we turned for the enrichment of the church and for the presentation of the Bible stories. Early painting and glass preserved at Canterbury Cathedral show how richly even the Norman churches were decorated, but not even Canterbury or York can give as true an impression of what the stained glass could do for a parish church as surely as one in Gloucestershire which has miraculously preserved its original set of windows. We refer to Fairford Church – a 'wool' church rich in mediaeval stained glass. Tourists come from miles to gaze at its magnificent ruby reds, its deep blues, and its gentle yellows across which the mediaeval painter drew his flexible brush. The sensitive point follows the sinuous lines of the dark lead, giving rhythmic swirls to the robes of saints, the flowing hair of the happy souls who had come to claim their reward in heaven, and emphasising the anguished contortions of the damned as they plunge headlong to the torments of Hell, pursued by painted demons with pitchforks.

When we describe Fairford Church as a typical 'wool' church, it must be understood that it is a generalisation only as true as that of 'the average man.' Every church was unique. Visit Northleach, Cirencester, or Winchcombe in Gloucestershire, or Long Melford or Lavenham in Suffolk, and you will find that they have much in common, but there is a local dialect in architecture as in any other means of expression, and although all have the insistence on a strong upward line, and flattened arches to the wide windows, it is always difficult to define a typical Perpendicular church. Many were built entirely afresh, the older shabbier structure being 'cannibalised' to provide material for the grand new church. Others – and Fairford is one of these – still bear traces of the earlier church as though the builders were reluctant to destroy the fabric which had been so laboriously fashioned by their forefathers. They felt it necessary to graft the new structure on to the old building, with reticence and restraint, even though it meant considerable modification of their own plans.

Fairford Church is typical therefore of many 'wool' churches in having an imposing West porch, a magnificent timbered roof, a carved rood screen, now destroyed, which used to span the chancel arch (a parish church equivalent of the screen or pulpitum normally found in a cathedral or abbey church) and a set of widely arched windows with the familiar grid pattern produced by the mullions and transoms. The columns which support the roof have shallow mouldings and simple, rather small capitals, and the widely projecting buttresses, seen from outside, proclaim the presence of the arches within whose thrust they convey to the ground. As in all 'wool' churches, there is an emphatic statement of structure. The bones of the building are not hidden behind a mass of superficial detail (unlike so many buildings of our own time where the steel structure is dressed up in pseudo-Georgian columns which support nothing) but are frankly accepted and possess a functional beauty. To look at a church of this period recalls a phrase which was used to describe the features of a Red Indian in *The Inheritors:* 'And you could see the bones – and the bones were beautiful.'

The pinnacles which decorate the buttresses have also a functional purpose – they provide additional weight and pin the buttress more firmly to the ground. A 'wool' church is like a great stone birdcage, and the walls, so massive in a Norman church, are now but slender frames to contain the mighty windows. Walk into a church of this period, if you can, in full moonlight and you will wonder at the proportion of space to structure which has endured so long.

Fairford is also typical of many churches of this time in having been built with money provided by a pious and prosperous wool merchant; in this instance a certain John Tame whose coat of arms, a wyvern and a lion, are to be seen in the main porch and again on the memorial brass which is let in the slab which forms the top of his tomb.

Memorial brasses are by no means confined to the Perpendicular period, for it had been the custom for nearly three hundred years to engrave a plate of *latoun* (or *latten* – a mediaeval alloy somewhat resembling brass) with a symbol of the knight and his lady inlaid to form a decoration to the top of the tomb in which they were lying. The symbols – for they made no pretence of being portraits of the deceased – provide the most authentic record of costume, armour and heraldic devices from late Norman times to the seventeenth century, and many parish churches still retain a limited number of these figures. As the warrior knight began to be superseded by other rulers, they too are represented in brasses, and scholars, lawyers, merchants and even architects appear with their wives on the tomb covers. Churchmen of course are represented at all times in the full dignity of their robes. Finally, those men who were dubbed knight for services to the Court or State, but who had never drawn a sword in battle, are nonetheless represented in armour: such men as Sir William Harpur, at one time Lord Mayor of London, and the founder of Bedford School, show that the old nobility which bled itself to death in the Wars of the Roses, was being replaced by others in the government of the country. A new middle class was taking the reins of government and shaping the pattern of English history.

Many of the brasses and the stained glass show Flemish influence, for strong trade connections with Flanders and the religious persecution which sent Flemings to seek refuge in this country all helped to enrich the native artist's tongue with a continental vocabulary. The craft of brick-making, almost extinct in this country from Roman times was revived by the craftsmen building the manor houses and developed by Flemish émigrés. Of this we shall say more later. From time to time you will find tombs erected on the south wall of the chancel, their sides carved with the representation of Christ emerging from his tomb, stepping over the sleeping soldiers who are supposed to have been guarding his body, and flanked by adoring angels. This kind of tomb, often with an elaborately carved canopy, is known as an Easter sepulchre and formed the central feature of the ritual which the mediaeval church conducted every Easter. An image of Christ, (which might be a carved or painted representation of Our Lord) was veiled and placed upon the flat top of the tomb. Monks kept constant vigil with it until the dawn of Easter Day. The whole village would assemble very early in the morning and as the veils were removed from the image, to symbolise the risen Christ, the doors of the church were opened to admit the worshippers, rejoicing at the triumph of Christ over death. Easter sepulchres can still be seen in some parts of the country, at East Kirby, Honington and Navenby in Lincolnshire, at Hawton in Nottinghamshire, at Bampton in Oxfordshire, at Cobham in Kent (which also possesses a superb collection of monumental brasses) and elsewhere.

Still more elaborate tombs are to be seen in other churches. Wherever local stone and craftsmen were available, full length figures appeared carved in the round and glowing with colour enclosed in beautifully screened chapels. Bright with heraldic ornament, they followed much the same pattern as the magnificent tomb of Edward the Black Prince which is still one of the glories of Canterbury Cathedral. The nobleman, or merchant – for it could now be the same man – was carved in robes of office or clad in full armour, lying beside his wife, their eyes fixed on Heaven, their hands pressed together in perpetual prayer. Often the tombs were designed with canopies above supported on columns of contemporary architecture, and vaulted with a lierne or fan vault which reproduced, if only in miniature, the lofty vaulting of the church in which they were housed.

Whilst it was feasible to have the interior of the churches of this period enriched with colour and with gilding, it was not, of course, so easily done on the exterior, where this climate of ours would seek out and destroy anything but the most permanent form of ornament. A very lovely form of decoration was therefore introduced by alternating different types of stone, giving an enriched draughtboard pattern to the walls themselves. This was not confined to church architecture. The Guildhall at Norwich shares this alternation of stone and flint with the many remarkable churches of the city, and it appears too, in King's Lynn, to mention only a few of the many examples available. A still more lovely version of this pattern work is to be seen at Long Melford, in Suffolk, in one of the most notable of the 'wool' churches. The windows themselves form a grey pattern against the stone, their Perpendicular tracery endowing the wall with a lace-like texture. A wall which for practical reasons could not be pierced with windows, would, if left blank, jar badly in so harmoniously designed an elevation. The builders of Long Melford church have therefore continued in stonework a pattern very similar to that provided by the real windows, but the 'window' tracery is built from an ordinary stone, and the 'glass' is suggested by inlaying the areas with grey flint. This device combines blank wall and real windows into a beautifully unified design.

Before we leave the 'wool' churches – the last churches to be built before the catastrophe of the Reformation – mention must be made of the magnificence of their towers. With such notable exceptions as Louth Church in Lincolnshire, the majority of the churches of the Perpendicular period abandon the spire in favour of a mighty square tower, rising majestically in beautifully proportioned stories, diminishing as they ascend, and topped by a lacework crown of pierced and fretted battlements. The same accent on the vertical, the same lightness of carved panelling, the same airy transomed windows are to be seen in the towers as within the church, and the powerfully constructed buttresses at the corners proclaim their functional purpose even as they enhance the decorative beauty of the panelled wall whose weight they contain. These splendid towers are to be found in almost every county in England – each with its own peculiar charm. One of the loveliest is to be seen dominating the market place at St Neots in Huntingdonshire, but no doubt readers from Somerset would stoutly uphold the superiority of the tower at Huish Episcopi or St Cuthbert's at Wells, Devon men vote for West Alvington, and Gloucestershire men maintain the mighty tower at Cirencester against all comers.

As has been shown, many of the 'wool' churches were built wholly during the Perpendicular period. There is a unity of style both within the church and without – nave, aisles – roof, columns – all are of the same style of architecture. Nevertheless, for various reasons, many churches far too solid and admirably maintained to be pulled down and rebuilt, received considerable additions at this time. The squat Norman tower would be redesigned and strengthened with new buttresses to receive light graceful windows, an extra storey or two would be added to house the new peal of bells endowed by some local merchant, and the top of the tower crowned by some of the fine pierced and fretted battlements so popular at that time. The deep-set Norman door would be enclosed in a modern porch, with a vaulted roof to carry the lofty chamber above in which a guild might meet, and the narrow lancets which graced the aisles might be replaced by the wide flattened arches of the transomed Perpendicular windows.

The early fragmented glass would give way to the clear light areas of the more ambitious sheets now manufactured some distance away and brought at great expense to enrich the old church.

Within, the old Saxon or Norman font would receive its new steepling font cover, carved by the same craftsman who had replaced the flat timber roof with a magnificent new hammerbeam construction, its flutter of gilded angels gazing down on the wondering congregation, its weight being borne by the Early English columns, but held by a new system of buttresses which frame the new aisle windows, outside. A fine new chapel, also with a carved and gilded screen, would enclose private pews for the family worship of one of the wealthy merchants, or a colourfully ornamented tomb. If the church had possessed an old Norman apse, or slender lancet windows behind the altar, these might all be swept away to give place to a superb Perpendicular East window embodying perhaps the coat of arms or the trade mark of the man who had furnished the money for so splendid an addition to their parish church.

Thus the parish churches, whether wholly new or skilfully rebuilt reflected the richness of invention and the fertility of design of the architects and craftsmen of the period in which they flourished immediately before the Reformation. It is a sad reflection on modern society that these churches are, in many cases, in danger of disappearing from lack of adequate funds to protect their fabric from the ravages of dry rot, the death watch beetle, and the relentless erosion of industrial fumes. If we are to preserve these precious examples of our architectural inheritance, we shall have to make a more significant contribution to their upkeep than a series of valiant 'Bring-and-Buy' stalls or 'Beetle' drives, or a furtive copper in the freewill offering box before the coach resumes its journey to the holiday camp. The parish churches of England suffered grievously during the Reformation and the Civil War, but they did survive. It would be ironical if our apathy should succeed in destroying them where the most fanatical of Reformers and Puritans so signally failed.

The same richness of invention shown in the parish churches is even more apparent in the additions to the great abbey churches and cathedrals at this time, where their greater wealth and the influence exerted by the powerful churchmen in control, enabled them to call upon the services of the best craftsmen and designers in the country. Many of them were only enriched by details added to the main structure – a splendid chapel or a new East window – but some notable examples underwent considerable reconstruction.

We have already commented on the beauty of the church towers of the West country, but we have left until last one which is certainly the most inspiring of them all – that which graces Gloucester Cathedral. Earlier than the famous Lady Chapel, it has the same graceful panelling in stone and the same *ogee* or *ogyval* arches enclosed by the rigid geometry of the buttresses. It is so beautifully proportioned that it is difficult to realise that any of the pinnacles with which the corners are surmounted would itself be large enough to form a whole tower on an ordinary parish church. (*Frontispiece.*)

A similar perfection of proportion may be observed in the central tower of Worcester Cathedral, in the Chapter House at Wells, and in the new retrochoir at Peterborough, to name only a few of the additions to our cathedrals made within a few years of each other, at this time.

At Norwich, the architects were confronted by a mighty Norman nave, upon which they proceeded to erect, with extraordinary skill and sensitivity, a modern lierne vault, making it spring quite naturally from the 300-year-old structure, effecting a complete harmony between the old and the new parts of the building. A little later – about 1472 – the apse at the East end behind the altar was reshaped, an upper storey of Perpendicular windows appearing above the existing Norman ones, and the whole was crowned with an intricate lierne vault, forming an almost dome-like roof.

Perhaps the most beautiful of all these later additions, however, is to be seen at Canterbury where the new 235-foot tower still dominates the whole impressive interior, and indeed the whole city. This tower had been under discussion for some time, and preparations to enable the existing structure to bear the additional weight had already been made early in the fifteenth century, but it was not until August 4th, 1433, that work to the designs of John Wastell actually began.

We quote from a letter written by Prior Selling to Cardinal Archbishop Morton published in *Portrait of Canterbury Cathedral*. It reads: 'Most reverend father in God, the master-surveyor and I have communed with John Wastell, your mason, bearer hereof, to preserve what form and shape he will keep in raising the pinnacles of them. . . .'

This graceful tower, known as the Angel Steeple because of the gilded angel which originally surmounted one of its pinnacles, is as lovely today as it was five hundred years ago, when it was the first glimpse of Canterbury seen by pilgrims as they breasted the hill just outside the city, and saw its noble finger pointing heavenwards from out of the misty valley below. Although the shrine of St Thomas would be their main objective, no doubt many found time to pause at the charming little chantry chapel ordered by Henry IV, where two priests would sing and pray for the peace of his soul, but only of interest today because it has the earliest fan vault in the cathedral.

To see a fan vault in its full beauty, however, we should go not to

Canterbury, but to Cambridge, to King's College Chapel, which has probably the most perfect fan vault in this country. There are others more intricate, but none more exquisite. It is believed to have been designed by John Wastell, fresh from his triumph at Canterbury, and to have been built between 1446 and 1515. The fan vaulting spreads out in a series of web-like patterns as though the exquisite craftsmanship of a giant spider had been petrified, retaining its geometry, but translating the gossamer threads into durable stone. As in most buildings of this period, the wall areas are pared to the bone, the vast windows bathe the interior with light, and stain the floor with their ruby reds and diffused blues, the shallow mouldings hold a rich display of carved heraldry, and the slender columns lead the eye inevitably to the glory of the vault above. (*Plate 14.*)

Other notable examples of the fan vault are to be seen at St George's Chapel, Windsor, at Henry VII's Chapel in Westminster Abbey, in Oxford Cathedral, and at Sherborne and Bath Abbeys.

At Windsor there is an odd lack of harmony between the flat girder-like arches and the filigree like fan vaults between them, and the construction is smothered with repetitive decoration as though the builders had somehow become ashamed of it. The vault lacks the inevitable flow from column and wall to arch, and despite its great height, the roof has a curiously depressed look. There is much for the student of architecture to enjoy in this building, and the view of the exterior from the Horseshoe Cloisters is truly magnificent, but the fan vault within is in no way comparable to that of King's College Chapel.

At Westminster Abbey a new addition is to be seen to the more simply designed fan vault, for here conical protuberances hang down like gigantic stone icicles, and the vault is pierced and fretted into an elaborate series of patterns, a little over-rich for our taste, but not impairing the overall splendour of the mighty arches, which, more acutely pointed than those at Windsor, rise to a triumphant climax from the banner-bedecked walls of the chapel.

These icicle-like decorations (for they have no structural significance) also appear in the fan vault at the cathedral church at Oxford, but they are clumsily attached, and the arches from which they hang have a reedy quality uncomfortably out of harmony with the more robust structure of the earlier building.

Away in the West country, both Bath Abbey and Sherborne Abbey have fine fan vaults, and indeed, the former, with its splendid central tower, its flying buttresses and the restraint of the fan vaulting inside is perhaps the loveliest of these smaller buildings to survive the Reformation. The clarity of pattern and the purity of line in this less pretentious building may well be preferred to the over-elaboration of vaulting in its Royal predecessors at Windsor and at Westminster.

Along with the classical learning of the Renaissance – although Gothic art had maintained a continuous if unobtrusive contact with classical art – comes an increasing flow of classical details, embedded in Gothic structure. This alien note appears in small details in some of the tombs of the learned churchmen (the chapel of Bishop West in Ely Cathedral, for example) and is particularly obvious on the tomb of Henry VII in Westminster Abbey, where the lovely little angels, modelled by the Italian sculptor Torrigiano are pure Renaissance, but the screen enclosing them is as characteristically Perpendicular Gothic.

As the creative impulse of the Gothic period waned (its final *coup de grâce* being administered by the savage fury of the Reformation), its place was taken by non-English ways of design and planning. These were not wholly absorbed into our architecture for something like three hundred years, a fact which accounts for a great many of the incongruities and awkwardness in much of the Tudor and Elizabethan work.

Of the many causes which led to the Reformation in England we are not here concerned. They were complex and the relative importance of them difficult to assess. It is ironical, however, that at least one of the causes of the movement which was to have such disastrous results on our own architecture should have been the erection of one of the architectural treasures of the Western World. Away in Rome, vast sums of money were needed to build the mighty church of St Peter, and to equip the libraries, apartments and other buildings on a princely scale.

One device for raising money was by the sale of indulgences, where the sinner, instead of doing penance for his sins might, in effect, pay a fine. A Dominican friar named Tetzel arrived in Saxony for the purpose of selling indulgences to finance the building of St Peter's, Rome, but found his work bitterly opposed by Martin Luther, the teacher of theology at the new university of Wittenberg. It was the conflict over the indulgences which led finally to the Reformation, and to the dissolution of the English monasteries and the destruction of much of our architectural heritage. We are not concerned here with the moral issues – only with the tragic impact which the Reformation had on architectural development in this country. Its effect was two-fold. The obvious and most immediate result was the wholesale looting and destruction to which reference has already been made. The second was the severance of England from the main source of the Renaissance – Italy – which resulted in architectural ideas reaching us in a roundabout way through the

D

more acceptable French and Flemish writers with the inevitable adulteration and distortion which this second-hand route entailed.

The destruction of the monasteries and the pillaging of their treasures caused irreparable damage. That there were corrupt and worldly churchmen there is no doubt (Geoffrey Chaucer had not spared them in his *Canterbury Tales* written nearly a hundred and fifty years before) but when once the attack on the monasteries was mounted, little attempt was made to discriminate between the really holy man and his wayward brother. Once the mobs were out for loot, it mattered little whether they bore the Royal cypher on their surcoats, or wore 'a horrid suit of the camp.'

At Canterbury, where the offerings of the pilgrims totalled as much as £1,000 a year (perhaps £25,000 in present currency) the shrine was despoiled, Thomas à Becket's bones scattered, and the jewels and precious metals carried away to the Royal Treasury. We are told that the loot totalled nearly 5,000 oz. of gold, 4,000 of silver-gilt, and over 5,000 oz. of pure silver, whilst 26 carts more were needed to carry away what remained of the treasure. So far as possible, all traces of the martyr's shrine were removed and St Thomas's name erased from the calendar. Similar destruction took place in every part of the realm. Tombs and chapels were desecrated, rood screens hewn down and burned, and the splendid stained glass windows lay in glittering ruin on the church floors. Particular care was taken to destroy every piece of painting, every mural decoration, and as much of the sculpture as possible, for the Roman Catholic Church having been the most powerful patron of the arts, all art was suspect from now on. If pictures and sculptures meant Popery, they must all go, and wherever a lout with a hook could reach it, the lovely mediaeval sculpture was toppled down, to be smashed in a frenzy of 'reforming' zeal.

So rich in sculpture were some of our cathedrals that it took many months of systematic destruction before the work was completed to the satisfaction of the Reformers – the Lady Chapel alone at Ely, for example, possessed some hundreds of statues – and as late as 1541 Archbishop Cranmer was still at work ferreting out any possible offenders in the cathedral churches in his own province. His order ended thus '. . . and if any shrine, covering of a shrine, table, monument of miracles or of pilgrimage do there remain, to cause it to be taken away so that there do remain no memory of it.' This disposed satisfactorily of a number of early tombs of archbishops which had survived the first onrush of vandalism.

Only the Royal Chapels or churches under special protection could survive, and many churches were left as empty shells and crumbling ruins. The Abbey lands were confiscated and, parcelled out to followers of the King, founded the family fortunes of many members of the House of Lords today. The very titles betray the origin of some of our 'stately homes'. Lacock Abbey, Buckland Abbey and Nostell Priory were all originally church buildings, and were part of the rewards given to loyal supporters of the King. Not only were the lands annexed, of course, but the very fabric of the abbeys and convents was taken to provide building materials with which the new owner might fashion a great house more suitable to his newly acquired distinction.

The wave of destruction and desecration which followed in the wake of the dissolution of the monasteries not only put a stop to church building, but canalised all the creative skill of architects and craftsmen into quite a new direction.

As we have indicated, the government of England and the power by which that Government was sustained had been passing slowly into different hands. The new masters of England were rising from a different stratum of society. As they grew in wealth and power, these men were able to offer an alternative patronage to the architects and craftsmen, and to replace what in the past had been almost a monopoly of the Church.

Where the merchants paid for the erection of the 'wool' churches, or additional chapels, or built a splendid church porch to provide accommodation for their guild meetings, there was no open clash of interests between the old patron of the architect and the new.

But the building of fine manor houses, the endowment of schools and colleges by laymen, and other secular buildings which necessitated the diversion of men and materials away from ecclesiastical buildings – all these show a growing rivalry between the patrons. After the Reformation virtually all architects and craftsmen, no longer able to rely on the patronage of the Church, were dependent for their livelihood on those members of the Court whose heads were still firmly attached to their shoulders, and on the wealthy middle class whose manor houses were now outnumbering the grim and comfortless castles of the nobility.

The last phase of this chapter on the Perpendicular period must therefore deal with the increasing emphasis on domestic architecture and with the impetus this kind of building received from the Reformation. In domestic architecture we might well include the University buildings, for they too were homes as well as places of learning for the scholars who came from all over Europe to study here.

The architect and master mason in the Perpendicular period might perhaps be compared to a juggler, who at the height of his music hall turn, is keeping several plates in motion at once. One plate might be labelled 'Castles,' the second 'Cathedrals,' the third 'Parish Churches' and the fourth 'Other Buildings.' After the fifteenth century, the 'Castle' plate is allowed to wobble to a standstill, and after the Reformation those labelled 'Cathedrals' and Parish 'Churches' need but a little twist to keep them just in motion for the next two hundred years. Our architect/juggler is then left with but one plate – 'Other Buildings' – but it is with this one plate that he is to perform some of his most dazzling feats, and judging by the delight of the visitors to our stately homes and university towns, they still enthral a world-wide audience.

Before we turn our attention to the architecture of the English house, we must warn our readers that the houses which we shall describe, and which have survived, are not those in which the vast majority of our fellow countrymen of the Perpendicular period lived or could have afforded to live.

As Professor Bindoff reminds us in *Tudor England,* 'Most Englishmen lived on a diet which was often meagre and always monotonous, and was little calculated to promote resistance to disease; wore coarse and ill-fitting clothes which harboured dirt and vermin; lived in hovels whose squalor would affront the modern slum-dweller.'

The cruck construction of the ordinary peasant house had made some progress at least since Saxon times, for the builders had contrived to increase the headroom by erecting the crucks on walls, but even if the wooden framework was sturdily built, the houses as a whole were extremely flimsy, and consisted of but one room, with a central fire, and with a louvre in the roof from which the smoke eventually emerged. The men at work in the open air suffered less than their womenfolk at home who had perpetually inflamed eyelids, chest trouble and other discomforts brought about by the reek of the fire.

With little enough of his own, the peasant gathered his precious livestock in with him, at the close of the day, partly for warmth and partly for their protection – a practice which is still with us in some of the more remote parts of Europe. (We remember walking down a side street of a small town in Southern Italy, in the early morning, and watching what must have been a common enough sight in fifteenth-century England. The woman of the house emerged first, driving the fowls before her, to be followed by a huge sow with a squealing litter, a few more hens, and finally a donkey.)

The walls of such a hovel would probably be of cob (straw and mud mixed) or of wattle-and-daub, neither of them very durable materials, although it is surprising that until the unusually heavy floods in the Spring of 1960 a cob church was still standing in the west country.

Architecture proper, however, may be said to begin with the

manor house, for the squalid hovels of peasants, even when they did consist of more than one room, were little better than the cattle sheds of which they were often a part.

Normally manor houses were built of local materials by local craftsmen, a fact which contributes a great deal to their beauty, for they fit into the landscape so snugly because they are fashioned from the same raw materials as the landscape itself. Where suitable stone could be quarried, the manor houses are of stone. In well-wooded country the houses are timber-framed, and roofed with oak shingles, or thatched with local sedge, reed or straw. In East Anglia a dearth of suitable building stone encouraged the revival of brick-making – a craft which had disappeared with the departure of the Romans. The re-discovery of bricks was undoubtedly stimulated by the arrival of Flemish bricks, at first carried as ballast in the ships which plied regularly between East Anglia and Flanders. Little Wenham Hall, a moated house in Suffolk erected about 1260 is one of the earliest examples of brick building in this country. Here Flemish type bricks are used extensively. Flemish refugees brought valuable technical information and assisted in spreading the technique of brick making and of building in brick still further afield. Indeed, by the middle of the fifteenth century, the Flemish influence was so strong that it would be possible to insert photographs of some of the East Anglian houses of this period into a guide book on Belgium without much fear of detection.

Few manor houses can be found to rival the splendour of the parish churches of the Perpendicular period, for the lofty vaulting, the multi-coloured windows and the richness of carving would have been considered ostentatious in a secular building. Nevertheless such houses as Ockwells Manor, in Bray, Berkshire, built about 1465, and Cothay Manor, in Somerset, built about 1480, have a quiet beauty and a reticent charm of their own.

As with the more ambitious houses built for the nobility the core of Cothay Manor is still the great hall, entered by a porch at one end, from behind the protective screen. Immediately to the rear of the screen, doors lead to the kitchen, the buttery and the pantry. At the far end of the hall, which occupies the entire height of the house, is the parlour, with the solar above. A large square court surrounding the house is reminiscent of the bailey of a castle, with its curtain wall and sturdy gatehouse, but the protective aspect of these defences is more superficial than functional, although it is possible that they would have enabled its occupants to beat off any attacks from de-mobilized mercenaries.

The plan of the house has evolved quite naturally from the needs of the household, and its beauty arises from the right use of the lovely material and the innate good taste of the builders rather than from any conscious design for a beautiful building.

An examination of Barrington Court in the same county, however, built from the lovely Ham Hill stone some forty years later, shows a marked contrast to Cothay Manor. Although they are but twenty miles apart, and separated by but forty-odd years, Cothay Manor and Barrington Court demonstrate entirely different methods of approach. Cothay Manor is essentially mediaeval in its planning and growth, whilst at Barrington Court you may see one of the earliest of English Renaissance houses.

Although the materials and the purpose of Barrington Court are much the same as at Cothay Manor, the later building has clearly been designed consciously, and with an intentional symmetry.

The plan of Barrington Court is E-shaped, the wings forming the cross bars of the 'E', carefully symmetrical; the porch is placed exactly in the centre of the front of the building. The porch is, in fact, a central point about which the house is balanced. The chimneys rise exactly on either side of identical gables; the wing on the left has one small and two large windows precisely over its central axis, reflected as in a mirror by those of the right-hand wing. From outside, apart from its conscious symmetry and a certain alien quality about its chimneys, the house is a typically English manor house. Within, however, there is one more important detail which makes its appearance for the first time – a detail which was to become one of the important features of the English Renaissance house. As we have said, the plan is 'E' shaped. On the second floor, running the whole length of the spine of the letter, is a long gallery – one of the first to be built in this country. Here, then, in a house built about 1514–20 for one of the military commanders of Henry VIII, we find the beginnings of the English Renaissance – a mediaeval house no longer, but the somewhat humble predecessor to some of our loveliest English houses.

A great many houses, of course, could not be built entirely in this new fashion, and many landowners preferred to make additions and modifications to their mediaeval houses. Perhaps the most beautiful of all the houses we have visited in which a gradual transformation has taken place is Haddon Hall, near Bakewell, in Derbyshire. Here we have a great house which has evolved slowly and gracefully from the closing years of the eleventh century to its virtual completion in the seventeenth century. Some restoration has taken place, of course, but it has been carried out with such skill and sensitivity by the successive occupants that one is scarcely aware of it.

The earliest part of the house dates from the eleventh century and was sited high up the hillside, no doubt to form a defensive position overlooking the valley of the Wye and the bridge which crosses the river at that point. After a few troublous years, however (whether by good fortune or by political adroitness it is difficult to say) the family was left to develop its estates in peace, deriving a good deal of its wealth from lead mines in the area.

The sloping ground on which the house is built obliged its owners to plan it at different levels, and the ingenuity with which it adapts itself to the contours, and the varied skyline which results from this is not the least of Haddon's charms. The kitchen, too often a temporary outhouse in the Middle Ages, here is an integral part of the buildings which group quite naturally round the Great Hall – the nucleus of the house. The Hall itself is rather less imposing and more intimate than that at Penshurst Place to which we have already referred. There is indeed at Haddon an intimate domesticity, a liveable quality throughout which feels particularly attractive after some of the more freezing qualities of other 'stately homes.' Later generations added a beautifully panelled dining room to the rear of the Great Hall (in the sixteenth century) with a Great Chamber above, still later to be enriched with fine Elizabethan plasterwork, and earlier parts of the building were demolished or embodied in the fabric of a magnificent Long Gallery, 17 feet wide and over 100 feet long. The Long Gallery, lit on three sides by wide bay windows, its panelling decorated with classically derived pilasters and Renaissance details, must have been the most modern room of its day.

With its slow evolution through five hundred years, Haddon Hall makes nonsense of any attempt to divide the history of architecture into rigid periods, and it is partly for this reason that we have dealt at some length with this remarkable house. However, if any visitor to this country, with limited time at his disposal, wished to study the earlier stages of the growth of domestic architecture in England in a single building, he could do no better than spend a day at Haddon Hall. The Great Hall, with its deep fireplace, the kitchens with the bake-ovens and wooden troughs for salting down meat still intact, the Chapel with its lovely mural painting unsullied by Reformer or Puritan – these and much else besides reflect the life of the community at Haddon for five hundred years. The 'inevitable' quality of the plan, and the craftsmanship with which the plan was carried out from generation to generation, embodies all that is best in the English tradition of architecture.

It is not only in stone-built houses, however, that one finds evidence of the beauty of English domestic architecture. Some of the most notable examples are to be found among the timber-framed houses – a growth which, running parallel with the evolution of the splendid timber roofs of the 'wool' churches, continued to develop long after the skill of the craftsmen had been diverted by the Reformation from ecclesiastical buildings to houses, guildhalls and other secular buildings.

As we have said, the early cottage or small house was built with a cruck construction – a simple and primitive beginning, but one which contained the germ of the completely timber-framed house of the Elizabethan period. A typical example of a timber-framed house, built for a Sussex yeoman, is still to be seen, slightly modified, at Bignor, not far from Bognor Regis. The central room, or hall, was originally two stories high, with a wing slightly projecting on either side. Each wing contained two rooms, each half as high as the hall, the whole being under one single span of thatched roof. The frame of the house would be assembled on the site – a cage of timber erected on a low stone base of Sussex flint. The uprights would be mortised and tenoned into the baulks of timber lying horizontally on the stone wall, pegged for strength with heart-of-oak pins. When all was ready, the entire village probably turned out to haul the framework upright, and just as we still occasionally find today, there would be 'drinks all round' on completion of the main structure. The building now has an in-filling of brick – probably a later addition. Where wattle-and-daub walls were used they would have been made by springing upright hazel sticks into notches cut for the purpose in the timbers, and then weaving a cross-pattern of brushwood in and out of them like a modern hurdle. The daub substance with which this basket work was rendered weatherproof varies from district to district, but the formula is basically a mixture of clay and cowdung, with chopped straw added to help the mixture to bind as it dried out. The central window of the Bignor house once extended to the roof of the main room, but when the room was divided horizontally in two so that it should correspond to those comprising the wings, the window was altered, and the space filled in with brickwork. Some of the bricks inserted in the timber-framed panels are built in zig-zag courses vertically across the panel – a most attractive arrangement called nogging and one which was to be exploited decoratively with great success in the Elizabethan houses. In this yeoman's house we have a number of different methods of filling in the wall spaces of a timber-framed house – with brick, with wattle-and-daub and with local stone. Their textures, combined with the patina of time, the weathering of the wood and the soft contours of the thatch, have combined to make this house, and many others like it, a favourite subject for artists, but we must remember that to some extent this aspect is a superficial one, which can all too readily slip into a sentimental reconstruction of the past which bears very little relation to facts. It is this superficial enjoyment of exterior qualities which has

Fig. 16.   The herringbone pattern of a brick in-filling known as 'nogging'

led to equally superficial imitation of them in wholly different materials and on quite unsuitable buildings – to such anachronisms as 'Tudor' garages, 'Elizabethan' railway buffets and all the dreadful aspects of 'Merrie England' for tourists with which we are still bedevilled. It cannot be said too often or too emphatically that the best buildings of each period are usually ones which were essentially modern in their own day – ones in which the best use was made of the techniques and materials available at that time to meet the functional demands of the building. We have seen that this was so with the mediaeval vaults and the planning of the abbeys and castles, and we shall find it permeating even humble houses like this one in Sussex.

At Coggeshall, near Colchester, in Essex, there is an even more splendid example of domestic architecture of this period. This is the house of one Thomas Paycocke, a wealthy cloth merchant who had it built in the closing years of the fourteenth century from the proceeds of the wool trade. A devout churchman who gave generously to the abbey near by and to his own parish church, Thomas Paycocke nevertheless enriched his house with panelling and carving befitting a prosperous middle-class merchant. With no right to a coat of arms, he placed his merchant mark where a nobleman would have used a heraldic device – on the carved beam on the outside of the house for all to see – and on the fireplace which warmed his high, timber-roofed hall. The upper rooms, as in most houses of this period, project slightly over the street, a device known as *jetting* which enabled town houses on a restricted site to have larger upper rooms and also afforded some degree of protection from the weather for the foot-passenger below. It is achieved by arranging for the floor joists of the upper rooms to project beyond the ceiling of the lower storey, and resting the next tier of framework on those ends. As the joists of the mediaeval house were laid plankwise (and not edgewise as in modern houses) the additional weight of the upper storey stabilises the floor which otherwise had a tendency to 'whip' when a number of people move about. A very lovely form of panelling, known now as *linenfold* panelling, decorates his front door, and a somewhat similar design enriches the panelled walls of the rooms as well. The whole house suggests a refinement of life and a graciousness of living among the new merchant class scarcely achieved even by the nobility in the previous century, although manners and habits must have still been crude by our standards, if the contemporary books on behaviour are to be believed.

One of the many timber-framed manor houses which demonstrate a more relaxed form of dwelling, less concerned with the need for defence, is Ockwells Manor House in Berkshire. Although the owner, Sir John Norreys, built it actually during the Wars of the Roses, between 1446 and 1466, its wide areas of window and its generous porch make it militarily quite indefensible. Perhaps a clue to the sense of security may be found in the magnificent heraldry set in the windows which give light to the lofty Great Hall. A nobleman who could proclaim heraldically his association with Edmund, Duke of Somerset, Richard, Bishop of Salisbury, Henry Duke of Warwick, King Henry VI and his Queen, Margaret of Anjou, would obviously be a dangerous man with whom to interfere, and the huge stained glass windows, interpreted aright, really gave more protection than more obvious forms of defence. (*Fig. 17.*)

The interior of the Great Hall at Ockwells is panelled as high as possible, as were most of the halls of this kind. Where he could afford it, the landowner would import tapestries and woven cloths from Flanders, from Ypres, Ghent and Arras (you will recall that Hamlet killed Polonius as he stood concealed behind the arras), or painted cloths if the Flemish work proved too costly. There was certainly not the weird display of ironmongery which adorns the walls of some of our less stately homes – a man who had need of his helm, his breastplate, his mace or his spurs, did not hang them to get rusty from inaccessible hooks forty feet from the floor. The original pins for carrying a number of pikes, still in place at Cothay Manor, show that weapons were immediately to hand.

As the Perpendicular period merges into the Tudor period, foreign influences become more and more pronounced. This is shown by the increasing use of brick, and the importation of terracotta with which some brick buildings were enriched. As early as 1430 brick was being used to build Tattershall Castle in Lincolnshire (*c.* 1431–1349), Hurstmonceux Castle in Sussex (*c.* 1445) and Caister Castle, near Yarmouth. Not only was the material still somewhat foreign, but Caister Castle, for example, was deliberately designed on the

Fig. 17. Drawing of an unfortified manor house known as 'Ockwells' (from a photograph). The huge expanses of glass would make it militarily indefensible. Built 1446–66

French pattern. Its owner, Sir John Fastolf, fighting at the battle of Verneuil had captured the Duc d'Alençon, and the unfortunate Frenchman had been obliged to have Caister Castle built in the French style for his captor as part of his ransom. By the end of the fifteenth century the castle was obsolete but the Perpendicular style was still vigorous, as we can see by studying King's College Chapel, Cambridge, or Henry VII's chapel in Westminster Abbey.

It is in great country houses such as Compton Wynyates, in Warwickshire, or Layer Marney, Oxburgh Hall and Hengrave Hall in East Anglia, or in the splendid palace of Hampton Court that new developments in architectural form and decoration can be seen.

The plan of such houses is still basically mediaeval, the constructive principles being those of the Perpendicular period, but the decorative details increasingly foreign, as craftsmen and artists from abroad introduce Renaissance ornament into England for the first time. This strange mixture, somewhat modified by the innate conservatism of the English craftsman, is to be seen in many of the Tudor mansions, in some of the colleges of Oxford and Cambridge founded at this time, and in alien-looking tombs which begin to appear in Gothic churches.

Many of the new houses are carried out in brick, a material which by the beginning of the sixteenth century was becoming rapidly assimilated into our architectural vocabulary, especially in the Eastern Counties. Bricks of this period tend to be slightly shallower than the modern brick, although this narrowing is partly due to the depth of mortar in which they were embedded. No great variation was possible in the width of the brick, for this is dependent on the span of a man's hand, and a larger brick could not be handled comfortably and might weigh too much when soaked in water before use.

Brick houses could be assembled with surprising speed, (as recently as 1924 a bricklayer at Treeton near Sheffield laid 809 bricks in one hour) and the English craftsmen soon became as adept as foreign workmen in shaping the bricks by cutting or rubbing to produce the fantastic shapes and beautifully fashioned chimney stacks which are such a notable feature of the Tudor house. Large areas of blank wall are relieved by patterns of different coloured brick, somewhat timidly at first, as at the tower of Bishop Fox at Farnham Castle built about 1500, and finally with confidence some twenty years later on the gatehouse of Layer Marney Hall in Essex.

Gatehouses, no longer a defensive necessity, became an excuse for ostentation. At Layer Marney Hall and at Oxburgh, they are vast erections completely dwarfing the main structure, tricked out with castellated turrets, parapets and all the superficial trappings of a feudal castle.

The 'carpet' knight of the Tudor Court, his honours freshly conferred but often without ancient lineage or hereditary castles of his own, hastened to make good these deficiencies. It is a kind of 'One-Upmanship' which occurs again and again in England – we shall see it at its most blatant among the industrial barons of Victorian England, and architecturally it is usually disastrous. Other writers, perhaps more charitably inclined, attribute it to a romantic love of the past, prompted at this time by the publication of Thomas Malory's *Morte d'Arthur* which was printed by Caxton in 1485.

At Layer Marney Hall, the mullioned windows and parapets were fashioned from terracotta by Italian workmen, employed by Lord Marney, no doubt on the advice of his fellow-Privy Councillor, Sir Richard Weston, whose country house, Sutton Place near Guildford, was also being embellished by terracotta ornament. At Sutton, they cast their terracotta details in both Gothic and Renaissance moulds, and the fusion of these cultures was surprisingly successful, although the mass-production of ornament was a sad introduction to an England which hitherto had only known the crispness and variety of hand-cut stone. The gatehouse at Sutton Place was destroyed in 1782 and we must confess that if it were as hideously disproportionate as that at Layer Marney Hall, the house has probably gained rather than lost by its disappearance.

The first half of the sixteenth century saw an outburst of building activity almost comparable to that which produced the 'wool' churches of the Perpendicular period, although the architectural quality is hardly as great. Rufford Old Hall, near Southport (now the South Lancashire Folk Museum), Coughton Court in Warwickshire, Holcombe Court in North Devon and Hengrave Hall in Suffolk are typical examples of the great Tudor houses which emerged in every county of England. Many of them have been altered by the later occupants and even abandoned, as at Cowdray House in Sussex, whilst others – notably Thornbury Castle in Gloucestershire – were left incomplete when their builders had their political and architectural ambitions cut short by the headsman on Tower Hill.

Undoubtedly the finest building of this period still surviving, however, is Hampton Court started in 1515 by Cardinal Wolsey and later to become a Royal Palace, its original splendour rivalling that of the King's own residences of St James's and of Greenwich. This gigantic manor house, with two courtyards and a moat, had no less than 280 rooms to provide accommodation for the Cardinal, his retinue of nearly 500 and such distinguished guests as the French Ambassador and his followers. The buildings are of rosy Tudor brick with applied decorations of terracotta, painted and gilded.

The house is virtually mediaeval in plan – indeed it is easy to overstress foreign influence, for the sum total of alien work is extremely insignificant when compared with the wealth of native craftsmanship. Once over the bridge which spanned the moat, visitors to the Cardinal entered by the main gateway, a tall gatehouse flanked by symmetrically placed turrets, and reached the Base Court. This looks now very much as it did in the sixteenth century. A second gatehouse, now called Anne Boleyn's Gateway, stands in the centre of the opposite wall, and it is through this gate that the visitor gained admission to the Clock Court, the main courtyard of the Cardinal's house. Considerable alterations have been made to this court since it was first built, and the Great Hall which occupies the whole of the Northern side was built by Henry VIII shortly after he had been 'given' the manor by an apprehensive Cardinal Wolsey. A few of the rooms on the opposite side of the court still bear traces of Tudor decoration, but can give very little idea of the sumptuousness of the original rooms. Linked to the Great Hall by a lofty room called the Watching Chamber is the Chapel Royal, and still farther to the North, within easy reach of the Great Hall, are the kitchens and similar offices. The whole of the Eastern wing of the Clock Court has been extensively rebuilt, but here again a few Tudor rooms, notably one called Wolsey's Closet, give some idea of the interior of the house as it was in the sixteenth century. One feature of the original plan which has disappeared and one of which Thomas Wolsey spoke with particular satisfaction, is the Long Gallery. We do not know its exact position, but it could well have occupied the site now covered by the Eastern wing of the Clock Court. Other galleries are known to have existed.

Records exist of the actual Englishmen who built this huge manor house, each tradesman apparently designing his own particular contribution – the masonry, the woodwork and so on. The vast brick structure was enriched by terracotta decorations, made specially in London by the Italian modeller, Giovanni da Maiano, and the shallow brick mouldings and flattened Tudor projections provide an admirable foil to Maiano's roundels on the gatehouse, from which Roman emperors, in high relief, glare disdainfully down upon the iced lollies and dangling cameras of the present-day visitors.

The gatehouses, with their beautifully executed coats of arms clearly designed upon an Italian model, were functional as well as impressive, for they were designed to be the principal guest chambers, a tradition which survived from those early mediaeval days when the gatehouse of a monastery was reserved for distinguished guests of the abbot. At Hampton Court the main room of each is lit by an elaborately decorated *oriel* window. This kind of window projects from the wall, and is supported by carved and moulded corbels. It became increasingly popular during the Tudor period, although a fine example can be seen at Glastonbury, projecting from the upper room of the Abbot's Tribunal House and built about 1515. The oriels at Hampton Court and Hengrave Hall form an admirable focal point – a centrepiece for the whole design of the gatehouses there. The symmetry of the gatehouses at Hampton Court is emphasised by the octagonal turrets flanking them and when Henry VIII accepted the incomplete house from Cardinal Wolsey in 1525 he immediately developed the whole West front, building an identical wing on either side to achieve a satisfactory balance about the central architectural feature.

Contemporary writers record the sumptuous interior of Wolsey's house. The rooms were wainscoted with carved panelling to two-thirds of their height, and the remaining frieze was decorated with paintings by foreign artists. Ceilings were enriched with elaborately modelled ornament in plaster and the timbers supporting the ceiling were overlaid with more ornament fashioned from plaster and papier-mâché, richly gilded and painted. The walls of the 280 rooms were hung with splendid tapestries and the Cardinal's own chambers were draped with hangings of richly coloured velvet and with cloth of gold. Foreign ambassadors, anxious to placate so powerful a states-man, showered on him rare and costly gifts for his palace – gold and silver plate, thick Oriental carpets for his rooms, magnificent Venetian glass and a host of other fabulous bribes. The value of the gold and silver plate alone was estimated at one and a half million pounds in Tudor currency by one foreign ambassador. Velvet hung in thick folds about the Cardinal's wide bed, and his pillows were hemmed with silk and embroidered with fleur-de-lys of gold thread. His very chairs, tables, chests and footstools were enriched with cloth of gold.

Having taken over Hampton Court, the King had the Cardinal's Great Hall demolished and built himself the one we see today. It embodies no new constructional principles, and, apart from the carved decoration and the flattened Tudor arch, could have been erected a hundred years before. Although the forest of chimneys at Hampton Court reveals the number of fireplaces within, the Great Hall was warmed by a large open fire in the centre, and the smoke escaped through louvres in the roof. A carved fan vault, its pendants hanging down like elaborately fashioned stalactites, roofs the large bay window by which the dais and the high table standing on it was lit. The remainder of the hall was lit by huge Perpendicular windows on either side with a slightly more elaborate one on the wall over the screens.

We have scanty information about Henry's own huge palace, the Palace of Nonesuch (or Nonsuch) in Surrey, and as it has entirely disappeared we do not propose to spend long in speculating on what it was like. The drawing by Joris Hofnaegal, now in the British Museum, shows that the lower storeys were of stone, the upper ones of half timber. Lavish modelled decoration filled the spaces between the upright timbers, and the skyline is restless with turrets, pinnacles and those clumsy little *cupolas*, like the top of a sugar-dredger, of which the Tudor architect was so fond. Sometimes these cupolas were decorated with mediaeval-type crockets, as at Hampton Court and Hengrave Hall, and sometimes they were plain, as at the Tower of London where they perch incongruously on the severe Norman turrets of the White Tower. The palace appears to have been an uneasy hotch-potch of styles – the main fabric of the building being erected in 1538 by Englishmen and the applied ornament being left to the individual whims of a number of craftsmen from the Low Countries, from France (for Henry was anxious to emulate Francis I), and from Italy. Its ostentation was to have an unfortunate influence on the architects and their patrons in the next century, and we may deplore that this monstrous building survived until the Restoration for its very presence encouraged much which is vulgar and superficial in Elizabethan decoration.

After the rupture with the Pope, Henry and his ministers sent the Italian craftsmen packing, and from now on the chief foreign influences on our architecture were either to come to us via the Low Countries, or were brought back by the few Englishmen who were not only able to travel to Italy but were sufficiently interested in architectural problems to make records of what they saw there. The same movement which dismissed Italians brought the German, Hans Holbein, to the Court and this ingenious and versatile artist is believed to have had a wide influence on architectural decoration, although no actual buildings can be traced to his hand. The so-called Holbein Gateway which used to straddle Whitehall was certainly not designed by him, but may have been used as his lodgings towards the end of his life.

Of the other Royal Palaces undertaken in the reign of Henry VIII, only St James's now remains, for Greenwich was entirely rebuilt, and Whitehall Palace was destroyed by fire in the seventeenth century.

But although palaces may show coming trends in architecture, we must remember that in a sense they are freaks, and it is to the ordinary house of the ordinary person who had neither the wealth nor perhaps the inclination to indulge in such fancies that we shall find the true quality of architecture of any period. Away from the Court, largely untouched by foreign influences, seemly little houses, of wood, of stone and later of brick, were being created and developed by humble English craftsmen who would certainly not have aspired to the title of architect. Every village had masons, joiners and smiths who could adapt their traditional craft to domestic needs and if glass was too precious a commodity to be used, the villagers made shift with 'fenestrals' – paper or linen stretched across the window, with a lattice of wickerwork, and shutters which could be unfolded or slid across in bad weather. We must remember this architectural common denominator which existed in every period, in case we get an entirely distorted picture of English architecture when we are engaged in studying buildings which were in fact ahead of their time.

We end this chapter on the Perpendicular period – the longest in the book – as we began it, with a quotation from Shakespeare which not only expresses the prevailing quality of the closing years of the period, but anticipates the next as well. Portia's description of her English suitor in Act 1 of *The Merchant of Venice* symbolizes the confused state of the architectural scene by the middle of the sixteenth century and also serves to underline the muddled state of Elizabethan design. Describing the incongruities and lack of harmony in the Englishman's dress, Portia exclaims '. . . How oddly is he suited! I think he bought his doublet in Italy, his round hose in France, his bonnet in Germany, and his behaviour everywhere.'

With a little adjustment, this criticism might be applied with equal truth to the design of many of the Elizabethan houses.

Chapter Seven

ELIZABETHAN AND
JACOBEAN ARCHITECTURE 1547-1625

I T is difficult to assign any particular dates to a period of archi-
tecture. During the final phase of Gothic architecture – the
Perpendicular period – a Tudor king was reigning in England, and
such buildings as King's College Chapel, normally considered
Perpendicular in architecture, might with equal truth be labelled
Tudor.

Elizabeth herself was a Tudor monarch, and many of the buildings
erected in her reign show no new features but only developments
from those already familiar in mediaeval times, so that the chapter
headings and the dates which accompany them should never be
taken too literally. Architectural growth is too diffuse and too
varied to be confined within such narrow limits.

The timber-framed buildings so generally recognised by the laymen as Elizabethan are in fact but natural developments from the
building construction current during the Middle Ages. Where there
was a strong local tradition in districts remote from fashionable
Court circles, it was inevitable that the craftsmen should continue to
erect traditional buildings long after other forms of construction and
decoration had been evolved elsewhere. The basic construction of
such familiar Elizabethan houses as Little Moreton Hall in Cheshire,
of Speke Hall in Lancashire, of inns such as The Feathers at Ludlow
and even of such market halls as that at Ledbury in Herefordshire
(built in 1633) is much the same as that of earlier mediaeval buildings,
even if it has become more sophisticated and self-conscious in the
course of time. As the timber roofs and the framework of the walls
became integrated, the spaces between the timbers of the wall tended
to become wider – especially as brick, a stronger material, replaced
the lath-and-plaster, and a more economical use of timber was possible. Nevertheless, this tendency was counteracted by some Elizabethan builders, who, seeing the decorative possibility of the woodwork, added many structurally superfluous timbers, enriching the
wall surfaces with a riot of pattern. It is as though a modern architect

had multiplied the number of girders required to support a building by five in order to produce an 'interesting' effect. The smaller Elizabethan houses still to be seen at Lavenham, in Suffolk, at Chiddingstone in Kent and in villages in many parts of the country, built sincerely and with a natural grace, are infinitely preferable to those larger and more ostentatious exercises in black and white timbering which continue to attract the tourist. The top-heavy clumsy gables of Little Moreton Hall, for example, look vulgar and self-assertive by comparison with the restraint and the economy of woodwork in some of the more humble buildings of the same date. It seems that the very word 'Elizabethan' has a hypnotic effect on some visitors, and as soon as it is known that such and such a building was erected in the reign of Good Queen Bess all critical faculty is suspended forthwith. Every period can show fine, well-proportioned, seemly architecture and every period can show clumsy badly pro-portioned examples as well. The fact that a building has survived for several centuries does not necessarily mean that it is far better, architecturally, than one which has been erected within the last ten years.

It is unfortunate that so few town houses of this period have survived and that we shall have to concentrate in the main on the isolated country houses standing in their own estates. It means that we have to rely upon written descriptions of Elizabethan townscape, and can only get an occasional glimpse in our towns today of the way in which the houses were originally grouped at this time to form a unified street. A few surviving houses in Chester, Warwick and Shrewsbury and the famous group of jetted houses and shops which form the side of Staple Inn in Holborn give some idea of the appearance of an Eliza-bethan town, but we should probably form a more complete idea by going to such German towns as Goslar, south west of Berlin where whole streets of timbered houses have been preserved, in order to vis-ualise the appearance of one of our own towns in the sixteenth century.

The picture is not an impressive one and indeed foreign visitors to London expressed surprise that '. . . these English have their houses made of sticks and dirt.' An Italian, used to the splendours of Florence, its palaces occupying the whole of one side of a street would have found the varied gables and individual houses which made up the English thoroughfare both primitive and quaint. Certainly no town in England could show such magnificent planning as the city of Vicenza, in North Italy. Here buildings were already being designed and supervised by Andrea Palladio which later were to have such a profound effect on the appearance of our own towns, and on many others on the mainland of Europe. London, however, still clung to its rambling haphazard mediaeval pattern – a fact which did

Fig. 18.   The exuberance of Elizabethan timberwork. Little Moreton Hall,
Cheshire, *c.* 1559. (From a photograph)

not fail to impress so acute a visitor as Fynes Moryson who, in his
Itinerary of 1617 wrote '. . . Now at London the houses of the citizens
(especially in the chief streets) are very narrow in the front towards
the street but are built five or six roofs high, commonly of timber and
clay with plaster. . . . But withal understand that in London many
stately palaces, built by noblemen upon the river Thames, do make a
very great show to them that pass by water; and that there be many
more like palaces, also built towards land, but scattered and great
part of them in back lanes and streets, which if they were joined to the
first in good order, as other cities are built uniformly, they would
make not only fair streets, but even a beautiful city. . . .'

But the houses in our towns and cities have all too often declined
to be joined together in good order, and their owners have been
unwilling to make that surrender of individuality however small
which is necessary if the whole street is to retain a sense of architectural unity. Because of this self assertion, our streets are still mainly
straggling lines of separate houses and the resultant skyline has a
kind of 'architectural hiccough' which afflicts much of our townscape.

This lack of unity in our streets springs from many causes, but one which may be largely responsible is the tendency to study our historical architecture in isolation and unrelated to the peculiar needs of a town. Because these magnificent country houses standing in their own parklands have no architectural allegiance to other buildings they have persuaded us that our town houses can behave in the same way. The lack of awareness of the basic difference between the country house and the house which is but one unit in a whole street, which is still common enough today, was obvious to the foreign visitor as early as the sixteenth century.

One of the most important reasons for the lack of a rigid plan to our cities was of course our sea-encircled island. On the Continent many countries were obliged to build a series of star-shaped fortress towns to survive invasion from more powerful neighbours. In England, the fortified town, like the castle, was soon extinct, and such town planning as we had was to be found in the graciousness of the collegiate cities of Oxford and Cambridge, their compact buildings grouped round their courtyards – a series of interlocking units with large areas of green in the very heart of the city.

Perhaps the best authority to consult for many aspects of Elizabethan life is William Harrison, whose *Description of England*, written just before the defeat of the Spanish Armada gives a vivid picture of life at that time. Extracts from this remarkable document and many others besides are to be found in *Life in Shakespeare's England* by Professor J. Dover Wilson – a fascinating collection of extracts from the writings of the Elizabethan period.

It is to the Elizabethan country mansion, erected for the new merchant-aristocracy that one turns in order to study the main developments in the architecture of this period, for, with the exception of that at Woodham Walter, in Essex, erected about 1563, no churches were built. In the Perpendicular period, much of the architecture was built to the glory of God. In the Elizabethan period it was built mainly to the glory of the owner – and sometimes to the glory of the great Queen.

The desire for a symmetrical plan which we observed as early as 1514–1520, in Barrington Court, and later at Hampton Court, now becomes the dominant factor in the design of every great house. Houses no longer evolved almost organically around the life of the household. Plans were now drawn on paper as interesting geometrical designs and all too often the fascination of playing with shapes on paper appears almost to be a pursuit in itself. The fact that this interesting pattern really represented a house in which someone was to live seems scarcely to have been considered. (This mistake is by no means confined to the Elizabethans.)

Often the owner was his own designer, calling in an architectural draughtsman to draw *platts* and *uprights*, as plans and elevations were then called, to his own specification. The desire to impress, and the prestige which was attached to the erection of an imposing house is all too apparent when we study some of the drawings and the buildings which resulted from them. The owner/designers were inspired from a variety of sources, and were liable to 'borrow' architectural ideas from any available pattern book. During the first half of the reign of Elizabeth, the châteaux of the Loire valley, in France, and the building of Fontainebleau appear to have exercised a strong influence on the design of our houses, although, as Italians were also at work in France, there is an Italianate flavour too, if only second hand. A more direct source of Italian Renaissance ideas, however, was a book published by an Englishman, John Shute, in 1563. Shute was sent to Italy by the Duke of Northumberland. '. . . to confer with the doings of the skilful masters of architecture, and also to view such ancient monuments thereof as are yet extant.' His book, *The First and Chief Groundes of Architecture*, starts with 'The fludde of Noe' (the story of the Flood in the Bible), touches on the architecture of Egypt and Greece, and then deals at some length with the writings of the Roman author, Vitruvius. He probably made measured drawings of some of the ancient buildings of Rome, although some authorities believe that he owed more to the writings of the Italian architect, Sebastiano Serlio, than to his own research. Shute's book includes detailed drawings of the five Orders of Architecture, the measurements of shaft to entablature and so on, a handy reference book for the man who aspired to build his own house.

But visits to Rome and, indeed, even Italian acquaintances were liable to be dangerous politically, and it was wiser perhaps to consult writers from France, from the Netherlands, or even from Germany. One of the most important of French writers on architecture was Philibert de l'Orme. He was not only very familiar with the writings of Vitruvius and the ancient architects – he produced a thoroughly practical book on building construction, with particularly concise and detailed diagrams on the design and production of timber roofs. (One type of trussed rafter roof named after him is still to be found in modern books on building construction.) It is not surprising that so valuable and so practical a guide should be in demand by Elizabethan noblemen. We find no less a person than William Cecil, the First Lord Burghley, and Lord High Treasurer to Queen Elizabeth, writing to the English Ambassador in Paris, asking him to obtain a copy of de l'Orme's book to help him with the construction of Burghley House, near Stamford.

Of the many other writers on architecture available to the Elizabethan builders, mention must be made of the books produced by the French architectural draughtsman, Jacques du Cerceau who produced a succession of books, culminating in his most important works in 1576 and 1579.

Early in the 1570s, however, Elizabethan England shows a growing interest in the architecture of Protestant Flanders. After our own unhappy experiences during the reign of Mary, our sympathies lay with the Flemish refugees who flocked here both before and after the Massacre of St Bartholomew in 1572, and Flemish architects, craftsmen, and their works were eagerly sought by Elizabethan gentlemen anxious to build their country houses in the most fashionable style. Of these Flemings perhaps the most important was an Antwerp artist named Vredeman de Vries. His designs are more notable for their ingenuity and imaginative decoration on paper than for their attention to practical detail. Many of the patterns were wholly unsuitable for carrying out in third dimensional wood and stone. They are extravagant flights of fancy – ingenious architectural doodlings, and where they were taken seriously had a calamitous effect on architectural details.

Still more unfortunate were the coarse, heavy handed designs published by a German, Wendel Dietterlin of Strasbourg who was obsessed by writhing human and animal forms. Some of the most unpleasant work in Elizabethan houses may be traced to this draughtsman.

Although the Elizabethan house evolved from that of the Perpendicular and Tudor periods, nevertheless it exhibits a number of important developments by which it can be quite easily recognised.

The plan of the Elizabethan house may be 'E' shaped, or 'H' shaped, but it was in any case absolutely symmetrical, and the main entrance was to be found in the centre of the front. The Great Hall, still the core of the house, was not, however, used by everyone for eating and sleeping. The filth and noise of which Erasmus complained, and which caused Cardinal Wolsey to hold a scented orange under his nose so that he could cross his own hall without inhaling the stench from the floor, were by now less apparent, as other rooms took the inhabitants away to their various devices, and gave them some privacy. The wall fireplace in every room – easily detected from the outside of the house by the multiplicity of chimneys – became not only a means of heating but the focal point of the room, a position which the fireplace has held until recently. (Now it looks as though it might well be ousted by the television set.) Because of its importance it was frequently most elaborately and ostentatiously decorated, with a lavish use of different coloured stone and high

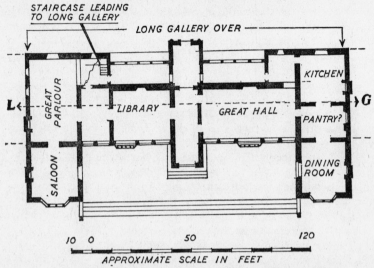

Fig. 19.   The plan of a typical Elizabethan mansion. This is an 'E' plan but could well develop into an 'H' plan. Notice the design about a central axis, and the 'Long Gallery' which occupies the whole width of the upper storey

relief ornament to impress the visitor with the wealth of the owner of the house.

The mediaeval screen, topped by its minstrels' gallery was usually but lightly carved. This was now replaced by another, more fitting to grace the house of the merchant prince, and all too often the rival of the fireplace in providing an excuse for a riot of swollen carved forms in high relief copied from one of the foreign pattern books, or even perpetrated especially by an imported craftsman.

Early in the period, the roof of the Great Hall was still the familiar hammerbeam or raftered roof of mediaeval times but later halls tend to be reduced in height and many finally were but one storey high, with rooms overhead. As the Hall shrank, its place was taken by specially designed rooms, the dining parlour and so on, and the extended plan provided accommodation for the servants of various status in the household, to become the 'servants' wing.'

Rooms were almost invariably panelled, with thin partitions of oak providing an alternative to the tapestries which covered the cold bare plaster. Where wood was plentiful it was naturally far cheaper as a wall covering than the imported tapestries, and the important rooms were enriched with veneers of such decorative woods as cherry, laburnum and holly, cut into intricate geometric patterns, and giving a warmth and richness to the sparsely furnished rooms. The more wealthy the owner the more elaborately carved the panelling, and although the Elizabethans preferred the natural woods to be exploited, we find that the Jacobean householder often indulged in painted and gilded woodwork. Although furniture is perhaps hardly architecture, it must be said that some of the bulbous carving and heavy limbs of bed and table created in this period harmonises hideously with the excess of ornament to be found on the chimney pieces and screens and reminds us somewhat irreverently of the less desirable present-day products of the multiple stores of Tottenham Court Road.

Ceilings provided yet another surface to be enriched with ornament, this time in plaster. There is a restless and vulgar display in some of the houses of this period comparable to the worst excesses of the Victorian industrialists or the post-First World War profiteers.

One notable addition to the design of the house was the introduction of the staircase as an architectural feature of some importance. It was not now merely a flight of stairs or a ladder by which one might reach the upper rooms. It was a processional way which the Elizabethan ladies with their wide-hooped skirts and the gallants with their padded breeches might ascend with dignity and safety. The stairs were shallow, the treads ample and wide, and the whole unit was designed as an integral part of the carefully contrived plan.

Of the rooms above certainly the most important was the Long Gallery which normally occupied the entire width of the house – the spine of the 'E' or the crossbar of the 'H'. Many Long Galleries are therefore of considerable length, well over 100 feet, but the corridor-like quality is usually avoided by building bay windows at intervals, the actual bay being so large that each constituted a fair-sized room. The Long Gallery had many uses. It is difficult for us to imagine what the long cold months of winter meant to the Elizabethans. Bad roads made travelling difficult and dangerous, and the absence of mackintoshes, Wellington boots or any light, effective waterproofing severely limited movement during bad weather. The Long Gallery was therefore a room in which exercise could be taken – a dance hall, a concert hall, a skittle alley, as well as a social club room where spinning and other domestic pursuits could be carried out. The very tapestries hanging from the walls could have been woven there and Elizabethan ladies, even of Royal blood, spent many hours in the Long Galleries embroidering the heavy curtains which surrounded the huge four-poster beds. Ancestral portraits made a brave show along its walls (and if the newly made nobleman had no ancestors of whom he could boast, some were quickly invented and painted for him!)

From time to time you will find a Long Gallery called 'the Cartoon

Gallery.' The term cartoon has, of course, nothing to do with an Elizabethan Walt Disney. It is also used for a full-sized drawing for a tapestry, for a stained glass window, or for a painting of some sort. An artist may design a stained glass window, working out his ideas in a number of detailed or rough sketches, but finally he has to produce a full-sized working drawing, and this alone is the cartoon. Working drawings of this kind are to be seen in the Victoria and Albert Museum, where the cartoons for tapestries drawn by the Italian artist, Raphael are on view. The Cartoon Gallery at Hampton Court houses a series made by another Italian artist, Andrea Mantegna, and quite a number of our great country houses have galleries built to display the collection of cartoons acquired by one of the former owners whilst touring the continent.

One of the big disadvantages of some Elizabethan houses is an arrangement of rooms which lead directly from one into another. It is no doubt convenient today for a guide escorting tourists around, but it must have been intolerable for the original occupant of a centrally placed room, for the traffic of servants and others to their rooms on either side must have afforded very little privacy or quiet.

Very few of the houses of this period have rooms set aside for bathing and none possessed lavatories, and although Queen Elizabeth had a 'bathing room' at Windsor Castle, her other requirements were met by a 'close stool' (still to be seen at Hampton Court) – the equivalent of the commode used today by invalids or by old people too enfeebled to leave their bedrooms.

Visitors to country houses open to the public are familiar with the claim that 'Queen Elizabeth slept here,' and, indeed, this much-travelled monarch, by her journeys, inspired her noblemen to build larger and more impressive houses, worthy to offer accommodation and entertainment to so distinguished a guest. A letter written to Sir Christopher Hatton, by Lord Burghley, refers to two houses, Theobalds and Holdenby (now destroyed) as being built to the greater glory of their Queen, and end with these words 'God send us both to enjoy Her, for whom we both mean to exceed our purses in these.'

It is clear that the planning of such houses involved a great deal more than merely providing accommodation for the owner and his household. Where prestige is involved, no expense was spared that the house should be designed in the very latest fashion, embodying many of the ideas set forth in the flood of pattern books imported from the continent. Where the owner was himself a man of taste, or allowed himself to be guided by a trained mason or architect, the result could be delightful. Such houses as Parham Park, in Sussex, where the classical details from abroad have been successfully and sympathetically absorbed into the fabric of a Tudor house seem to us to display all that is wholly admirable in the architecture of this period. There are unfortunately many houses where the builder has collected detail upon detail from a wide variety of sources, adding them to the building with rather less taste and intelligence than that with which the caddis worm collects odds and ends from the bottom of the pond to embellish her dwelling.

The demands of Elizabethan clients upon their builders could be very odd – as capricious as some made by the film stars of today in Beverly Hills. A deep belief in the Holy Trinity impelled one eccentric nobleman to build his own house on a triangular plan, and even John Thorpe, himself a surveyor and architect, whose folio of drawings is preserved in the Soane Museum in London, drew a plan for his own house based on his own initials. The drawings in the Soane Museum show the final house to have Flemish gables and the entrance in the centre linking the 'J' shaped half of the house to the 'T' shaped wing which it balances. The house was never built, apparently.

Various scales were used by Elizabethan architects, including one of 8 feet to the inch still commonly in use, and there is no doubt that in addition to plans, elevations, perspectives and so on, models were normally used to enable the client to visualise the final building.

More cultivated clients were, of course, quite capable of seeing that the master mason, or builder, designed the house strictly in accordance with the rules laid down by the classical authorities. Sir Henry Wotton, a diplomat who, during his service in Venice, had made a close study of ancient and modern architecture, gave first hand information of the methods current in architectural workshops. His book 'The Elements of Architecture . . . from the best Authors and Examples' was intended to be a guide book to the increasing number of noblemen who regarded a knowledge of architecture as an essential part of the education of a cultivated man. His demand for buildings to be erected with 'Commoditie, Firmness and Delight' is as important today as it was when he first published his book in 1624. One passage in his book says 'Let no man that intendeth to build, setle his Fancie upon a draught of the Worke on paper, how exactly soever measured or neately set off in perspective; and much lesse upon a bare Plant thereof . . . without a Modell or Type of the whole Structure, and of every parcell and Partition in Pastboord or Wood. Next that the said Modell bee as plaine as may be, without colours or other beautifying, lest the pleasure of the Eye preoccupate the Judgement;' Sound advice indeed, especially for the young married couple of today too often putty in the hands of the house agent or the speculative builder!

One of the first great houses of this period to be built under the personal supervision of its owner, was Longleat House, near Bath, which still preserves a great deal of its original appearance from without, but suffered considerable alterations within, during the last century. The building as it now stands was erected in 1568, although for thirty years after, minor additions were made, and it seems possible that the final top storey was not added until after the visit of the Queen in 1575. The plan is symmetrical, and almost square, the North front being about 350 feet across, and the sides measuring approximately the same, giving the effect of a four-sided palace, built on the site of a manor or grange wrested from the Carthusian monks who owned it during the Reformation.

Its owner, Sir John Thynne, employed a team of Scottish free-masons to build it from stone quarried at Haslebury, near Box, and even when he was away at Parliament, kept a strict eye on the progress of his house by a voluminous correspondence. There seems to be considerable doubt as to the actual architect, although possibly one Robert Smithson (or Smythson), of whom we shall hear later, was concerned with the later stages of the construction of the house.

In the meantime, away in Stamford near Peterborough, another great country house – Burghley – was in course of construction, and again on the site previously occupied by a monastery. William Cecil, the first Lord Burghley, was conversant with the architectural text-books written by the Frenchman, Philibert de l'Orme, and a good deal of the planning of Burghley House is reminiscent of the French châteaux. This house, too, is approximately symmetrical and its principal front is over 200 feet wide, balanced about a huge central tower, three stories high, and with massive turrets crowned by cupolas. The restless skyline is very like the reconstructions we have seen of Nonsuch Palace, and Flemish ornament, either imported or carved by Flemish workmen brought over specially for the task is apparent everywhere. Nevertheless, the clock tower dominating the inner courtyard is clearly derived from Philibert de l'Orme's work at Anet, in France, and the stone vaulted staircase, too, is more French than English or Flemish.

Horace Walpole, that inveterate old gossip of the eighteenth century who haunted country houses with the zest of a Chicago tourist determined to 'do' England in a week, was by no means pleased with what he found at Burghley. He wrote, 'The taste of all these mansions was that bastard style which intervened between Gothic and Grecian architecture, or which perhaps was the style that had been invented for the houses of the nobility when they first ventured on the settlement of the kingdom after the termination of the quarrel between the Roses, to abandon their fortified dungeons and consult convenience and magnificence.'

Magnificence of a kind he would certainly have found at Burghley, but it is doubtful whether convenience was ever much considered in the planning of this huge house. Nevertheless, despite some incongruity of ornamental detail, there is at Burghley a refined quality almost entirely absent from Wollaton Hall, an enormous mansion built shortly after the completion of Burghley House, for a wealthy coal merchant named Sir Francis Willoughby, whose ancestors had changed the family name from Bugge in the thirteenth century.

The stone for this house was carried from Lincolnshire by packhorses from the mines from which Sir Francis derived his wealth, and, ever an acute man of business, the mineowner arranged for the animals to make the return journey laden with coal.

The house is square in plan, with an enormous central hall rising some 50 feet, imposing its huge mass on the whole house and on the country around. The wings surrounding the hall are two stories high, and the towers which are set squarely at each corner add yet one more storey. The keep-like central tower, its corners ornamented with circular turrets, rises to a triumphant crescendo of four stories. The building is a romantic fantasy, as unreal in its own way as a Walt Disney castle, and had it been left in naked Ancaster stone, it might have achieved a certain grandeur. Unfortunately Sir Francis Willoughby was spending £80,000 and was determined to have full value for money. A memorial tablet in the church says that it commemorates one 'Robert Smythson gent architector and surveyor unto the most worthy house of Wollaton with diverse others of great account . . .' It would be kind perhaps to regard this tablet as the memorial to the unfortunate architect, and the house as that to his relentless client.

Pattern books from Flanders were ransacked to provide a riot of decorative motifs for the house. Here we see Flemish gables with strapwork writhing over their stone faces and wreathing their sides. Classical orders are piled one above the other, and the very chimney pots sprout from classical columns. The wide, mullioned windows are framed in classical pilasters, and the pilasters, in turn, are separated by niches channelled to receive nearly two hundred statues, whilst any bare wall space which remains is punctured by classical 'portholes' from which busts of Hercules, Diana and a dozen more mythical deities gaze across the Nottingham landscape. In the roof of the Great Hall, the timber construction is painted to resemble stone, and light is supplied to the lofty room only by the windows piercing the high central tower. The kitchens which serve Wollaton Hall are almost underground, an arrangement more reminiscent of 1888 than 1588.

A house is largely a reflection or an extension of the personality of the owner. At Hardwick Hall in Derbyshire, the effect of the personality of the owner was no less marked than at Wollaton, but the indomitable Elizabeth of Shrewsbury (better known as 'Bess of Hardwick'), was such a cultivated and able client that the final result was very different from that achieved at Wollaton. That she dominated the whole splendid conception there is no doubt, and the architect, whoever it may have been, was entirely subordinate to the owner. This was by no means her only experience of architecture. Her successive marriages had given her ample wealth and opportunity to indulge her passion for building but of all the great houses with which she was associated, Hardwick Hall, one of the most beautiful houses of this period, alone remains. Worksop was burned in the eighteenth century, Oldcotes has long since disappeared, Chatsworth is entirely transformed, and Hardwick Old Hall, now in ruins beside her splendid new house, was looted to provide material for this, her most remarkable production.

It seems probable that Robert Smithson, the architect of Wollaton, also worked at Hardwick, but there is no doubt at all that his designs would have been rigorously scrutinised by his ruthless and intelligent client, and that he would have had little freedom of planning. Such an unorthodox arrangement as that of placing the Great Hall at right angles to the main axis of the building may have been the architect's idea, or that of the owner, but it suggests that neither had much use for stereotyped plans.

Nevertheless, the plan is emphatically symmetrical and the high pavilions which appeared at the four corners of Wollaton, are to be seen here not only at the corners but in the centre of each end elevation as well. Here any resemblance to Wollaton ends. There is no indiscriminate plastering of the surface with a riot of ill-digested motifs from Flemish pattern books. The long horizontal lines of the front, punctuated by the clear vertical rhythm of the huge grid-iron windows give a sense of serenity and repose. The house has that clarity of shape, and an acceptance of purposeful construction which one associates with good modern architecture, and the reticent mouldings and comparatively untroubled skyline all contribute to the dignity and personality of the great house.

The low ripple of balustrading which crowns the upper storey is beautifully subdued in order to give just that slight prominence to the monogram, E.S. (Elizabeth of Shrewsbury), which forms the central motif to each tower, a quiet but firm reminder of the creator of this mighty house.

The same firm reticence is to be seen within. The screen in the Hall – a light airy series of columns very different from the solid mediaeval version – is beautifully proportioned, and the decoration over the fireplace, with heraldic stags enmeshed in flat Tudor strap-work, is discreetly modulated to the scale of the Hall. The designs which decorate the plaster ceilings and the carved fireplaces through-out the buildings are all by local workmen and although they betray the foreign origin of the basic details, they are interpreted with the sensitivity of a true craftsman. The feverish and restless decoration, all too common in some Elizabethan houses, finds no place at Hardwick, and although we are not entirely in agreement with one distinguished writer who described the High Presence Chamber at Hardwick to be '. . . the most beautiful room, not in England alone, but in the whole of Europe' it is nevertheless a superb room, and one moreover which demonstrates the peculiarly English genius for taking alien ideas and so blending and modifying them with our own that they become part of our own architectural vocabulary.

The coloured plaster reliefs which adorn the upper part of the High Presence Chamber are typical examples of the natural ability of the native craftsmen to take two quite different sources of design – the classical and the mediaeval and to reconcile them with such intuitive skill that they form a coherent unity. The plasterwork at Hardwick is far more ably controlled than that at Burton Agnes in Yorkshire, for example, where it has a 'nouveau-riche' quality scarcely less objectionable than that which permeates Wollaton. Plasterwork of the quality of that to be seen at Hardwick Hall and at Montacute House in Somerset represents to us the very best of Elizabethan 'folk art.' It demonstrates the fusion of native craftsman-ship and foreign ideas to form an entirely original product.

Before we leave Hardwick Hall, mention must be made of the Gallery, which, some 150 feet long, stretches across the whole of the Eastern front. As we have already indicated, the Elizabethan Long Gallery played an important role in the household, and here at Hardwick it seems possible that it not only provided ample accom-modation for the usual activities of dancing, music making, and so on, but was also designed to display the superb set of tapestries we can still see adorning its walls. In a house which is singularly rich in tapestry and embroidery, perhaps the finest complete set of tapestry there is that acquired from Sir Christopher Hatton for £326 some four years before Hardwick was built, and the size of which may account for the unusually lofty dimensions of the Gallery. It is of course impossible to mention all the houses of this period possessing nobly-designed Long Galleries, but few can compare with that at Hardwick. (*Plate 17.*)

By 1607, shortly after the completion of Hardwick, that monu-ment in stone to its indomitable mistress, plans were already afoot for the erection of another ambitious house, this time of brick, by another powerful family of the Elizabethan Court. This is Hatfield House, just north of London, built by Robert Cecil, the son of the Lord Burghley whose mansion at Stamford we have already considered earlier in this chapter.

Hatfield House was a modern building erected on the site of and with materials partly derived from a former Royal Palace. Of this Palace, the Great Hall is the only part which survives. The new house is of rosy red brick, with stone features embodied in it forming a core to the refined symmetry of the whole design. It is unfortunate that the public are not normally able to see its most imposing façade – that facing the garden, for they are only admitted from the other side. The plan is 'H' shaped, with a most elaborate central feature crowned by a tower and forming a stone centrepiece, flanked by red brick wings which are decorated with square turrets topped by the familiar sugar-sifter cupolas. Apart from the curved Flemish gables, the roof line is carefully controlled by a restrained balustrading which serves to emphasise the stability and dignity of the disciplined façade below it. The Great Hall is again at the centre of the plan, but its screen is rather more ornate than its mediaeval ancestor, and the ceiling, instead of being of exposed timber construction, is almost flat, and panelled with the usual Flemish strapwork motifs in finely worked plaster.

It is in this house that we encounter the Elizabethan staircase as a decorative and prestige-enhancing feature. Despite the attention lavished on the staircase at Hatfield, it is perhaps more curious than beautiful. Robert Cecil took great delight in the building of his house, and employed a Dutch craftsman named Janivers to design and construct the staircase. It is an odd mixture of Dutch pattern book details, of motifs derived somewhat remotely from the Italian Renaissance and of classical notions wrongfully employed and only partly understood. The naked Cupids adorning the newel posts, had they been carved by an Italian, would have been light and graceful. As they emerge from under the Dutchman's chisel, they have a suetty quality – a heavy Germanic solidity very unlike the Italian examples from which they were derived. The classical pilasters on either side of the newel posts contain an incongruous mixture of Roman urns, swags and carved gardening tools. The very post on which each Cupid stands is a debased form of column, tapered in reverse, being far wider at the shoulder than the base. Nevertheless, the staircase is clearly an important feature architecturally in this great house, and as such heralds an important addition to domestic architecture.

To study the staircase of this period at its very best we should visit Knole Park in Kent. Built about 1604–1608, the superb staircase in this house is more mature and evolved in its design than any built so far.

Knole Park, a complex house which developed over a number of years, embodies many features with which our readers will be familiar by now, and although hardly a fraction of its rooms are as yet available to the public, it is still a memorable house to explore. The Great Hall is a lofty room about the dimensions of a tennis court, with an ornately carved screen, a restrained Tudor fireplace and a delicately modelled plaster ceiling. The staircase leads directly out of the Great Hall, and after walking up and down it a few times one can experience to the full the exact rightness of proportion of tread to rise, and understand the relationship of the banisters set at precisely the most comfortable height under the hand, and the logical and generous proportions of the landings, lit by ample windows, with which each flight of stairs ends. The staircase is supported by beautifully fashioned classical pillars, economically decorated, and relying more for their beauty on delicacy of proportion than on applied ornament. The panelling is decorated in 'grisaille' – a series of silvery toned paintings in grey.

Carving is restrained, except on the newel posts, where the sculptor has concentrated all his energies on the magnificent Sackville leopards which squat with tense and sinuous grace at the head of each banister. By 1604, the art of heraldry had deteriorated sadly, but here at Knole, most unexpectedly we come upon leopards so brilliantly carved that they would take their place as heraldic art with the finest of those blazoned on the stall plates and banners in Windsor Chapel Royal. The rotund phlegmatic little cupids at Hatfield are poor indeed when compared with these vital leopards at Knole. (*Plate 20.*)

Knole Park has several galleries. One is known as the Cartoon Gallery, but as the cartoons hung in it were drawn by a Dutch artist named Mytens who was not in England until 1618, it would seem that the gallery was not specially built to accommodate the cartoons, and received its name later. Because of its complexity and its slowly evolved pattern Knole Park is not typical of the great houses of this period, however. There was an increasing tendency to plan a great house theoretically on paper, sometimes with little regard for its function.

It is perhaps for this reason that Sir Francis Bacon, who produced essays on so many subjects, opened the one 'Of Building' with the following words 'Houses are built to Live in, and not to Looke on: Therefore let Use bee preferred before Uniformitie . . .'

All too often his advice was to be disregarded, not only by his contemporaries, but by later architects. Not all the houses of this period were as beautifully designed as Montacute House, or Parham Park, or displayed such sensitive handling of brickwork as that to be seen at Blickling Hall or Bramhall. Where ostentation replaced reticence either outside the buildings, as at Wollaton, or within the building as at Audley End or Aston Hall, the results could be lamentable. Such fireplaces as that to be seen in the Long Gallery at Aston Hall are a sad commentary on the taste of the craftsmen who designed it and on that of the nobleman who commissioned it. Here masks, grotesques, scrolls and strapwork sprawl in profusion over the chimneypiece – 'fairground' Elizabethan at its worst – and the marble studs which project from the stone like monstrous winegums do little to improve the general effect. (*Plate 18*.)

The same incongruous profusion of ornament can be seen in some of the tombs in cathedrals and churches of this period, surrounding the architectural framework in which the Elizabethan or Jacobean lord and lady lie at rest. Some of the effigies follow the traditional design, and are portrayed lying face upwards, their hands pressed together in prayer. Others adopt a new and far more casual attitude, their heads propped nonchalantly under their hands, and their eyes fixed, not on Heaven, but on their fellow men. This was so marked a departure from the normal procedure that we find the dramatist John Webster commenting on it in his play *The Duchess of Malfi* where one of the characters says:

> 'Princes' effigies on their tombs
> Do not lie as they were wont, gazing on Heaven,
> But with their hands under their heads, as if
> They died of the toothache; they are no longer fashioned
>   With their eyes fixed upon the stars, but as
> Their minds were wholly bent upon the world,
> The self-same way they seem to turn their faces.'

This reclining position is actually derived from Italian sources, for it first appears in a church in Rome, introduced by the Italian architect, Sansovino.

But if some of our ancestors no longer gazed upon the stars, the actions which resulted from their being absorbed with the world around them were by no means without merit. Since the Reformation, the void left by the disappearance of those churchmen concerned with the education and welfare of the underprivileged, the aged and the sick, had been filled by many worthy laymen. If, as Webster has said, 'their minds were wholly bent upon the world' they were at least determined that the world as they saw it should be a better and more kindly place for their having passed through it. To this end they founded university colleges and grammar schools, and endowed

E

almshouses and hospitals, accepting the responsibilities which accompanied their new-found wealth as well as the benefits it conferred upon them. Many of our grammar school boys and girls, now attending the complex and airy schools provided by the Welfare State wear on their blazers the crests of the seventeenth century gentlemen who originally founded those schools. At the annual Founders' Day Service they listen to the quaint and often lovely English of the Bidding Prayer in which are remembered the names of the men and women who endowed the schools, and to the superb passage from Ecclesiasticus which starts 'Let us now praise famous men, and our fathers that begat us.' As the splendid sentences roll on perhaps even the least attentive in that congregation must detect some link between the vast concrete and steel construction which they call school and the humble little brick-gabled building with its handful of reluctant scholars from which it has all evolved.

The syllabus at such a grammar school in the beginning was, of course, restricted and could be taught in one room, for there was no need for specialised rooms, the laboratories, the domestic science rooms and so on which are essential to modern education. The school was a house which provided accommodation for the master, and usually one large room for teaching purposes. From such a humble building emerged eventually even such famous schools as Harrow, founded in 1611. Shakespeare himself went to just such a grammar school, and the many classical allusions to be found in his plays imply that his audience were at least sufficiently well grounded in the classics to understand the 'hydra-headed multitude,' the fate of one of his characters who was borne 'Like Orion on the dolphin's back' and other references which are apt to be lost on the modern audience.

Fragments of these seemly little buildings are still to be seen all over the country, their Flemish brick gables and crumbling stone heraldic plaques carrying the debased Roman lettering so dear to the Elizabethan or Jacobean gentleman, now quite overshadowed by more recent buildings and often to be found disused and neglected in the less fashionable parts of our industrial cities.

Considerable additions were also made at this time to our university buildings. Some of the most characteristic are the delightful little fountain at Trinity College, and the Gate of Honour at Caius, both in Cambridge, the Tower of the Schools with its Five Orders of Architecture piled one above the other, at Oxford, and, of course, the entrance to Wadham College at the same University. These are examples of the most modern architectural expression of the first quarter of the seventeenth century, although it is worth noting that the builders of most of Wadham College, masons from Somerset, fashioned it in their traditional mediaeval style, and the great hammerbeam roof which spans its Hall is equally old fashioned in its construction.

The piety of the philanthropists also found expression in the many almshouses and 'hospitals' founded at this time. Some were a direct continuation or expansion of those which had lapsed during the troublous times following the Reformation; of these, Leycester Hospital refounded by the Earl of Leicester in Warwick about 1571 may be regarded as typical. Others, such as Penrose's Almshouses in Barnstaple, Devon, founded about 1627, were new foundations established to continue the charitable work which had formerly been the monopoly of the Church. Few were as magnificent architecturally as the Abbot's Hospital at Guildford, but even the more unobtrusive which still continue to serve the old people in many a country town are well worth our consideration. There is a humane warmth about their soft brick courtyards and flagged paths, a decency and intimacy of layout and proportion which all combine to make them homely and non-institutional. We are faced today with caring for a larger number of elderly people than at any other time in our history, and although it would not be wise merely to copy the architectural forms of the Elizabethan almshouses in modern materials, there is much to be learned from the intimate and friendly scale of these buildings.

A widespread erection of market halls in the new style followed the increase in trade and accumulating wealth of this period, and here again local craftsmen produced a great many comely buildings from the local materials. At Chipping Campden in Gloucestershire and at Rothwell in Northamptonshire, for example, they are of stone, the strong local architectural tradition imposing a discipline on the imported classical forms and combining them with grace and dignity to conform with the other buildings around. At Ledbury, in Herefordshire, however, the Market House has little to do with the new style, and apart from a few details, its timber construction could belong to the century before, although it was actually built about 1633. There was, however, widespread concern at the enormous wastage of wood involved in the construction of timber-framed buildings as a whole. The multiplication of the number of rooms in the house, the clothing of these rooms with wainscot and panelling and the increased number of articles of furniture meant serious demands on the store of seasoned timber – a store which was also being depleted by the needs of the Navy. The ships and their escorts were thrusting in every direction to the limits of the known world and beyond, and the manufacture of the very cannon with which they were armed devoured more and more wood as the furnaces of the Weald of Kent smelted the iron and cast their formidable snub muzzles and a hundred and one other items of naval equipment. Timber was moreover a dangerously inflammable material from which to build houses in a tightly congested town area, and the expression 'to spread like wildfire' had an unpleasantly real meaning to the seventeenth century citizen, whose only means of lighting and heating his house was a naked flame.

It was for these reasons that a number of royal proclamations decreed that London houses should have brick and stone fronts, but timber houses nevertheless continued to predominate and this disregard of the royal decrees was to have disastrous results later in the century. London mansions such as Old Somerset House and Northumberland House which had considerable effect on the style of architecture of their day have since disappeared entirely, whilst others are but ruined shells. Of the latter, two of the most important are Cowdray House, in Sussex, and Kirby Hall, in Northamptonshire. Enough still remains of Kirby Hall to enable the architectural student to reconstruct detective-fashion the many sources from which its architect drew his inspiration. Whoever designed Kirby Hall extracted some details from a Flemish textbook published in Zurich in the middle of the sixteenth century, combined them with those from the writings of Sebastiano Serlio, the Italian, and together with others from French sources succeeded in welding them into a surprising unity.

A romantic interest in the mediaeval past gave rise to a number of Elizabethan and Jacobean buildings in a pseudo-Gothic style. Of these, Bolsover Castle in Derbyshire is one which is well worth a visit. For all its appearance of military might, however, it was helpless to prevent the devastation of the valley below by the barons of iron and coal, and its walls only stand now through the care and supervision of the Ministry of Works.

Other Elizabethan houses were either considerably altered by their later occupants, as at Lacock and Osterley, Audley End and Castle Ashby, or were even demolished and sold piecemeal, fireplaces, staircases, panelling and other architectural details being incorporated into the fabric of houses in other parts of the country, or as with the remains of Warwick Priory, transhipped to the United States and re-erected there.

The unusual developments in the design of the house are as characteristic of the sixteenth century as that of the parish church in the preceding chapter, and it is for this reason that it has been dealt with at some length. We have traced the development of the idea of the symmetrical plan, the emphasis on the Great Hall, the evolution of the Long Gallery as an integral part of the 'E' and 'H' shaped plan, the introduction of the staircase as an architectural feature in its own right; and we have indicated the sources from which the design of screens, fireplaces, ceilings and so many other features were derived. If in its early days the great house justified the quotation from Shakespeare with which we ended the last chapter, by the end of the century there emerges a more coherent picture, and the recognition of the need for a unified control of the whole complex operation of designing, planning and decorating a house. This unified control was difficult all the while the final decisions were in the hands of many people – the patron who was obliged to instruct his mason/architect from long range or with insufficient technical knowledge to make his orders architecturally intelligible, or the mason/architect well able to execute his own work, but finding it difficult to co-ordinate all the other activities. By the beginning of the seventeenth century, however, there emerged one of the first great architects, as dominant in his own sphere as his brilliant contemporary, Shakespeare, was in the theatre. This was Inigo Jones, an architect of such genius that his work was not only to have a profound effect on the design of buildings in the seventeenth century, but on the entire course of architecture in England. The next chapter therefore must open with an examination of the work of this remarkable man, and the architecture of the century which followed.

Chapter Eight

THE SEVENTEENTH CENTURY

IT is remarkable to observe the persistence with which the human race has sought for perfection throughout its long history. The manifestations of this search are as rich and as complex as life itself, ranging from the noblest of religious aspirations to the quest for a bikini-clad female of such exquisite proportions, such vital statistics that she alone might be worthy to stand crowned the 'Cotton Queen' of the current financial year at the Ideal Home Exhibition.

In architecture, however, the quest has usually been directed to the most minute examination of the measurements and proportions of buildings accepted by common consent to be the most beautiful examples of their kind, and then, by analysis of the proportions thus studied to evolve rules from which other buildings might be created. This attempt to reduce beauty to a comprehensible formula – a sort of mathematical 'Philosopher's Stone' by which the base metal of building might be turned to the richest architectural gold has indeed had some odd results. Where the architect employing the formula has been an artist of sensibility, the resulting buildings have been lovely things, but where he was not, the products have been all too often worthy but dull. In exactly the same way, the rules which govern Harmony and Counterpoint handled by a Beethoven or a Mozart have produced noble music. In less sensitive hands they have produced little more than a deplorable exhibition of musical pedantry.

The canons of proportion expounded by Vitruvius in the first century B.C. were rediscovered by Renaissance scholars and architects in Italy during the early years of the fifteenth century and revealed to them the order and discipline which permeated classical architecture. With tireless enthusiasm they squatted in the hot sunshine or grovelled in the cool caverns of the excavated past, checked and re-checked the eroded remnants of column, capital, architrave and cornice, committed them to paper in a host of meticulous drawings and published their findings with scholarly pride.

134

Both classical buildings and those derived however remotely from them have two important factors in common – the use of the Orders of Architecture and the module dependent upon them. The module is not a recognisable measurement such as a foot or a yard. It is usually the radius of the column employed in the Order, and just as the type of Order – Doric, Ionic, Corinthian, etc. determines the exact proportion of column to capital, column to entablature and the relationship of each part of the building to the whole, so the module determines their size and dimensions. It must be remembered that Renaissance architects were employing classical proportions and details on a variety of buildings quite unknown to their Roman ancestors. The Roman villa, for example, bears little relation to the villas erected all over the north of Italy during the sixteenth century, and certainly the great churches designed for Christian worship bore only a superficial resemblance to the pagan temples whose details they so clearly adapted.

Having recognised the mathematical basis on which all classical architecture had been established, the Renaissance architects pursued their search for mathematical perfection. They sought for a system of related proportions until it became something of an obsession only equalled today perhaps by those gamblers who are still convinced that there is a mathematical system somewhere awaiting discovery by which they will break the Bank at Monte Carlo or win vast fortunes on the football pools.

During their exploration of the architectural possibilities of geometrical patterns, and the harmonies of mathematical progressions from which these patterns could be evolved, many of these writers developed most involved philosophical theories which to the modern mind at least seem to have little to do with the very practical business of architecture. One important theory they had in common, however, which is as valid today as it was when the Renaissance architects first deduced it from their classical studies, is the one defined by Leon Battista Alberti. From the writings of Vitruvius he extracted the truth that beauty is '. . . the harmony and concord of all parts achieved in such a manner that nothing could be added or taken away except for the worse.' A building must in fact be conceived as a completely integrated unit, in which even the smallest detail must contribute to the harmony of the whole, and this rational mathematical interpretation of beauty produces a clarity and lucidity of architectural design which is characteristic of all fine buildings. More important from our point of view than the writings of Alberti, however, are those of one of his successors, the Venetian architect Andrea di Pietro, better known as Andrea Palladio. His theories of architectural design and the beauty of his buildings were to have considerable influence on the English architect, Inigo Jones, and somewhat later, in eighteenth-century England, on that select group of architects and their patrons who were proud to call themselves Palladians.

Andrea Palladio (1518–1580) was born in Northern Italy in Vicenza, a city which he later returned to and beautified when he had become a trained and accomplished architect. He intended at first to become a sculptor and made his way to Rome, but, inspired by the beauty of buildings being erected there by Michelangelo's great rival, Donato Bramante, and by the splendour of the ruins of ancient Rome, he determined to become an architect. In 1554 he published the results of his extensive researches into classical antiquity in a book called *The Antiquities of Rome*, but his most influential book, by far, was published in 1570. This monumental, four-volume work was his famous *I Quattro Libri dell'Architettura*. The first volume dealing with the principles of architectural design was clearly derived from the writings of Vitruvius. The second volume, however, was concerned with Palladio's own original theories, and with constructive principles which were the result of the author's own practical experience. The third book dealt mainly with problems of town planning, and the fourth with the layout and design of pagan temples and to a limited extent with the design of Christian churches. Together these four books became a kind of architectural bible – a holy writ to which many architects were to turn again and again for guidance and instruction. The effect of the treatise was all the more permanent because not only were the theories in it stimulating, but the author himself was a practising architect whose buildings could be seen to demonstrate and to vindicate the theories and arguments set forth in his book.

Andrea Palladio was the architect most admired and respected by Inigo Jones, although during his travels the Englishman spread his intellectual net very wide and his study was by no means confined to this particular writer. His books – many of them now preserved in the library at Worcester College, Oxford – and the variety and sources from which he drew ideas for his own buildings, show that Inigo Jones availed himself of every possible source to enrich his architectural and artistic education. His was no blind acceptance of a current architectural theory, but a penetrating and critical analysis of architectural method, not only from drawings and writings, but from the original buildings and the classical sources from which many had been derived. He studied first hand the work of Bramante, looking at his charming Tempietto in Rome with a critical eye. He examined drawings and books by Serlio, the works of Raphael the great painter and architect, and even of the Frenchman Philibert de l'Orme, subjecting their drawings to the most minute analysis, working over them again and again, dividers in hand, to check and compare and to assess their architectural worth. The result of this painstaking and scholarly research must be sought not only in his writings but in the architecture he created here in England.

The early years of this most remarkable man are something of a mystery. A creative artist in those days was almost wholly dependent on noble patronage for his livelihood, unless he happened to be a member of a wealthy family. Of Inigo Jones's family we know very little, but it is certain that the child who was christened on July 19, 1573, in the church of St Bartholomew-the-Less, Smithfield, inherited little money from his clothworker father. Of his upbringing, education and training for the first thirty years of his life, there is little record. Nevertheless, his precious copy of Palladio's *Quattro Libri dell'Architettura* in which he jotted down so many personal observations is inscribed '1601 In loccato Ven' so that by the time he was 28 years of age this young Englishman had somehow contrived to travel to Venice and to lay the foundations of a considerable collection of books and drawings to which he added from time to time in the course of his successful and rewarding career. Some authorities state that he had in fact also journeyed to Denmark, possibly in the retinue of an English nobleman such as the Duke of Rutland, but whatever the truth we can be sure that Inigo Jones emerged first publicly not as an architect but as a theatrical designer – the artist responsible for the décor for the Twelfth Night production of Ben Jonson's *Masque of Blackness*, produced in 1605. The freedom and grace of his costume designs, the imaginative liveliness of his drafts for theatrical sets testify to the supple and creative mind behind the drawings. In the years to come Inigo Jones was to design the settings and costumes for no less than twenty three Court masques, and a considerable number of those lovely drawings can still be seen in the Duke of Devonshire's library at Chatsworth House in Derbyshire. Profiting by his visits to Italy, Inigo Jones was able to introduce movable scenery and what we should now call backdrops into the masques at court, and since many of the masques were performed by amateur actors, members of the aristocracy, they were quick to realise the talents of this young theatrical designer.

By September, 1613, Inigo Jones was back again in Italy, this time with Lord and Lady Arundel, acting as his Lordship's adviser in the purchase of works of art for his collection, but also pursuing his own investigation in architectural matters. He visited Palladio's beautiful Villa Capra, talking to the aged Scamozzi (a former pupil of Palladio) and making sketches not only from architecture, but also from painting and sculpture. Two busy years thus passed with visits to Rome, Naples, Genoa and to France where he drew the Pont du Gard, scrutinised the Maison Carrée at Nîmes, and examined the famous double staircase at the Château de Chambord, in the valley of the Loire.

Shortly after his return to England in 1615, Inigo Jones accepted the post of Surveyor-General of the King's Works and Buildings – an appointment which he was to fill with distinction until like many another loyal servant of the king he was to pay for his devoted service with imprisonment and loss of his property at the hands of the Cromwellians. Despite his lack of practical experience in architecture, there can have been no man in England better equipped to build for his Royal client. Although his creative work had been confined to theatrical design, it is evident that he had been absorbed by purely architectural problems for many years and his career has been most ably summarised in his own words. 'Being naturally inclined in my younger years to study the Arts of Design, I passed into foreign parts to converse with the great masters thereof in Italy; when I applied myself to search out the ruins of those ancient buildings which despite of time itself, and violence of barbarians, are yet remaining. Having satisfied myself in them, and returning to my native country, I applied my mind more particularly to the study of architecture.'

It is illuminating to compare Inigo Jones's own words with those of Andrea Palladio for whom he had such admiration. In the preface to his famous treatise, Palladio says 'My natural inclination leading me, from my infancy, to the Study of Architecture, I resolved to apply myself to it: and because I ever was of opinion, that the ancient Romans did far exceed all that have come after them, as in many things so particularly in Building, I proposed to myself Vitruvius both as my Master and Guide, he being the only ancient author that remains extant on this Subject. Then, I betook myself to the Search and Examination of such Rules of ancient Structures as, in spight of Time and the rude hands of Barbarians, are still remaining; and finding that they deserved a much more diligent Observation than I thought at first Sight, I began with the utmost Accuracy to measure even the minutest part by itself; ... to publish to the World the Designs (or Draughts) of those Edifices, which with equal Expence of Time and Danger to my Person, I have collected; and briefly to set down what seem'd to me most worthy to be considered in them; and further to give those Rules which I have hitherto follow'd in Building, and which I still follow, to the end that they who shall read my Books, may be able to practise whatever they find useful in them, and to supply what is wanting, as many such things there may be.'

The phrases are occasionally almost identical, and the intention of each very similar. Inigo Jones also agrees with the Palladian rules of proportion for the most beautiful shapes for a room, viz. '. . . round, square, diagonal proportion, a square and a third, a square and a half, a square and two thirds or two squares.'

But we should be doing Inigo Jones a grave injustice if we were to imply that he was merely an English echo of an Italian voice. As R. H. Wilenski has observed in writing about Rembrandt, the painter – a great Dutch contemporary of Inigo Jones – 'A small man uses another man's work to make good his own creative inability. A great man uses another man's work as a jumping-off point for an enlargement of his own experience.' Inigo Jones had ample creative ability, and we can only regret that of the score or so buildings which he designed only eight survive today, and of these only four are sufficiently well preserved to give us some idea of his genius. Many buildings have been attributed to him because they were either built during his lifetime or bore a superficial resemblance to his style. Others have now been assigned to his faithful assistant and biographer, John Webb, who, overshadowed by his master, has only of recent years been acclaimed as a creative architect in his own right.

The four with which we are most concerned are the Queen's House at Greenwich, the Banqueting House, Whitehall, Marlborough House Chapel, and finally, Wilton House near Salisbury, in Wiltshire.

The emotional effect of architecture, as with any other art, varies considerably. Some buildings repel us, some attract us, whilst others seem to have no discernible effect at all. But occasionally – and it is an all too rare experience – we see a building which gives us such a sense of exaltation, such a lifting of the heart, that we know for certain that we are confronted with great architecture. Prolonged acquaintance with this quality of architecture only intensifies our first impression. We have always regarded the saying that 'Familiarity breeds contempt' as one of the sillier half-truths, and we suspect that if familiarity does indeed breed contempt, the object of the contempt can have been worth little else from the start. Familiarity with such buildings as King's College Chapel, the Senate House at Cambridge, the Lantern at Ely, and a few other examples we could mention has not bred contempt, but only a deepened sense of wonder at their perfection. Among the select group of buildings which still evoke this kind of response after a number of years we would certainly include the Queen's House at Greenwich. Whether we see it from the precipitous slopes of Greenwich Park, or from the noisy clangour of the main road which severs it from the Naval College, and despite certain additions made to it in the early nineteenth century, it is still a memorable example of fine architecture.

It was designed by Inigo Jones in 1616 – the year after his great contemporary, William Shakespeare, died – to be a more worthy gatehouse than the existing one which spanned the main road to enable the Queen to cross into the Park. Queen Anne, the Danish wife of James I, had already employed Inigo Jones to design her masques for her, but the Queen's House, and work on the now vanished palace of Oatlands in Surrey, were among the first architectural commissions undertaken by the newly appointed Surveyor-General. (*Plate 23.*)

The house, as Jones designed it, was 'H' shaped in plan, the crossbar of the 'H' being the bridge across the Deptford–Woolwich road. One side of the house, 115 feet long, containing the Hall, faces the river, the other faces the rising ground of Greenwich Park. It was not until after the architect's death that his assistant, John Webb, added two further bridges and converted the plan to its present square. In plan, therefore, the house differs but little from any other house of the period. In every other way it is quite different. Instead of a mediaeval house with inept additions picked at random from a pattern book, the whole building is designed, logically and beautifully, in the classical manner, following the rule of the perfect relationship of part to part to produce a completely integrated whole. The elevation is clear, untroubled and serene. The roofline in this period, too often a conflicting array of gables, chimneys and sculpture, in this building is controlled by a balustrade which conceals a flattened roof. Two exactly placed chimneys give a vertical emphasis to the centre of each wing. The elevation facing the river stands on a low terrace, reached by a charming little symmetrical pair of staircases, and is divided into three parts – a central feature a little wider than its flanking wings with a very slight projection to provide a discreet emphasis, and with two rows of three windows to complete its domination of the wings. They have two rows of but two windows each. The lower storey is made to look a little more massive than the upper by skilful use of rusticated stone, a sheathing to strengthen the effect of the whole building which is actually built of plastered brick.

The second half of the building facing the Park also has a dominant central feature, but its upper storey is a charming loggia, with a low balcony and six Ionic columns. Nothing like this building was known in England, and the interior was even more remarkable to its Jacobean visitors than the outside. Gone was the hall with the dark panelling, the hammerbeam roof or the heavily encrusted ceiling. In its place was a light airy room two stories high, with plastered walls which reflected the light, a balustrade above giving access to the rooms on either wing, and reached by a graceful spiral staircase. The floor was of marble with a geometrical pattern which emphasised the absolute symmetry of the room. True to his findings from Palladio and the other Italian masters, Inigo Jones made this main room a cube of 40 feet, and the lesser rooms a square and two thirds in proportion. The house was once known as the House of Delight – a name as suitable now as it was then. It is a house which must be moved in and examined to realise its full worth, and although it has been sadly maltreated in the past, it is now beautifully restored, if a little empty. The Maritime Museum maintains it well, hanging its walls wherever possible with contemporary painting, but it sadly needs furniture and fabrics if it is ever to be more than a lovely shell.

Just before the death of Queen Anne of Denmark, work on it was halted, so that it was not completed until 1635, when Henrietta Maria, the Queen of Charles I, commanded that it be finished. Because of this interruption in its construction, it is not actually the first house in England to be built in the new style, for the Banqueting House in Whitehall, started three years after the Queen's House, was completed by 1622. Despite the ravages of London smoke the Banqueting House is still one of the most impressive buildings in London. Jones evidently had great difficulty in deciding on its final appearance, for the entrance had to be at the narrow end, and to have a Palladian elevation at all it would have to be on the longest sides – the one facing the river or the other stretching along White-hall. The drawings in Chatsworth show two versions which Jones visualised before settling on the final one we see today. Of the plans for a vast palace in Whitehall which Inigo Jones and John Webb drew up this building is the only surviving part. It will be observed that in everything he did, Jones was sure of encouragement and understanding from his patrons. Without the right kind of intel-lectual climate the creative artist, although he will survive, can never develop to his full stature, and his work will never reach complete maturity. Fortunately for him and for us, the Court of both James I and Charles I with all its political failings had a very clear idea of what constituted fine art and the vital role it should play in both private and public life. Inspired by such books as *The Compleat Gentleman* by Henry Peachum, published in London in 1622, and by the example of the King, the Court not only represented an aristocracy of power, but an aristocracy of culture as well. No gentleman could consider himself truly complete unless he under-stood the principles of the arts and sciences. This is borne out by the description by William Lilly of King Charles 'He had many excellent parts in nature, was an excellent horseman, would shoot well at a mark, had singular skill in limning (painting), was a good judge of pictures, a good mathematician, not unskilful in music, well read in divinity, excellent in history and law; spoke several languages and writ well, good language and style.' Small wonder that such a man demanded nothing less than the best of those he employed – Van Dyck to paint his portraits, Peter Paul Rubens to decorate the ceiling of his Banqueting House and a Surveyor-General such as Inigo Jones.

When completed in 1622, and even some twenty-seven years later when on that bleak January day, Charles I stepped out of it on to the scaffold, the Banqueting House looked somewhat different from the building which now faces the Horse Guards. Now it has glazed windows overlooking Whitehall. Originally the windows on this side were blocked in, and not all of those on the river side were glazed. The sash windows we now see were not used in England until towards the end of the seventeenth century, and those designed by Inigo Jones had mullions and transoms of stone. The serene and dignified front which was to be the inspiration for a great deal of Georgian street architecture was originally composed of three different types of stone – tawny Northamptonshire stone for the base, grey stone brought from Oxfordshire and from Yorkshire for the main storey (the piano nobile) and white Portland stone for the balustrading. All this subsequently suffered so severely from air pollution that it had to be entirely recased. (*Plate 22.*)

The interior of this magnificent building is a double cube measuring 110 feet long, 55 feet broad and 55 feet high. (A good deal bigger in floor space than a tennis court, which measures only 78 feet by 36 feet). It was enriched with paintings by Peter Paul Rubens in 1634.

Between 1623 and 1627, Inigo Jones was principally engaged on the design and construction of his first church, although his duties as Surveyor-General did not prevent his continuing to design costumes and settings for the masques, or acting as advisor to Lord Arundel and to the King on the purchase of works of art. The church, now Marlborough House Chapel, was originally designed for the Roman Catholic Infanta of Spain, but when she failed to come to England, it was used by Henrietta Maria, and still later, after its pillage by the Cromwellian forces, it was restored and used by Queen Catherine, the wife of Charles II.

The Chapel (one of the first churches we have referred to since those passages dealing with the Reformation) demonstrates once again Inigo Jones's preference for the proportions laid down by Andrea Palladio, for it is a double cube, 56 feet long, 28 feet wide and 28 feet high with a superb coffered ceiling, itself derived from *The Four Books of Architecture.*

One respect in which Inigo Jones differs from Andrea Palladio is in his attitude towards decoration. For the Italian, it was necessary that decoration should arise from the constructive units of the building.

Inigo Jones, whilst he emphasised that decoration should be restrained and controlled, particularly on the outside of a building, was
prepared to superimpose such units as columns and pilasters for
their decorative effect, and not because there was any constructional
need for them. Nevertheless, he asserted that '. . . The outward ornament is to be solid, proportional according to rule, masculine and
unaffected.'

The exterior of the Chapel is indeed somewhat plain – (almost dull)
but the interior, now beautifully restored, is very fine, with its
magnificent coffered ceiling, and what is considered to be the first
example of a Venetian window in this country. This type of window
which was to appear very frequently in eighteenth-century buildings,
consists of a central window over which is a semicircular arch, with a
flat topped window on either side.

The second church with which Jones was concerned was but one
unit in a whole scheme – a tentative approach to town planning – the
design of Covent Garden about 1631 on the pattern of an Italian
town square or 'piazza.' This scheme was the direct outcome of a
control of private building which Charles I ordered his Surveyor-
General to enforce. It was the first example of its kind in England,
and although it is difficult to visualise it from the present condition
of Covent Garden, a trace of his original scheme – a nobly proportioned doorway in the North Arcade – is still to be seen.

The Church of St Paul's, Covent Garden, the wonder of the
Palladians of the eighteenth century, has been rebuilt and refurbished
so many times that it is really no longer Inigo Jones's work, and even
if it is an accurate reconstruction of the original, its heavy overhanging portico and generally forbidding air makes it one of the
least pleasant of his buildings.

Nothing now remains of the extensive repairs and additions he
made to the tottering fabric of the old cathedral of St Paul's, for all
this was destroyed by Sir Christopher Wren after the Fire of London.
In any case, before all the repairs were completed, Inigo Jones's
career was interrupted by the Civil War, a catastrophe which not
only brought his brilliant career almost to an end, but was to im-
poverish him severely, and break him in health. During the Civil
War, Inigo Jones, an intimate and trusted servant of the King,
suffered imprisonment after having been taken at the siege of Basing
House in 1645. Although later the Cromwellians fined him heavily
and released him, he was by then a tired and sick old man, scarcely
able to direct and instruct his faithful assistant, John Webb. Between
them they were able to produce what is probably one of the most
beautiful suites of rooms in any house in this country – that still to
be seen at Wilton House, near Salisbury.

A disastrous fire had broken out at Wilton during 1647, destroying most of the old Tudor building, and its owner, Lord Pembroke commissioned Inigo Jones to rebuild it in the new modern style. Neither Lord Pembroke nor Inigo Jones lived long enough to see the completion of the house in 1653, but it is clear from drawings found during the last few years, annotated both by Jones and by his Assistant, Webb, that the older man designed and supervised the whole rebuilding operation, until his death in 1642. Considerable alterations were made later to the house by James Wyatt (between 1800 and 1811) but the magnificent suite which contains the famous 'double cube' and 'single cube' rooms still survives, together with the superb set of paintings by Anthony Van Dyck, still inset in the places Inigo Jones had designed for them.

Sufficient of the Tudor house survived the fire evidently for Inigo Jones to retain the basic plan for his new mansion, and he even kept corner towers as in the old house, but gave them a very different quality architecturally as we shall see.

The South front, which contains the State Rooms which are the glory of the house, is balanced symmetrically about a magnificent Venetian window – a feature we have already encountered in his design of the Royal Chapel at St James's – and this window, with its crowning sculpture, forms the focal centre of the piano nobile. The whole of the South front is spanned by a classical balustrade reminiscent of that which surmounts the Queen's House, almost concealing the roof from ground level and acting as a horizontal link between the towers at either end and the main block. To harmonise these towers (which are an un-Palladian feature) with the rest of the classical detail, Inigo Jones has surmounted each with a classical pediment where the ordinary architect of the period would probably have used the familiar sugar-dredger cupola. This original contribution to the architectural vocabulary of England was to be seized upon and used extensively as a Palladian feature by the followers of Inigo Jones in the next century, but it was in fact his own way of reconciling the towers on the Tudor plan with his own rebuilding programme.

The house appears to be dignified and a little restrained from the outside, and certainly the visitor is not prepared for the splendour which he encounters within. It is the interior of Wilton House, the perfection of its proportions and the magnificence of its ornament, which make the visit such a memorable experience.

You will recall that Alberti defined beauty as '. . . the harmony and concord of all the parts achieved in such a manner that nothing could be added or taken away or altered except for the worse.' Few buildings in England demonstrate this classical ideal as clearly as

17. Hardwick Hall, Derbyshire, the Long Gallery, *c.* 1595. A splendid example of the Elizabethan Long Gallery, measuring about 166 feet long and 22 feet wide. The bed canopy on the left is not part of the original fittings

18. The fireplace in the Long Gallery, Aston Hall, Birmingham, 1618–35. Compare this with the severity of Parham Park, in the next illustration

19. Parham Park, Sussex, 1570–90. The Great Hall seen from the 'squint' window in the solar above. A beautifully proportioned hall with exquisite refinement of detail. Note particularly the restraint of the ceiling and the classical detail of the hall screen

20. Knole Park, near Sevenoaks, Kent. The Great Staircase, c. 1605, a beautifully combined mixture of mediaeval and Renaissance forms. Note the grisaille painting on the walls, and the heraldic newel posts

21.   Wilton House, Wiltshire. The Double Cube Room, designed by Inigo
Jones, *c.* 1648 and carried out with the assistance of John Webb. The
portraits by Van Dyck are essential parts of the decoration of this superb
room. It measures 66 feet long, 33 feet wide and 33 feet high. More
recently it was used by the General Staff in which to plan 'D' Day, 1945

22. The Banqueting Hou[se] Whitehall, 1619–21. Designed by Inigo Jones, it is all that now remains o[f] the Whitehall Palace built for Charles I. It was from this building that the King walked to the scaffold

23. The Queen's House, Greenwich, the first classical Renaissance building in England, designed by Inigo Jones, 1619–35. The front facing the river. Note the severe roof-line, the symmetrically placed chimneys. The colonnades are later additions

24. The Royal Naval Hospital, Greenwich, by Wren, after 1698. The Painted Hall is in the right-hand block, the Chapel opposite. In the distance is the Queen's House

25. St Bride's Church, Fleet Street, London, *c*. 1680. A Wren City Church, with galleries. Compare the classically detailed roof with that of King's College Chapel. This photograph was taken before bomb damage necessitated extensive repair work

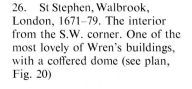

26. St Stephen, Walbrook, London, 1671–79. The interior from the S.W. corner. One of the most lovely of Wren's buildings, with a coffered dome (see plan, Fig. 20)

27. Mompesson House, Salisbury, 1701, showing the perfection of English domestic architecture on a small scale. Given after restoration by its owner, Denis Martineau, M.A., A.R.I.B.A., to the National Trust

28. Blenheim Palace, Woodstock, 1705. An exterior view of Sir John Vanbrugh's mighty memorial to the Duke of Marlborough. The courtyard is about the size of the Cup Final pitch at Wembley

29. The Grand Salon, Holkham Hall, Norfolk, *c*. 1744. William Kent, the Palladian, reduced the grandeur of a Roman palace to a scale suited to the house of a country gentleman. Note the deeply coffered ceiling, and heavy pediment to the door

30.　Syon House, Isleworth, *c.* 1762. The Dining Room. Robert Adam, its designer, said that such rooms should be 'finished with stucco, and adorned with statues and paintings, that they may not retain the smell of the victuals.' Notice the original treatment of the ceiling and compare it with that in Holkham Hall

31. Chiswick House, 1725–29, by Richard Boyle, third Earl of Burlington, and William Kent. Modelled somewhat on Palladio's Villa Capra

32. The gallery, Strawberry Hill, Twickenham. Horace Walpole started his Gothick house in 1750, using mediaeval details in an entirely non-mediaeval manner. Compare with King's College Chapel

Copyright: 'Country Life'

33. The Pagoda, Kew Gardens, 1762–3, by Sir William Chambers 'of Chinese renown'. The bizarre Oriental flavour came as a relief from an excess of classical formality

the Double Cube Room at Wilton House. Inigo Jones used this double cube proportion in several of his buildings. Here the room is 60 feet long, 30 feet broad and 30 feet high, a huge portrait group of the Herbert family by Sir Anthony Van Dyck measuring 17 feet by 11 feet occupying the greater part of the end wall. A great many portraits by this remarkable painter have been built into this room and integrated into the scheme of decoration, and although Sir Anthony Van Dyck died in 1641, there is no doubt that Inigo Jones who knew and admired him was determined that the Double Cube Room should not only do honour to the family which was employing him, but should be worthy of the great artist whose paintings were to be displayed in it. (*Plate 21*.)

The prevailing colour scheme of the room is ivory and gold, and a magnificent fireplace and overmantel occupies the centre of one side, balancing the Venetian window of which we have spoken on the other wall. Oddly enough, the fireplace was not placed centrally, and it seems possible that a fireplace already there forced the architect to adjust the position of his own, although he has accomplished this so cleverly that it is not apparent that the design is in fact not symmetrical. Decorative carvings with fruit and classical swags in high relief echo the splendour of the sculpture over the main door and on either side of the fireplace. The tame ordinary doors of an ordinary house open to admit ordinary people, but the doors at Wilton are so splendid that through them one is inclined, as an actor would say, to 'make an entrance.'

The Double Cube Room is undoubtedly the finest room at Wilton, but the others – the Single Cube Room, which follows it, and the others which precede it, are in their own way, extremely lovely.

It is difficult to determine how much this great house owes to Inigo Jones and how much to John Webb. Scholars have lately been more inclined than writers of earlier generations to allot credit to John Webb, and many buildings formerly attributed to Inigo Jones are now believed to have been designed as well as drawn by the younger man. Webb had hitherto been assigned the role of Sancho Panza to Jones's Don Quixote, but it became clear after his master's death that this particular Sancho Panza was by no means an unoriginal humble draughtsman overshadowed by a great man, but an able and sometimes inspired architect in his own right. His role was no longer confined to carrying out in precise architectural terms the larger and freer drawings of Inigo Jones's brilliantly imaginative ideas, and his work at Lamport Hall in Northamptonshire for the Isham family shows him to have had considerable ability. We now know that the early Georgian Group who so enthusiastically embraced the Palladian ideas were largely responsible, by their adulation of Inigo Jones, for the neglect of John Webb and his work, but events immediately following the Restoration show that Webb's own contemporaries had little time to spare for him. Despite his unswerving loyalty to the Crown which often put him in danger of his life, Webb was shabbily treated at the Restoration. He was obliged to see the Surveyor-Generalship he coveted and which he had been promised pass to Sir John Denham (a political and not a professional appointment) and later to another amateur, Sir Christopher Wren. Webb appears to have been a victim of that particularly English prejudice which prefers the amateur to the professional and the Gentleman to the Player. It must have been small consolation in the closing years of his life that his Charles II Block in Greenwich Palace (later the Naval Hospital and now the Naval College) dictated the overall design and that Wren himself willingly subordinated his plan to that of his assistant.

Before we turn to Sir Christopher Wren, however, we should mention, in passing, such craftsmen-architects as Nicholas Stone (1586–1647) who not only worked in close collaboration with Inigo Jones but was also responsible for the design of the charming little York House Water Gate almost on the Embankment in London, and for the flamboyant entrance to St Mary's, Oxford, and Robert Lyminge who worked at Blickling in Norfolk. It would be tempting to investigate more fully the influence of the oddly named Sir Balthazar Gerbier, the friend of Peter Paul Rubens, and of Rubens himself, but this book must guard against being too diffuse and must be content to draw the reader's attention to but one building which we know to have been erected during the Commonwealth and which must suffice to show the type of house designed during that (architecturally speaking) sterile period. This is Thorpe Hall, near Peterborough, designed by Peter Mills in 1653–1656 and one which shows an odd fusion of architecture based on the book by Peter Paul Rubens on the Palaces of Genoa, and with details derived from old Flemish pattern books and the designs of Wendel Dietterlein, the German. Mills is best known for his disciplined street architecture (Great Queen Street, Lincoln's Inn Fields) and for his work of surveyor directly after the Great Fire of London. With the Fire of London, however, we are committed to the study of one of the greatest architects England, and perhaps Europe, has ever produced – described in 1654 by the diarist, John Evelyn, as '. . . that miracle of a youth, Mr Christopher Wren.' As this book is concerned with Wren's remarkable impact on English architecture, we must pass all too quickly over his brilliant career prior to his emergence as an architect.

Christopher Wren, the son of a well-connected clergyman, was born on October 20th, 1632, at East Knoyle in Wiltshire. He grew up in the troublous times of the Civil War and his father, who was by then the Dean of Windsor, suffered from the displeasure of the Roundheads. Wren was himself at Oxford University in 1649, having already had admirable instruction in scientific matters from Dr Charles Scarborough, an eminent scientist who so stimulated this brilliant youth's interest in scientific research that he retained it all his life. It is of little value perhaps from the architectural point of view that Wren experimented with the injection of fluids into the blood stream of animals, that he produced elaborate drawings to illustrate a book on the human brain, or that he is supposed to have produced an artificial eye, except that it shows the extraordinary versatility of the man. No less an authority than Robert Hooke, the famous seventeenth-century scientist, who was later to become associated with Wren as an assistant surveyor, declared his opinion of Wren in these words: 'I must affirm that since the time of Archimedes there scarce ever met in one man so great a perfection, such a mechanical hand and so philosophic a mind.' This then was the man who, having become the Professor of Astronomy at Gresham College, London at the age of 25, and four years later Savilian Professor of Astronomy at his old university, in his early thirties turned his attention to architecture.

It seems possible that this very first architectural design was that of the chapel of Pembroke College, Cambridge, in 1663, but certainly his first major work, and one which showed his genius was the Sheldonian Theatre at Oxford, the following year. This was not a theatre as we understand it today but a building in which the university ceremonies might be carried out.

The ceremonies, which had previously been performed in the university church, required that everyone taking part should be both clearly seen and clearly heard, and that no columns nor pillars should obscure the view. Basing his design on Sebastiano Serlio's description of the classical theatre of Marcellus at Rome (for he had not yet been abroad), Wren designed an ingenious trussed rafter roof which needed no internal support for the whole of its seventy-foot span. Despite alterations to the original made some time after Wren's death, the Sheldonian Theatre is a noble building and a remarkable achievement indeed for a scientist untrained in architecture.

A more powerful influence in the formation of Wren's architectural style than the Italian, however, was his interest in modern French architecture. His visit to Paris in 1665 and his encounter there with the aged Bernini was to some extent to determine the direction in which his personal and very individual architectural designs were to develop. It might be as well to stress at this point that although throughout the whole of this chapter we have mentioned a number of sources from which creative architects have derived their information, this should not suggest that they were mere copyists who rehashed or reconstituted ideas from this variety of sources. No artist works in a vacuum, and to cite the sources from which Shakespeare, for example, derived the original story of *King Lear* or *Hamlet* in no way diminishes the quality of those plays. Sir Christopher Wren went to Paris quite frankly to obtain information – it was the way in which he used the knowledge he obtained that demonstrated his genius. His letters show a wide range of architectural interests. '. . . Bernini's Design for the Louvre I would have given my Skin for, but the old reserv'd Italian gave me but a few Minutes View; I hope I shall give you a very good account of all the best Artists of France; my Business is to pry into Trades and Arts . . .' He visited a number of French buildings, both modern ones under construction and much earlier ones such as those at Ecouen and Chantilly, and the results of his research are not only to be found in such buildings as St Paul's Cathedral but in his domestic architecture as well.

Shortly after his visit to France, which lasted for about six months, and whilst Wren was actually engaged on the renovation of the old Cathedral of St Paul's, the devastation of the city by the Great Fire presented him with the greatest opportunity of rebuilding and redesigning a city for which any architect could hope.

The City suffered grievous damage. In the 436 acres of charred ash lay the smouldering embers of 89 churches, over 13,000 houses and 200 streets. Four short days after the Fire, Wren presented his plan for the rebuilding of London, with every hope of its being accepted. An atmosphere far more favourable to the arts had returned to England with the Restoration, for during their exile abroad, members of the Court, however impoverished, had spent their time in cultivated circles in which painting, sculpture and architecture were not frowned upon as they were in the dour Roundhead community in England. Prince Rupert himself was a practising artist who is credited with the introduction of the art of mezzotint engraving into England. The new King, had he been able to assert complete control, might have gone down to posterity as the monarch who had sponsored the loveliest city in Europe. Unfortunately, Wren's plan was never to be carried out. It was defeated by the selfish and short-sighted citizens of London who could see no further than the ends of their purses.

The shelving of the plan was all the more regrettable because, in London, Wren would have suffered from none of the limitations which so often restricted town-planners on the continent at this time. There they had to bear in mind the need for the military defence of the city – a restriction from which our cities had been free for two hundred years or more. Too often the star-shaped fortress determined the pattern of the Continental town, and its design was distorted by the need for large areas of barracks in which to house the standing army which every petty princeling needed to minister to his vanity and to retain his position. With wide areas devoted to barracks, to the arsenals, to huge parade grounds and to processional avenues on which to display his armies, the prince or king gave little thought to the needs of the civilian population. Such considerations as these could be ignored in Wren's plan for the City of London. Secure in our island, the citizens of London needed their city walls only to define the municipal boundaries and their city gates only to exercise some kind of control on the carts which, groaning with produce, poured into the area every day, jamming the winding mediaeval streets now proved to be incapable of dealing with the increased traffic.

Wren's design of the new city showed a breadth of vision and a largeness of conception which, however impracticable it may have seemed to the citizens of London confronted by the chaos and ruin of the fire-ravaged city, would in fact not only have solved many of their most urgent problems, but some of those with which we are grappling today. Nevertheless, we must admit that Wren's plan was a mathematical ideal, and took little account of any buildings which had survived. He started virtually from scratch, treating his city area as a giant blank drawing board, visualising a geometric city with broad avenues 90 feet wide, radiating web-like from the area of the Royal Exchange, and with two main thoroughfares converging on St Paul's Cathedral. The arrangement of streets had a grid-iron pattern oddly like some of the towns in Australia and America.

By 1669, ably assisted by Robert Hooke the scientist, and by Roger Pratt and Hugh May, Wren's work for the devastated city was well in hand, and much had been done in preparation for the erection of the new St Paul's. In the same year, despite a vigorous protest from the unfortunate John Webb, Wren was made Surveyor-General to the Works, and set out on his professional career as a practising architect – a career which from now on was to over-shadow his other scientific and academic interests.

The pattern of this career is somewhat involved, for not only did he design more than fifty city churches over a period of several years, but there were difficulties with the design of St Paul's. Several versions were submitted before the acceptance of the one we see dominating the City today. He was also engaged in work for Oxford and Cambridge Universities, and in many other important architectural problems.

In his excellent biography of Wren, Professor Geoffrey Webb divides Wren's career into four phases. The first, which contains his immature work may be said to close about 1670. The second, in which the majority of his city churches were designed if not actually completed, lasts from 1670 to 1687 and included early designs for St Paul's, Trinity College Library, Cambridge (1676), Tom Tower, Oxford (an essay in Gothic carried out in 1681), and Chelsea Hospital (1682).

The division of his career at 1687 is interesting. As Professor Webb points out, this date has been chosen because then there was a significant re-allocation of funds derived from the tax on coal which had been levied to pay for the re-building of the city. Up to 1687, £88,000 of the tax had been allocated to the rebuilding of St Paul's and three times that amount (about £264,000) to the city churches. After 1687 the funds were allocated in quite a different proportion. From 1687 to 1700, the third phase of Wren's career, St Paul's received £247,674 but the contribution to the city churches had dropped to about £53,000. This was the period in which Wren was to show his inventive genius by the remarkable variety of church spires which appeared in every part of the city. He demonstrated his ability to design domestic architecture by his work at Hampton Court and Kensington Palace, in 1689, and, some ten years later, in his superb design for Greenwich Hospital.

The last phase of his development, from 1700 until his death saw the triumphant completion of St Paul's despite the malicious interference and criticism from political opponents which marred the closing years of his life.

Before dealing with the remarkable contribution which Wren made to the development of church architecture, it would be as well to examine, in brief, the changes which had occurred in the churches during the troubled century which followed the Reformation. It was to be expected that few churches would in fact be built and that the majority of those would tend to follow established Gothic tradition. As we have said, where a strong local tradition is fostered by generations of craftsmen, the pattern of building is not likely to be affected very much by fashion or by foreign influences. The interior arrangement of post-Reformation churches, however, was considerably modified both by Reformers and by the Cromwellians, quite apart from the damage and desecration from which our churches suffered at the hands of both these parties.

To a visitor who had known a church in pre-Reformation days perhaps the most striking difference would have been the disappearance of the rood screen, or where it had survived, the substitution of the Royal coat of arms for the rood cross itself. He would

also have found the altar in different parts of the church according
to what monarch was reigning at the time of his visit, for its position
varied between the reigns of Henry VIII, Elizabeth and Mary.
There seems to have been considerable difference of opinion as to
whether it should or should not be enclosed with a rail to prevent it
from being used as a hatstand, a cloak room (quite literally) and
other unsuitable and irreverent purposes.

The pulpit, never a very important part of the Pre-Reformation
church, now became a far more imposing structure, and symbolised
a change in attitude to church-going which is common enough today.
Modern church-goers are liable to feel that their visit to the service
has been wasted if the sermon falls beneath their expectations, a
misconception of the reason for their attendance at church which
appears to date from the Reformation. With the increased emphasis
on the importance of the sermon, there was naturally greater
interest in the design of the pulpit which developed considerably in
size and in complexity until we reach the familiar 'three-decker' type
with its huge overhanging sounding board and its elegantly carved
flight of steps. In some churches (All Saints, Northampton, for
example) it was actually placed in a dominant position in the centre
of the entrance to the chancel, effectively masking the altar itself
from most of the congregation.

With the decrease in the relative importance of the altar area, and
the obligation to display the Ten Commandments (ordered in one of
the Canons of 1604 to be at the East end) that part of the church
assumed a different appearance. It now tended to be a more emphatic
area of panelling, but little more than a visual resting place for the
eye in a main decorative scheme. At the other end of the church, the
altar was balanced by the organ, where one was available. Certainly
an instrument of some kind was desirable to lead or to control the
congregational singing. There is a marked difference between the
role played by the congregation of the pre-Reformation church and
that assumed by the worshippers in a church during Wren's lifetime.
The pre-Reformation congregation tended to be passive spectators –
witnesses to a holy mystery conducted beyond the rood screen by the
clergy. The seventeenth-century congregation participated actively
in the conduct of the service – indeed, if Sir Roger de Coverley was
typical, almost too actively!

The introduction of the gallery in the church design at this time
was due to the need for the accommodation of a large congregation
in a restricted area. Even if land had been available, there was a
danger that if the floor area became too large, many of the congregation would be unable to hear the sermon. It was therefore necessary
to build part of the church in two stories, erecting seats on galleries

over the aisles. The university church of St Mary the Great at Cambridge shows the addition of such galleries to a mediaeval church, but naturally, where new churches were being built, these galleries could be an integral part of the design.

The high pews, oddly like horseboxes, presented something of a problem to the architect, whose finely proportioned columns were partly masked by their high walls. Wren overcame this difficulty to a certain extent by raising his columns on a high pedestal – but then Wren was not unduly worried about keeping rigidly to the classical rules – a trait for which we should be grateful, but one which was to contribute to his unpopularity later.

It would be an enormous task quite outside the scope of this book to undertake the analysis of the design of the fifty or more churches with which Wren adorned the City. Many of the most beautiful were destroyed during the air raids on London of the last war, and although a number have been skilfully restored, others still remain pathetic heaps of rubble overgrown with weeds and littered with cigarette packets, or stand gaunt skeletons against the glittering new office blocks with which the Londoner is becoming increasingly familiar. It would not be of much satisfaction to read a long description of a Wren masterpiece only to find that the original can no longer be seen. The essence of the enjoyment of architecture is the delight we get from personal investigation of the building, and it is for this reason that, wherever possible, we have confined ourselves to buildings which still survive, as far as possible in their original form, and which are available for inspection. (*Plate 25*.)

Although Wren experimented with a Gothic style in the design of four of his city churches, the bulk of them were wholeheartedly classical in design, usually with a symmetrical plan. If the irregular site made this impossible, Wren was adept in concealing this fact, and produced the illusion of symmetry by skilful proportioning of the various parts of the church. Apart from two modern examples of churches built by Inigo Jones which have already been described, Wren had no others on which to base his designs. It was a challenge to his inventiveness and originality to which he responded with considerable success.

He too consulted Vitruvius and Sebastiano Serlio for inspiration and St Mary-le-Bow, built in 1680, of which only the mighty spire now survives, was freely modelled on the Basilica of Maxentius in Rome. All kinds of plans were used by Wren. Some churches were based on a Greek cross (that is, a cross with arms of equal length like the symbol of the Red Cross). Others were simple rectangular basilica type rooms with or without aisles, whilst perhaps his most beautiful city church – that of St Stephen, Walbrook, has a superb dome

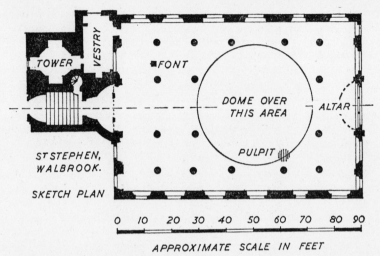

Fig. 22. Plan of St Stephen, Walbrook, one of Wren's most beautiful churches. Notice the apparent symmetry, and compare with the photograph

carried on eight equal arches. It is one of the most exquisitely pro-portioned church interiors in England, and although it too was bombed, it has now been beautifully and sensitively restored to its former airy grace – a little gem in the heart of the City. The dome is made of light wood and plaster and exerts but little pressure on the supporting arches and their elegant Corinthian columns. Its slightly recessed windows flood the whole structure with light and dispel the feeling of gloom which is all too easily associated with the interior of churches. St Stephen, Walbrook, designed about 1672 and com-pleted by 1687 is only a tiny church and in its design Wren had not attempted to grapple with the problem of accommodating a large congregation in a small area so that all might see and hear the preacher. Nevertheless it is at St Stephen's, Walbrook, that we see the germ of the idea which Wren's fertile brain was to seize upon and develop in later churches. He erected his slender Corinthian columns on high plinths so that their proportions should not be masked by the tall horse-box like pews. (*Plate 26.*)

In 1677 at Christ Church, Newgate Street (now a ruin), the plinths were raised even higher, converting them into supports for the fore edges of his galleries, and by 1680, in the church of St Clement Danes he exploited this idea even more, transforming the pedestals into square Doric columns on which to support his gallery. For Wren himself, the most satisfactory solution of a two-storied church with a gallery and a vaulted nave and aisles was to be seen in his design for St James, Piccadilly, completed about 1683. All these churches suffered heavy damage in the Blitz, but St James, Piccadilly, has been entirely reconstructed and the new church gives a fair idea of the ingenuity and the beauty of Wren's original design.

Only two of Wren's city churches were built in the Gothic style for, like most of his contemporaries, Wren had little liking for the mediaeval methods of building. One of his most successful essays in the Gothic style is the charming church of St Mary Aldermary, which has a delightful fan-vaulted roof. The money bequeathed for the building of this church, however, was only forthcoming if St Mary Aldermary, burned during the Great Fire, was rebuilt in its original Gothic style, so Wren had little choice but to build a 'mediaeval' church in 1681. His other Gothic city church was St Michael, Cornhill, and here the tower was based on that of Magdalen College, Oxford, and is skilfully welded to a semi-classical church.

It was perhaps fortunate that whilst many of Wren's city churches were built in the early years of his architectural career, the towers and steeples which were to be their crowning glory were frequently not added until later, when he had gained more experience and his personal style had matured. His steeples were striking evidence of his originality and the wealth of his creative ideas, for no two were alike and he had no examples in the past from which to derive his designs. The Italian painter, Antonio Canale (Canaletto) who came to London in the middle of the eighteenth century has left a wonderful record of the beauty of the London skyline in which Wren's churches and the dome of St Paul's were dominant features. (The original painting is at Windsor Castle.) Even before the last war, when the body of a Wren church might be largely concealed by the warehouses and offices surrounding it, the spire could be seen lifting itself high above the wreathing city smoke, its deftly graduated stories leading the eye inevitably upwards, lifting the heart, if only for a moment, from the squalor of the commercial pavements. The disappearance or masking of Wren's steeples has made a sad alteration to London's skyline.

But this brief reference to Wren's accomplishment in the design of church architecture must lead to the examination of his masterpiece, St Paul's Cathedral, one of the loveliest churches not only in England but in the whole of Europe. The original Gothic cathedral had been badly in need of repair for many years, and Inigo Jones, backed by Archbishop William Laud and the High Church party had made Renaissance additions to the old building. The whole structure was so seriously undermined by the Great Fire, however, that Wren was left with no alternative but to rebuild entirely. His design for Old

St Paul's, completed only six days before the outbreak of the fire shows that Wren from the start had visualised a domed building, and the scanty evidence which exists about his first design suggests that the dome was to be placed at the west end. The design was accepted in 1670, but three years later, Wren produced his famous 'Great Model' design – so called because of the splendid wooden model, large enough to hold a man, which is still exhibited to the public from time to time, in the present day St Paul's. This cathedral was an altogether more imposing building, a great Greek cross in plan about 300 feet square, with eight piers supporting a central dome about 120 feet in diameter, and rising to a height of 180 feet. The derivations of this design are involved, and although it is easy to read into it a similarity to the plan of St Peter's, Rome, there are differences which show that Wren was working out his problems for himself. The cathedral, however monumental it would have appeared, was not liked by the clergy. All cathedrals hitherto were built with a long nave, and on the plan of a Latin cross. The services, the ritual, the processions, all demanded a long vista culminating at the altar, and Wren's Greek cross would have curtailed all this. This design had to be abandoned, and only the model in the cathedral and the detailed drawings still preserved in the library of All Souls, Oxford, now remain.

A new design appeared by 1675 – one in which Wren appears to have tried to reconcile the need for an elongated cross with his wish for a central dome. This is the so-called 'Warrant' design, since the acceptance for it was embodied in a Royal Warrant in April, 1675. The plan of the final building was not unlike that of the Warrant design, but it is fortunate that Wren altered the remainder of the design very considerably. The central feature consisted of an odd saucer-like dome upon which was perched a drum, pierced with windows and strengthened with double columns at intervals to support a little cupola. The cupola was to be surmounted by a succession of little diminishing stages which tapered pagoda-like to a point. It was a grotesque design unworthy of the great man, and it has in fact been suggested by one writer that it was produced by Wren in a fit of temper after the rejection of his earlier plan. Perhaps a more reasonable explanation of this strange design is that it is the work of an inexperienced architect trying to reconcile the demands of his clients with the dictates of his own creative wishes. The modifications to the original plan were in fact so successful that once they were settled he could feel free to review the unfortunate appearance of the first elevation.

Because of the magnificent dome which finally evolved it would be as well perhaps to examine the structure of this beautiful building a little more carefully. Despite its external appearance, the cathedral is actually very traditional in its construction – with the exception of the dome. The thrust of the nave vaulting is transferred to flying buttresses but, unlike a mediaeval architect, Wren has concealed these behind a high screening wall which masks the real construction, but nevertheless provides a heavy dead weight to hold that thrust. The construction of the mighty dome, as well, is entirely hidden – in fact, the splendid dome which rides so triumphantly above the city smoke is not the one at which we gaze from the floor of the cathedral, and neither of them actually carries the weight of the lantern and cross. A dome which looks satisfactory from within the building might well appear flat and insignificant when seen from outside, and a dome built for external effect would be far too lofty when seen from inside. Wren therefore decided on two carefully contrived domes, both in fact dummies so far as construction was concerned, but both magnificent as architectural scenery. Free to evolve the most beautiful shape and proportions he wished without any weight-bearing to be taken into consideration, Wren 'drew' the silhouette of his outer dome in a cladding of wood covered with lead – as magnificent a piece of stagecraft as one could wish. Inside the building he designed a second, a saucer dome of masonry, the perfectly arched dome we see today. But the architectural feature doing the real work of sustaining the lantern is an invisible brick cone, pierced at intervals to admit light to the inner dome and conveying the thrust of the structures above to the piers. This thrust was contained still more surely by encircling the whole of the drum of the outer dome with an iron band (replaced and reinforced with chains in more recent times). Although St Paul's Cathedral is small by comparison with others on the continent, the cross on the dome of St Peter's, Rome, for example, being 452 feet from the ground, whereas that of St Paul's is only 365 feet, the lovely dome designed by Michelangelo is badly masked by the huge façade, whilst that of Wren is visible nearly all the way up Ludgate Hill. The dome of St Paul's is exquisitely proportioned – lantern to dome, dome to the encircling drums, and the whole central structure to the splendid façade and flanking towers – the latter an addition not in the original design.

Of the squabbles and malice which clouded the final years of Wren's career we shall have to speak later, but no professional jealousy and no political jobbery can now come between us and our admiration for this great memorial to his genius.

Wren's work as Surveyor-General was not of course confined to the re-building of the City churches and St Paul's, nor indeed to work in London. He was an immensely energetic and prolific worker, and whilst he was engaged on buildings all over London, found time to

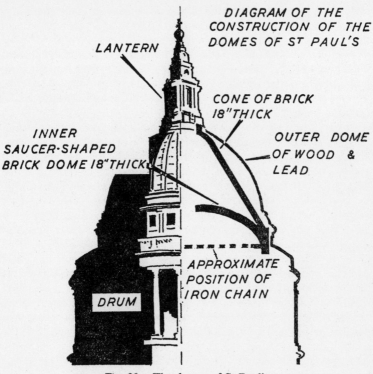

DIAGRAM OF THE
CONSTRUCTION OF THE
DOMES OF ST PAUL'S

LANTERN

CONE OF BRICK
18" THICK

INNER
SAUCER-SHAPED
BRICK DOME 18" THICK

OUTER DOME
OF WOOD &
LEAD

APPROXIMATE
POSITION OF
IRON CHAIN

DRUM

Fig. 20. The domes of St Paul's

design Emmanuel College Chapel, and Trinity College Library in
Cambridge. In 1679 we find him engaging an assistant named Nicholas Hawksmoor – a wise choice as it happened, for Hawksmoor was
an intelligent and able man, and three years after he had joined
Wren's staff at the age of 18, we find him entrusted with the bulk of
the work at Chelsea Hospital.

In 1682 Wren was back at Oxford, designing another Gothic
building – Tom Tower Gateway at Christ Church. His choice of a
Gothic design was the result of his wish for the new gateway to
harmonise with the older Tudor building, although the oddly domed
structure can hardly be said to resemble the sharp square-cut silhouette which most people associate with mediaeval architecture.
Nevertheless, Wren was confronted with the kind of problem still
with us today. If an addition is to be made to an ancient building, is
it better to fake the modern design so that it appears to have been
part of the original, or quite frankly to build the addition in the

style of architecture more suited to modern requirements and materials? There is no easy answer. At Oxford, Wren chose to design his gateway in the form of a past age. At Hampton Court, where he was making considerable additions to the old Tudor Palace he destroyed whole areas quite ruthlessly and replaced them with modern architecture – indeed had he been allowed to complete his scheme, very little of the Hampton Court we now know would be standing today. Instead we should be admiring an entire Wren conception – the most up-to-date building of the year 1689.

One delightful building which Wren was able to execute in its complete form, however, is Chelsea Hospital – that charming brick and stone building where the grand old men known as the Chelsea Pensioners now live. Its quality has been most aptly summed up by the Victorian writer, Thomas Carlyle, who lived within a stone's throw of it for much of his lifetime. He wrote '. . . I had passed it almost daily for many years without thinking much about it, and one day I began to reflect that it had always been a pleasure to me to see it, and I looked at it more attentively and saw that it was quiet and dignified and the work of a gentleman.' This is in fact a quality which permeates Wren's work throughout, and one which we find in the best of English buildings in every period. It is to be found in his small almshouses – Morden College at Blackheath, built in 1695, and particularly in the superbly proportioned Orangery just outside Kensington Palace, near the Round Pond. This little building is one of the minor gems of the architecture of London. It is also a splendid example of how fortunate Wren was with his craftsmen, for the quality of the rubbed and gauged brick of this period has probably never been surpassed. Wren was particularly sensitive in his use of brick and stone together. We see this at Chelsea, at Hampton Court, in his one brick City church, St Benet, Paul's Wharf, Queen Victoria Street and in many other minor buildings.

Nothing remains apart from drawings of Wren's work at Winchester Palace, and the fire of 1698 destroyed the somewhat ambitious Whitehall Palace; Hampton Court was only partly carried out, and we are left with Greenwich Hospital only by which to form an opinion of Wren's ability as a planner and a designer of secular buildings comparable perhaps to his achievements in ecclesiastical architecture. The history of Greenwich Palace – later the Royal Naval Hospital, and now the Royal Naval College involved a number of notable architects. It seems probable that the ill-used John Webb originally designed this impressive scheme, only to leave his building incomplete at his death in 1672, the whole scheme having been shelved some four years earlier. In 1694 interest in the buildings (the King Charles II block) was revived by Queen Mary who decided to incorporate them in the hospital for seamen, and she, supposing them to be the work of Inigo Jones, ordered that they should not be destroyed but that a duplicate block should be built on the opposite side of the court. From then on, Sir Christopher Wren and his assistant, Hawksmoor, Sir John Vanbrugh (Wren's great successor), and a number of lesser architects contributed to the superb pattern of buildings which form a natural frame to the exquisite little Queen's House. Visitors to the Naval College should approach it from the river – there is normally an excellent water-bus service from Westminster Pier during the summer months which enables visitors to see this beautiful group of buildings at their best, and to imagine what a splendid sight they must have been even to the Royal party as the great gilded State Barge (now housed in the Maritime Museum at Greenwich) rounded the curve of the river by the Isle of Dogs. The graceful twin cupolas, the rhythmic march of the colonnades and the impressive masses that confront the Thames still make a visit to Greenwich by water a memorable occasion. (*Plate 24.*)

Whilst we look at the superb achievements of Sir Christopher Wren at Greenwich, at Hampton Court, in the City churches, and at St Paul's, we must not forget some of his less monumental but very delightful smaller works, particularly those where he was to display his sensitive understanding of the beauty of brickwork combined with stone.

As we have said, there was a growing tendency for brick to replace wood as a constructional material throughout the whole of the century – and this was naturally given considerable impetus by the tragedy of the Great Fire. The appearance of the brick buildings was predominantly Dutch, for East Anglia, in particular, had always received both materials and craftsmen from the Low Countries, and apart from the period of tension caused by both English and Dutch navies trying to establish supremacy there had been free interchange of ideas and methods. As early as 1631, the house we now know as Kew Palace was referred to as the 'Dutch House' owing to its then unfamiliar style. By the time that Wren had reached his architectural peak, a host of exceedingly skilful bricklayers and brickcutters were at hand to carry out his designs. The lovely brickwork ornament on the Orangery could never have been carried out had there not been such a remarkable development of skill in carving and rubbing brick to produce the sharp clean lines of the mouldings, and the sweetly fashioned capitals and pilasters.

On a Tudor house the mortar joints were often as much as half an inch thick to take up the irregularity of the bricks. On the Wren buildings the bricks were laid so accurately and were so meticulously fitted that the joints may be as little as one-eighth of an inch, and their thin lines have little effect on the overall unity of the carved and rubbed ornament.

Roofs underwent a major change as well, for the gabled roof disappeared early in the century and was replaced in every major building by the hipped roof with dormer windows, although the gable was to linger on for some time in the rural districts. The charming little town house in Chichester, attributed to Wren, built about 1696, with its simple brick shapes quietly emphasised by stone dressings is characteristic of the seemly and well-proportioned house of this period.

The transformation which took place in the appearance of the English house during the seventeenth century is well demonstrated by comparing 'Batemans' at Burwash in Sussex, a gabled house of sandstone built about 1634, and later the home of Rudyard Kipling, and Fenton House in Hampstead, a brick country house of about the same size built some thirty years later, just after the Great Fire, and embodying all the most modern features of a house of that time. Both houses are open to the public and can therefore be inspected, although as they are not actually functioning as private homes, the visitor will have to use his imagination as well as his knowledge of the architecture.

The interior of the ordinary house showed the general increase in wealth and a higher standard of living – and as a natural reaction to the austerity of the Commonwealth a certain lavishness of decoration, especially in the houses of the nobility. Few people could afford to employ the famous carver, Grinling Gibbons, whose best known work is to be seen in St Paul's, but the great room at Petworth House, executed by Gibbons for Charles Seymour, Duke of Somerset, towards the end of the century, will give sufficient indication of the taste which prevailed at that time. The staircase provided also ample areas for the display of carving and that at Ham House (now an 'outstation' of the Victoria and Albert Museum), constructed early in the century and the one at Thrumpton Hall near Nottingham, made about thirty years later, show the tendency to elaborate carved ornament.

The founding of the famous Gobelin tapestry factory in France in 1677 soon induced some wealthy owners to cover the panelling of their principal rooms with its products, but the majority left their oak or cedar panelling plain, and relied upon the richness of light and shadow cast by the raised bolection moulding – a newly evolved moulding which projected well away from the face of the framing – to give variety to the surface. M. Marquet the Frenchman also introduced marquetry, and this enrichment, together with veneers of splendidly grained woods gave a wonderful variety of decoration to table and bookcase, bureau and cabinet. If the panelling was of pine, it was usually painted and the plain colour acted as a simple background to the intricately inlaid decoration of the furniture, and as a foil to the richly worked plaster ceiling with its swags and arrangements of fruit and foliage in high relief.

By 1702 at least, a variety of wallpapers was available in London, most of them frankly imitations and substitutes for tapestry, for chintz, for embossed and gilded leatherwork, and even for marble.

Unlike their Elizabethan counterparts, fireplaces were soberly designed, classically framed rectangles, although the fire-dogs and fire-irons were often lavishly and even luxuriously decorated. It is about the end of the seventeenth century that the corner fireplace begins to make its appearance.

Such then was the English house towards the end of the century, whether actually designed by Wren himself, or in the style which we now attribute to him. A surprisingly large number of houses of this period are still to be found, both in the town and in the country. Those which are particularly well preserved, and are open to the public include Denham Place, in Buckinghamshire, Owletts, in Cobham, Kent, some four miles from Gravesend, Gunby Hall, near Skegness, and perhaps the finest, Mompesson House in Salisbury, overlooking the Cathedral Green. (*Plate 27.*)

The elegance of the buildings of this period was not confined to houses and churches. We have already mentioned Wren's Chelsea Hospital and the Naval Hospital at Greenwich, but both of these are extensive buildings, and such minor works as the almshouses known as Morden College, Blackheath, and the Town Hall at Windsor, both attributed to him, are well worth a visit.

The Custom House at King's Lynn, built by a little-known architect named Henry Bell, and very much influenced by Dutch architecture is characteristic of the sober good taste and nicety of proportion of which the English builder of this period was capable. As Wren observed, casting a critical eye on his craftsmen – 'Our English artists are dull enough at inventions, but once a foreign pattern is set they imitate so well that commonly they exceed the original.'

Certainly English architecture of the seventeenth century, thanks to the changing political scene, had been subjected to all sorts of influences from abroad. By the opening years of the eighteenth century, however, the principles of architecture introduced into this country by Inigo Jones had been developed by his successors and so completely absorbed into the native tradition that a recognisably English style had evolved from them. Fickle public opinion, however, which had been so favourable to Wren in the past now changed in

F

favour of his critics. The ageing Surveyor-General was dismissed his post, and a new generation of architects arose to reshape the architectural pattern of England. It is with this new generation of architects and the buildings they created that our next chapter must be chiefly concerned.

Chapter Nine

THE EIGHTEENTH CENTURY

T HE end of the seventeenth century saw the meteoric rise of so extraordinary an architect that instead of the period tapering off into a kind of consolidation of the new architectural territory explored and claimed for England by Wren, architecture took a new and dramatic turn.

The sudden appearance of a new and dynamic architect at this stage of the passing century might be compared to the storming finish of a race in the Olympic games which brings the spectators to their feet in a wave of excitement.

The architect to produce this dramatic appearance was, appropriately enough, himself a dramatist, and already one of the most important figures in the Restoration theatre – Sir John Vanbrugh. He had already had an extraordinary career before taking up architecture. Born in 1664 the son of a wealthy sugar manufacturer, Vanbrugh had been an officer in the infantry in 1686, but on resigning his commission had gone to France, only to be arrested on the charge of being a British spy and to be held in the Bastille and other French jails for nearly two years. On his release he obtained a commission in the Marines, but whilst serving with the regiment (where his duties must have been merely nominal) he produced two of the most popular plays on the restoration stage – *The Relapse* and *The Provok'd Wife* and then, astonishingly enough, turned to architecture.

A staunch Whig, Vanbrugh found no difficulty in obtaining a patron – the Earl of Carlisle, for whom he built a magnificent country mansion in Yorkshire, Castle Howard.

It is characteristic of the man that he started his new career not by trying out his wings on a small tentative flight, but by launching out boldly (even rashly) on a vast project. Sir Christopher Wren had been a mature and experienced architect before he undertook the design of Greenwich Hospital. Vanbrugh's very first design was a mansion with a frontage which exceeded that of Greenwich by about 100 feet. Mere size had never had any great appeal for Wren, but it had a fascination for Vanbrugh who, with a fine sense of the dramatic, opposes vast masses of masonry with equally vast masses, handling the bold design with remarkable skill. It is not merely a question of the actual size involved – it is the breadth of conception of Vanbrugh's work which makes him such an impressive figure in English architecture.

The huge scale of his buildings makes it impossible for photographic reproductions to convey the impact they make on the visitor. To realise Vanbrugh's ability to design great masses of architectural forms and to weld them into a vast impressive unity it is necessary to stand dwarfed in their shadows or to creep pigmy-like within their great walls.

It must be added, however, that for all his soaring imagination, Vanbrugh could not have achieved this triumphant mastery if it had not been for his able assistant, Nicholas Hawksmoor, lent to Vanbrugh by Wren and with him for many years, no doubt exercising some restraining influence on the more extravagantly unpractical flights of Vanbrugh's fancy, and making it possible for the architect's castles in the air to be rendered in material of a more durable kind.

Hawksmoor was at Vanbrugh's elbow during the building of Castle Howard, but the whole project was never completed, and the building has in any case been damaged in a recent fire, losing the dome which was the crown of the main central block, so that it is to his next great building – and one open to the public – that we must go to assess the architectural ability of this remarkable amateur. This, Vanbrugh's masterpiece, is Blenheim Palace in Oxfordshire, built for the great Duke of Marlborough and later to be the birthplace of an even greater Englishman, Sir Winston Churchill.

Blenheim, a mighty monument to a mighty general, now remains one of the truly baroque buildings in England. This term baroque is by no means an easy one to define. It always implies a knowledge of the rules and discipline of classical architecture, combined with a freedom to disregard them, and in fact to flout them deliberately if they should impose undue restriction on the overall arrangement of the masses of the building. The deviation from classical rules and proportions in some of the baroque architecture on the continent can be so wide as to be eccentric; the English architect with his natural reticence avoided the freer flights of baroque fancy. St Paul's Cathedral may be regarded as a baroque building, if a restrained one; Blenheim Palace is a universally acknowledged masterpiece of English baroque. (*Plate 28.*)

The scale of this great mansion would make it impressive in any English landscape, but it is not only the scale, but the theatrically conceived proportions which emphasise and reinforce its dramatic

size. The three massive blocks grouped about the vast courtyard
appear almost to have been hewn from the solid rock like giant
sculpture, not built piece by piece. The central court is about 300 feet
across and 400 feet in length (just about the size of the Cup Final
pitch at Wembley) but the area is nevertheless completely dominated
by the massive buildings which enclose it on three sides.

The main suite of rooms is housed in the great central block, itself
about 300 feet across and 100 feet deep. It is connected to the kitchen
block on the east and the incomplete stable block on the west by
sickle-shaped colonnades which bind the whole into a unity, gathering the ends of the vast courtyard into a manageable shape and
enticing the visitor to the foot of the steps which lead to the high
central door.

In a classical building there is a sharp difference between the
grounds outside the house and the rooms within. No such rigid
division is to be found in a baroque building. There the masses are so
skilfully related and so subtly fused that you move quite naturally
and almost unconsciously from one to the other. Probably the most
familiar example of this baroque characteristic by which the outer
part of the building and its inner part are closely related is St Peter's,
Rome. The enormous square in front of the great church is partly
encircled by two crescent shaped colonnades which, as it were,
gather in the huge crowds assembled to hear the Pope, and guide
them to the portico and the vast interior of the cathedral beyond.

At Blenheim the spaces and the masses are so related that the
courtyard seems to be part of the house, and the house a dominant
part of the courtyard.

The main door admits the visitor straight into the Great Hall, a
most impressive introduction to the interior of the house, nearly 70
feet high, with the Royal Coat of Arms of Queen Anne carved in the
main keystone to emphasise that Vanbrugh's intention at Blenheim
was to design a mansion '. . . much more as an intended Monument
to the Queen's glory than a private Habitation for the Duke of
Marlborough,' although Marlborough too was to have his rightful
share of the glory which England had gained as a result of his
military genius. His victory at Blenheim, in Bavaria, from which
the house received its name, is celebrated by a painting on the
ceiling by Sir James Thornhill, who had worked on the decorations
of the dome of St Paul's for Wren, but his fee of twenty-five shillings
a square yard was considered exorbitant by the Duchess, and the
Italianised Frenchman, Louis Laguerre replaced Thornhill as mural
painter in other parts of the house.

Laguerre's painting in the Saloon introduces another aspect of
baroque – a form of mural painting known as *trompe l'oeil*. This type

of painting is not found very often in England, although it is almost invariably part of the decorative scheme of any baroque interior on the Continent. By skilful use of the normal lighting of the building, walls are painted with architectural forms – pilasters, mouldings, columns and even sculpture in such a way that they appear to be three dimensional. Often the illusion is so complete that it is with difficulty that one realises that the column or the moulding is not actually projecting. Clearly, if a wall surface can be used in this way, an entirely different impression of space and mass can be given to the room. The Saloon at Blenheim appears to be surrounded by a colonnade open to the sky, and crowded with spectators gazing down into the room. The ornate sculpture above the cornice and the very cornice itself are all an illusion – it is all *trompe l'oeil.*

The dismissal of Sir James Thornhill was typical of the continual battle waged by the Duchess of Marlborough against the mounting cost of the huge house. There seemed to be no limits to the ambitious plans of the architect. The history of the house is punctuated by furious quarrels between the Duchess and Sir John Vanbrugh. There is no doubt that as it progressed the house became far more grandiose than Vanbrugh's model and plans had suggested. He took advantage of her absence to pull down much of the new central block and to rebuild it entirely, adding the upper storey which dominates the courtyard today. His imagination fired by what was already rising above the scaffolding, Vanbrugh added detail upon detail, and expense upon expense. Roman generals used to display arrangements of helmets, breastplates, and other weapons captured from their enemies in their triumphal progress through Rome. Vanbrugh celebrated Marlborough's triumphs by decorating the building with carved groups of trophies of war, and employed Grinling Gibbons to produce a pair of marble lions each tearing at a cockerel (the symbol of France) on either side of the clocktower.

Yet another expense was caused by the erection of a magnificent bridge to span the marshy land in the valley below. The Duchess had consulted Wren (whom she would rather have employed) but Vanbrugh succeeded in having his way, and the present bridge was erected at a far greater cost than that proposed by Wren.

With estrangement between the Duchess of Marlborough and the Queen, financial troubles followed thick and fast, delaying the completion of the mansion by several years. Despite an inscription on the East Gate which refers to the house being built '. . . under the auspices of a munificent sovereign . . . and a grant of £240,000 towards the building of Blenheim . . .' the change of fortune brought about partly by political jobbery and to some extent by Vanbrugh's duplicity resulted in vast sums having to be found by the Duke himself for the completion of the Palace. In 1716 the Duchess dismissed the arrogant and self-willed architect and he was never allowed to set foot in Blenheim again, but Hawksmoor his assistant, not only remained but designed the great entrance gate through which visitors enter.

Blenheim Palace has been subjected to a barrage of criticism, much of it tinged with jealousy. Visitors today are often quick to dilate upon the vast distance between the kitchen block and the dining room, and fresh from their cosy semi-detached homes enlarge upon the inconveniences of so large a mansion. It is almost as though they had been shown Snowdon or Ben Nevis and had regretted that they were too large for the rockery at home. In any case their criticism is less wittily put than a similar one by Alexander Pope. His is in verse, and is entitled *Upon the Duke of Marlborough's house at Woodstock* and runs thus:

> "See, sir, here's the grand approach,
> This way is for his Grace's coach;
> There lies the bridge, and here's the clock,
> Observe the lion and the cock.
> The spacious court, the colonnade,
> And mark how wide the hall is made!
> The chimneys are so well design'd,
> They never smoke in any wind.
> The gallery's contrived for walking,
> The windows to retire and talk in;
> The council-chamber for debate,
> And all the rest are rooms of state.
>
> Thanks, sir, cried I, 'tis very fine,
> But where d'ye sleep, or where d'ye dine?
> I find by all you have been telling,
> That 'tis a house, but not a dwelling."

Blenheim nevertheless is the most important example of the work of this audacious amateur, for Seaton Delaval in Northumberland was damaged extensively by fire, and his work on the east side of Greenwich Naval Hospital is difficult to distinguish from that of the other architects who besides Wren contributed to this mighty building.

His assistant, Nicholas Hawksmoor, also worked as an independent architect and was responsible for St Mary Woolnoth in the City of London, one of the churches erected as a result of the Act of 1711. It is a strange craggy building in which Hawksmoor seems to have been influenced more by Vanbrugh than by Wren, but he was by no means a slavish follower of either, and at Oxford demonstrated his personal versatility by designing Queen's College in the baroque style, and All Souls' College in an equally distinctive 'Gothick' manner. He was in fact an individual artist and despite his close association with Vanbrugh and with Wren, could 'be himself' when the occasion served.

Associated with Nicholas Hawksmoor in 1713 and engaged on the building of one of the new churches was James Gibbs, a Scot but newly returned from Rome. With Gibbs we enter a new and important phase of English architecture.

The opening years of the eighteenth century had witnessed an increasing hostility to Wren, to Vanbrugh and to other architects whose baroque tendencies seemed to flout the sacred rules of classical architecture. In *Parentalia* Sir Christopher Wren had made his reply to such criticism . . . 'Modern authors who have treated of Architecture seem generally to have little more in view, but to set down the Proportions of Columns, Architraves and Cornices in several Orders . . . and in these Proportions finding them in the ancient Fabricks of the Greeks and Romans (though more arbitrarily used than they care to acknowledge) they have reduced them into Rules, too strict and pedantick. . . .'

Nevertheless, reaction to Wren grew rapidly, and by 1712 the Earl of Shaftesbury launched a scathing attack on the Surveyor-General in the words . . .

'Through several reigns we have patiently seen the noblest buildings perish, if I may say so, under the hand of one single Court architect, who, if he had been able to profit by experience, would long since, at our expense, have proved the greatest master in the world. But I question whether our patience is like to hold much longer . . . Hardly as the public now stands should we bear to see a Whitehall treated like a Hampton Court, or even a new cathedral like St Paul's.'

A new movement was already gathering momentum – a movement which demanded that 'modern' architecture should cease to tamper with those rules of construction and proportion laid down by Andrea Palladio and his great English disciple, Inigo Jones. The leader of this new movement which was to have such profound effects on our architecture was not, however, a professional architect, either, but a cultivated and intelligent young nobleman, Richard Boyle, whose wealth allowed him to travel extensively and to encourage architects and writers on architecture to spread the Palladian gospel.

Born in 1695 (when Wren was 63), Richard Boyle, Third Earl of Burlington, succeeded to estates in England and in Ireland. Although by the time he was 20 he had been appointed a Privy

Councillor, Lord Lieutenant of the West Riding of Yorkshire and Lord High Treasurer of Ireland, his political career was of far less importance than his passion for architecture.

No young nobleman in the eighteenth century who had any pretensions to education at all would have admitted ignorance of the rules governing architecture, but few can have had such a detailed and first-hand knowledge of classical architecture as Richard Boyle. His travels in Italy had led him to study the fine villas erected some two hundred years before by Andrea Palladio. His original enjoyment of these villas, reinforced by careful drawings of them and by drawings made by Palladio himself of Roman buildings, made him resolve that here in England he would erect buildings of his own which should faithfully echo the splendour of the Italian Renaissance.

He determined, moreover, that translations of Palladio's own books should be made available in English, and he financed the publication of the translation of *Palladio's Architecture* by the only Italian architect of the group, Giacomo Leoni, in 1715.

Of the architects who benefited from his patronage and his wealth and who, incidentally, contributed to his own architectural knowledge, it will suffice to mention three – Colen Campbell, William Kent and James Gibbs.

Colen (Colin) Campbell, who had already erected a Palladian villa at Mereworth in Kent – a villa based closely on the Villa Capra near Vicenza, built over a century before by Andrea Palladio – attracted Richard Boyle's attention by a splendid book on the modern architecture of the day. This book, called *Vitruvius Britannicus*, or *The British Architect*, published in 1715, contained 100 engravings of buildings in the classical style in Great Britain, and included many designs by Campbell himself, as yet unfulfilled.

Campbell from that time onward became both master and servant to Richard Boyle, teaching him much of the business of architecture and gladly accepting the task of improving Burlington House, the London family residence.

The second architect intimately connected with Richard Boyle's architectural interests was William Kent – an indifferent painter who withdrew from this particular art fairly early in his career to become an interior decorator, a landscape designer and finally an architect.

Kent incurred the contempt of William Hogarth, the great English painter, who resented the preference by such patrons as Richard Boyle for Italian art to the exclusion of the native born artist. He also resented William Kent being preferred to his father-in-law, Sir James Thornhill, when mural paintings were required at Kensington Palace.

With Colen Campbell's example of an English 'Villa Capra' before him, Richard Boyle decided to erect a Palladian villa for himself, near his house at Chiswick. This is a charming building now open to the public and known as Chiswick House. It was not, however, intended to replace his original house. He had no intention of living in it. It was rather to be a sort of Temple of the Arts – a refined and beautiful receptacle for his many art treasures and for his magnificent library. It was also to act as a meeting place for the many writers, artists and musicians he patronised – Alexander Pope, the satirist Jonathan Swift, and such musicians as Handel. It was in fact a temple in which the High Priest, Richard Boyle, paid homage to the Arts assisted by his faithful retainers. (*Plate 31.*)

Although Richard Boyle not only had Colen Campbell's example at Mereworth and the benefit of his advice at Chiswick, it must not be assumed that Chiswick Villa is merely a repetition of Mereworth, or for that matter of the Villa Capra. Although an amateur, Richard Boyle was a man of real understanding of architecture and his villa shows considerable personal feeling. Nevertheless, it would be as well to restate the principles of design which were to dominate domestic architecture for the next one hundred years at least.

The house is absolutely symmetrical – a line drawn down the centre would divide it exactly in half, each half a mirror image of the other. No departure from this rigidity was permissible.

It is evident from such a plan that a staircase on the left must have its twin on the right, and a range of windows on the left is repeated exactly by an identical one on the opposite side. The rooms at Chiswick are also grouped symmetrically round a central octagonal hall, which is lit by windows in the high dome.

The same exactness of balance seen within persists when the house is viewed from outside. By using the module of half the width of the base of the columns, the spaces between the columns, the height of those columns and the proportions of the entablature crowning them are all pre-ordained. The doorways bear an exact relationship based on the module to the windows and to the wall space surrounding them. The very panes of glass in the windows bear an exact and mathematical proportion not only to the windows, but in turn to the wall surfaces, and to the whole elevation. You will see how faithfully these Georgian architects followed the instructions of such writers as Vitruvius, Palladio and Inigo Jones in their quest for perfection. In such a house nothing was irregular, nothing was unforeseen. Everything had been calculated as logically and as beautifully as the structure of a fugue by Bach.

It is this feeling of order and exactness of balance which gives the sense of beauty. It is worth recording at this point, however, that the

villa was not just a fine building at which to look – although it is
certainly that. The ground floor, which by Palladian rules was
always more robustly designed, with emphatic use of stonework and
small windows, was used to house the library, whilst the main suite
of rooms, reached by the beautifully proportioned twin staircases and
known in all Palladian houses as the 'Piano Nobile' (the noble floor)
was used to accommodate the glittering assembly who came to
admire Richard Boyle's collection and to discuss the very latest
additions to the architectural scene.

William Kent was largely responsible for the decoration of the
interior of the villa, basing the design for the decorations and
fittings on drawings by Inigo Jones in the collection of Richard
Boyle. The magnificent overmantels and fireplaces were largely
borrowings from Inigo Jones and from his followers, but inspired
borrowings, brilliantly adapted and fitting beautifully into the
fabric of this splendid house.

Prolonged study of the Inigo Jones drawings was to result in a
publication of a selection of them, together with designs by Richard
Boyle and William Kent in 1724–7, adding yet another book to the
growing volume of Palladian propaganda.

William Hogarth, glowering in his little red brick house with the
mulberry tree, at Chiswick, must have watched the development of
this new villa and others like it with growing annoyance, until he
was forced to admit 'If an architect today had to build a palace in
Lapland, or in the West Indies, he would feel obliged to take Palladio as his guide and would not dare to make a move without con-
sulting his books on architecture.'

The Palladians were not only affecting the appearance of the house
themselves, but of their surroundings, the grounds in which they
stood – indeed the very countryside. Inspired by the paintings of
classical landscape as imagined by Claude Gellée (the French artist
spent the greater part of his life in Rome), English noblemen began
to lay out their broad acres in a classical manner. They created little
Roman temples in artfully-designed glades, dammed brooks to
provide sheets of water for charming little Palladian bridges, grouped
their trees to frame the severely classical porticos of their delightful
new houses.

Few of the owners can have lived long enough to see their dreams
realised, for trees will not be hurried, and the magnificent woodland
scenes which they visualised may well have come to maturity long
after their designers were laid to rest in their cold marble tombs, but
so great was their faith in their way of life and the England for which
they lived that they built and planted for the benefit of Englishmen
yet unborn.

William Kent's design for the gardens at Chiswick was but one of the first and by no means the most imposing of the new attempts to design house and landscape as a unity, and it is to Stourhead, in Wiltshire, now the property of the National Trust, that you must go if you would wish to share the delight of the Georgian gentleman in his lovely estate.

The Palladian mansion was built from 1721–24 by Colen Campbell and the design of the grounds followed some twenty years later.

It is at Holkham Hall in Norfolk that we see William Kent as architect as well as interior designer. At Holkham too you can see the experience and maturity of the Palladian architect producing something of permanent value, not a rich man's toy, a temple, a trifle, however charming, but a mansion in which to live.

William Kent's patron was Lord Leicester, who had met Kent and Richard Boyle in Rome when he was undertaking his Grand Tour, but it was not until 1734, when most of the lessons to be learned from Palladianism had been absorbed, and William Kent had served his apprenticeship, as it were, as an architect that building commenced.

The yellow brick exterior of the building is somewhat disappointing and gives little indication of the splendour of the interior. Splendour is indeed the keynote of this mansion. It is the splendour of the Roman emperors scaled down but a little to provide a home for a Georgian nobleman. The very entrance hall with its marble columns, its richly decorated frieze and its deeply coffered ceiling of plaster, would not have looked out of place as an antechamber to the Baths of the Emperor Caracalla, or in the Palace of Diocletian at Split. Handled with less skill, it could have looked vulgar and ostentatious but as it is, the proportions are so beautifully related, the workmanship so refined that it serves only to give the half-a-crown visitor a foretaste of the richness of the rooms to come. (*Plate 29.*)

At Holkham superb paintings by Claude and Poussin, the French seventeenth-century artists who spent most of their lifetimes in Rome emphasise the debt which the landscape designer owed to the landscape painter at this time. The classical landscapes which hang on the walls are echoed and re-echoed in the open air by a score of similarly contrived estates. They appear in every part of the British Isles, from places as far apart as Rousham in Oxfordshire, Hopetoun in Scotland, Shugborough in Staffordshire and Wakefield in Sussex.

One of the most important creators of eighteenth-century landscape was a former gardener, Lancelot Brown – more widely known perhaps as 'Capability' Brown. The nickname derived from his optimistic assumption that even the most barren estate was capable of conversion to a classical landscape of taste and beauty. He first became acquainted with William Kent at Stowe, but after 1749 embarked on a most successful career as landscape designer and even as an architect. His rise to fame incurred the displeasure of Sir William Chambers whom he had supplanted at Claremont House in Surrey, but 'Capability' Brown continued to delight his many clients with the re-modelling of their estates until his death in 1783. His influence on the appearance of our countryside was commemorated in verse by Cowper, as follows:

> ". . . The Omnipotent Magician Brown appears,
> He speaks; the Lawn in front becomes a lake;
> Woods vanish, hills subside and valleys rise;
> And streams – as if created for his use
> Pursue the tract of his directing Wand;
> Now murmuring soft, now roaring in cascades
> E'en as he bids . . .'

On Kent's death, 'Capability' Brown virtually dominated the scene – quite literally – and the matured results of his planning are still to be seen at Bowood in Wiltshire, at Compton Verney in Warwickshire and in many other parts of the country. Although many of his architectural designs are the outbuildings, stables, and so on, closely allied to the landscape, the great Picture Gallery at Corsham Court (now used by the Bath Academy of Art) is a fine example of one of his interior designs.

One of William Kent's country mansions is to be found, strangely sited, with the landscape compressed to a courtyard, in the heart of London. This is the Horse Guards, certainly the most famous of his buildings. Designed by William Kent but finished by Vardy after Kent's death in 1749, the Horse Guards displays all the familar Palladian characteristics, but the gatehouses which should mark the entrance to the classically designed grounds are now but sentry boxes for the Household Cavalry. The grounds are shrunk to a paved court where tourists jostle for a glimpse of the Changing of the Guard. Viewed from the Guards Memorial in St James's Park, however, the Horse Guards is much more readily imagined as a country mansion, and is a fitting companion to Inigo Jones's Banqueting House in Whitehall, the inspiration to so many Palladian architects.

About 1730 at the new health resort of Bath, John Wood the Elder was transforming a small country town into one of the loveliest cities in this country. This was no dilettante noble-man indulging in an extravagant architectural hobby, but a scheme of speculative building on a sound financial footing. The very term 'speculative builder' has an ugly sound to modern ears because of the appalling mess made of our countryside by the speculative builder of the 1930s. In eighteenth-century Bath, with a speculative builder who was a gifted and sensitive architect, and a financier with ample supplies of lovely Bath stone with which he could build, the result was very different from the rash of ribbon development and indiscriminate bungaloid growth which defaced our country before the last World War.

One of the first of John Wood's speculative schemes in Bath was Queen's Square, a square that shows the Palladian principles of symmetry and proportion applied to a whole street. The elevation which forms the whole side of the square is exactly symmetrical, a central, triangular pediment being balanced on either side by a square headed upper storey. At ground level, the mass of the construction is emphasised by the large rusticated blocks of Bath stone, punctuated at regular intervals by doors and windows. The piano nobile or first floor has more imposing windows, each with its crowning pediment, alternately rounded and pointed to break the monotony. This and the second storey, with its smaller squarer windows, are linked by attached columns with Corinthian capitals, or by pilasters, of the same order. A casual glance might suggest yet another Palladian mansion but it is, of course, actually a number of houses – in fact, a complete street, but a street designed as a unified whole, not merely a string of houses side by side. Just as Beau Nash was controlling the visitors to the Bath Pump Room, daring them to misbehave under pain of his displeasure, a displeasure which could mean social exile, so John Wood disciplined his houses. No vulgar clamouring for personal recognition, no architectural bad manners were permitted to disturb the serenity of the façade – all was a dignified, disciplined harmony – a harmony worthy of the Georgian gentleman-about-town.

Backed by Ralph Allen, who owned the quarries of honey-coloured Bath stone, John Wood acquired more and more land, extending his new houses farther and farther. He, too, built a fine country mansion overlooking the city for Ralph Allen, although a private quarrel stopped his completing the mansion, Prior Park, and it was finished by another architect.

John Wood had a most ambitious plan for Bath ... 'A Grand Place of Assembly to be called the Royal Forum of Bath; another place no less magnificent for the Exhibition of Sports, to be called the Grand Circus; and a third place of equal state with either of the former, to be called the Imperial Gymnasium of the City ...'

He did not live long enough to see the scheme carried out – indeed it is doubtful whether the latter part of the scheme could ever have been a practical proposition. One can hardly visualise the spindly rakes and pot-bellied old gentlemen of Rowlandson's drawings of Bath taking much active interest in the 'Grand Circus' as John Wood the Elder described it, or in the 'Imperial Gymnasium.' He did, however, work on the Royal Forum of Bath, and the North Parade in which scenes in *The Rivals* by Richard Sheridan were set, was the only part of the grand scheme he was able to complete. It was left to his son to carry on his work and to finish not only the King's Circus, as it was to be called, but to extend the plan to the Royal Crescent. The Circus, as it is now called, is again a unified street of 33 houses but circular in shape, and it was originally intended to be grouped round an equestrian statue of the king. (Wood may well have derived this idea from the Place des Victoires in Paris.) It was to a house in the Circus that many sedan chairs, bath chairs and carriages made their way for their occupants to sit for their portraits by Thomas Gainsborough, and a plaque now commemorates the fact in the Circus today.

The magnificent Royal Crescent is linked by a short street to the Circus and is the work of John Wood the Younger who proved to be as fine an architect as his father.

The Royal Crescent brims the lip of the bowl in which Bath is held, and is actually elliptical – possibly derived from the shape of the Colosseum in Rome, neatly cut in half. The crescent shaped street of 30 fair sized houses exhibits the same architectural good manners as Queen's Square and the Parade. There are the same series of carefully graduated proportions, although this time there is no central pediment, the rustication is missing from the ground floor, and the piano nobile is linked to the upper storey and the balustrade which crowns it by slender Ionic columns instead of the Corinthian work used by Wood the Elder. The pavement is wide, and the 'area' below ground level which admits tradesmen to the lower kitchen regions is sufficiently open and generously proportioned to allow the sunshine to penetrate to the flagged yard. The result is that instead of the 'area' being a green, insanitary sink with discouraged ferns sprouting dismally by the refuse bin, as in so many London squares, in Bath it is an open air room where canaries sing and fig trees flourish in the baking sun. It must have been a glad day in the servants' quarters when my lord announced that they were leaving London after the season was over and spending the next few months at Bath.

The development of the idea that a street should be a unified whole, so beautifully exhibited at Bath, was to have a remarkable effect all over the British Isles for the next hundred years. The Royal Circus was not widely imitated, although Oxford Circus and Piccadilly Circus may be derived from it. The Royal Crescent, however, was adopted all over the country and particularly in watering places like Buxton and Cheltenham, claiming Spa waters with healing qualities rivalling those of Bath.

Another Forum appeared in Dorset, where Blandford, almost destroyed by fire in 1732, was rebuilt in the Palladian style by John and William Bastard. The parish church was also Palladian in feeling but was built of brick with stone facings and not wholly of stone.

For the truly Palladian church, however, we must consider the work of the third of the architects who served Richard Boyle so well – the Aberdonian architect, James Gibbs.

Born in 1682, Gibbs was a link between the older architecture of Wren and the modern architecture of the Palladian movement which replaced it. Like his fellow-countryman, Colen Campbell (who thought well enough of Wren's architecture to include it in *Vitruvius Britannicus*), James Gibbs admired Wren. Comparison of his spire at St Martin-in-the-Fields with those of Wren's City churches showed how much the younger man owed to Wren's imaginative treatment of this architectural feature. It is worth remarking that the spire of St Martin-in-the-Fields was in turn to be copied and to arise as far away as the American Colonies. St Philip's Church and St Michael's Church, both built in Charleston about 1751, have clumsy provincial copies of the spire of St Martin-in-the-Fields.

It must be admitted, too, that James Gibbs, an M.A. of Aberdeen University, a widely travelled man who had studied architecture in Rome under a pupil of Bernini, was far better equipped to appreciate the Palladian principles of architecture, to modify them in the light of his wider experience and relate them to modern needs than some of his, architecturally speaking, illiterate contemporaries.

Although it is thought to be only partly by his hand, the Senate House at Cambridge built by Gibbs from 1722–30, and his own Fellows' House at King's College (1724), are together two of the most beautiful buildings in a city so rich in fine architecture. Not only are the proportions of the parts of the Fellows' building beautifully related, but the very mouldings are designed to catch the sunlight and to produce a ripple of shadows, emphasising the horizontality of the windows, and of the balustrade which separates the roof from the main body of the building. The central feature is gently projected to break the violence of the main archway with its flanking Roman Doric columns.

James Gibbs was, in fact, too big a man to be wholly confined within the Palladian movement, and his famous Radcliffe Camera at Oxford owed nothing to the rigid Palladian system. Although he built a number of country houses in many parts of the country, it was

Gibbs' own books *A Book of Architecture*, published in 1728, and *Rules for Drawing the Several Parts of Architecture* (1732) which had an even wider influence on architecture than perhaps his buildings.

The first was designed to enable any country gentleman of means to instruct a local mason and builder to erect him a house in the modern style – a sort of 'Do-it-yourself' manual.

There was an obvious danger to guard against in the prevalence of such books, of course, and even Alexander Pope, devoted to the Earl of Burlington and to the Palladian cause, doubted his Lordship's wisdom in making such publications so readily available. He wrote:

> 'Yet shall, my lord, your just, your noble rules
> Fill half the land with imitating fools,
> Who random drawings from your sheets shall take
> And of one beauty, many blunders make.'

Nevertheless, the number of books multiplied and their effect is to be seen, still, all over the country. Not all of them, of course, were written by men as expert as James Gibbs, whose *Rules for Drawing the Several Parts of Architecture* describes with many accurate drawings the uses of the various Orders of Architecture, the exact proportions to be observed when using them for whole façades, for doorways and windows, fireplaces, balustrades, domes and ceilings.

With such a book the harassed Mr Robinson, nagged by his wife to improve the house in order to keep up with the Georgian Joneses, could approach a good local craftsman and with him produce a very fair imitation in Derbyshire stone, or in Kentish brick, if not of a whole house, at least of a Palladian façade with the new sash windows, to replace the old-fashioned Elizabethan front with its lattice windows. The old Tudor fireplace could be demolished and a provincial version of the fashionable Gibbs fireplace erected according to his instructions. Plate XLIX, for instance, gives detailed scale drawings of six different chimney pieces and instructions, such as 'Chimney pieces are larger or smaller, according to the bigness of the Rooms for which they are designed. I have on this Plate given six draughts which are so marked that the proportion of their breadth to their height may be readily seen. The three uppermost are square, and their Architraves are one sixth of their openings; in those below, being larger, the Openings vary which the divisions plainly show. The upright scales show the proportions of their height, and of their Architraves, Friezes and Cornices.'

Almost all who could possibly afford the expense (and some who could not) were engaged in re-building their houses and re-designing their estates. A writer for *Common Sense* commented . . .

'Every man now, be his fortune what he will, is to be doing something at his Place, as the fashionable phrase it . . . One large room, a Serpentine River, and a Wood are become the absolute necessities of life.'

Of course only the wealthy or very foolhardy attempted schemes as grandiose or as ambitious as General James Dormer at Rousham, or Sir Rowland Winn at Nostell Priory in Yorkshire, but the Palladian transformation was at work in every county, and homes which are prized now as Ancient Monuments were being erected in the first half of the eighteenth century as the most advanced modern architecture of the day.

The twisted brick chimneys of the earlier periods gave way to the more severe classically moulded stacks emerging from behind the pedimented roofs. The new sash windows replaced the old diamond paned lattice windows, the heavy bulbous newel posts and clumsy staircase gave way to elegantly turned Georgian banisters, and the old formal knot gardens were ripped out and the grounds replanted in the new 'Picturesque' manner.

By the time the new style had been accepted by the ordinary public, however, the fashionable set were seeking something new – a relief from the Palladian severity. The reaction came from two main sources – one a return to the Middle Ages for inspiration was to be of much greater significance than seemed apparent at first. The other was so alien to our British shores that it could never survive for any time, save as a curio. With the first of these styles, 'the Gothick,' we shall deal later, and it is with the 'barbarous gaudy gout of the Chinese' as one lady of fashion wrote, that we shall concern ourselves.

The British Empire had been extending its boundaries both East and West, and its pioneers, many who had amassed vast fortunes in the Far East, returned laden with spoils. Explorers, accompanied by artists to record the results of the expedition, had returned with drawings of strange lands and peoples on the other side of the globe.

The Daniells, uncle and nephew, returned with remarkable engravings and drawings of the wonder of the architecture of the Indian sub-continent, whilst Chinnery's drawings of China and the Coromandel coast were the first records seen by many Georgian gentlemen of the Chinese civilisation. At first the Chinese mode was restricted to one room hung with hand-painted Chinese wallpaper and containing the lacquer cabinet and squat Chinese god. Later came complete buildings such as the Chinese Dairy built for the Duke of Bedford, at Woburn Abbey, and the Pagoda erected in Kew Gardens for the Royal Family. Authentic records were too scanty to cope with the demand for this new fashion and the furniture designers and interior decorators began to flood the market with

designs in the Chinese mode which came from no further East than
the East End of London. As the news-sheet *The World* said in 1753,

'According to the present prevailing whim, everything is Chinese
or in the Chinese taste . . . Chairs, tables, chimney pieces, frames for
looking glasses, and even our most vulgar utensils are all reduced to
this new-fangled standard; and without-doors so universally has it
spread that every cow's yard is in Ts and Zs, and every hovel for the
cow has bells hanging at the corners.'

The 'prevailing whim' did not prevail for long. It was to bankrupt
Lord Verney who spent a fortune on converting his house into a
dwelling more fit for a mandarin than for an English lord, at Clay-
don, in Buckinghamshire, and to leave its mark in less extravagant
ways in many other Georgian houses, and in the familiar 'willow-
pattern' plate.

Of the remaining buildings decorated in the Chinese mode, which
you can go and see today, the most important ones are probably the
Royal Pavilion, Brighton (a riot of Oriental fantasy built right at the
end of the Georgian period) and the Pagoda at Kew. (*Plate 33.*)

The architect of the Pagoda at Kew was Sir William Chambers, the
son of a merchant. Born at Stockholm in 1726 he grew up at Ripon,
but made a voyage to China at the age of 16 before studying architecture in Paris and in Rome. He was therefore the only trained
architect who had had first-hand knowledge of Chinese architecture.

Returning to England in 1755, Chambers quickly gained the
Royal patronage through the help of the powerful Earl of Bute, and
became architectural tutor to the Prince of Wales. He did, in fact,
design the Coronation coach in 1761 – the very coach seen by so
many millions of people on television and on film at the coronation
of our own Queen, and on the accession of George III to the Throne,
was made Royal Architect. His most important classical building
was Somerset House, designed to accommodate the newly formed
Royal Academy, of which he was a founder-member, but he was
also responsible for the lovely little Casino, near Dublin. The Irish
workmen would appear to have served him better than their English
counterparts, for portions of Somerset House began to fall down, an
event which was commemorated in a typically eighteenth-century
ode, written by 'Peter Pindar' in 1785, and which runs thus:

> 'Sir William! cover'd with Chinese renown,
> Whole houses are no sooner up than down,
> Don't heed the discontented nations's cry:
> Thine are religious houses! very humble,
> Upon their faces much inclined to tumble;
> So meek, they cannot keep their heads on high.'

His writings on Chinese architecture, notably *Designs for Chinese Buildings*, however, published in 1757, helped to popularise the Chinese mode, but his book on Classical Architecture, *Treatise on Civil Architecture*, written two years later did much to establish his reputation as a modern architect of the eighteenth century, working in the classical style. As an official spokesman of the academically-trained architects, he wrote scathingly of the 'architects' who, having started as bricklayers, plasterers and other tradesmen, attracted patronage and made sufficient money to set themselves up in business. This was indeed a common enough practice, particularly in the development of the London estates, where one writer observed that by the design of the houses it was possible to detect the origin of the builder, whilst another commented on the foolish assumption that to have been to Rome was to ensure success as an architect.

The second and far more important deviation from the Palladian taste was the revival of interest in Gothic architecture. This was by no means confined to the eighteenth century, of course, for we have given a number of examples of both Elizabethan and Jacobean buildings which exhibit Gothic features, but it was to assume a new significance in the hands of the Georgian aristocrat.

The names of many of the Georgian mansions betray their connection with the Gothic period – Woburn Abbey, Nostell Priory, Stoneleigh Abbey, Creech Grange, are all obviously derived from earlier mediaeval foundations, but the Georgian gentlemen normally regarded the buildings of the Middle Ages as products of a barbarous past. The very word 'Gothick' was a term of disgust. As late as 1771 Smollett, in his novel *The Expedition of Humphrey Clinker*, says: 'The external appearance of an old cathedral cannot be but displeasing to the eye of every man who has any idea of propriety and proportion' and then goes on to compare the ugliness of this 'Saracenical' or barbarous architecture with the modern architecture of the Assembly Room at Bath which 'seems to me to have been built upon a design of Palladio, and might be converted into an elegant place of worship . . . the company on a ball-night, must look like an assembly of fantastic fairies, revelling by moonlight among the columns of a Grecian temple.'

It was in fact a certain grotesque quality which Gothic architecture appeared to have in Georgian eyes, trained as they were to appreciate the classical symmetry of their own buildings, which gave it just that contrast they sought. Some of the noblemen whose fine new houses were built on the site of a mediaeval abbey, or whose old family homes had undergone a modern transformation, still had fragments of the mediaeval architecture about the grounds. These romantic fragments, reminders of an uncouth ancestry and warlike past, assumed a certain rugged grandeur overgrown as they were with lichen and ivy, and crumbling into picturesque decay – a grandeur enhanced by the writings of some of the Georgian novelists.

Other noblemen, less fortunate, but not to be outdone actually erected mock Gothic ruins, and did not scruple to loot early churches to provide authentic details for their carefully sited 'eye-catchers' as they were called. The 'eye-catcher' was often built on the crest of a hill, where the last rays of the setting sun would glare through its empty windows, or silhouette its ragged shape against a lowering sky.

Lord Kames, in his *Elements of Criticism*, discussed with the utmost gravity the respective merits of ruins built in the Gothick style, or in the Classical style. He concluded that it would be better to erect 'Gothick' ruins for that 'exhibits the triumph of time over strength – a melancholy but not unpleasing thought; a Grecian ruin suggests rather the triumph of barbarity over taste – a gloomy and discouraging thought.'

Of the noblemen excited by Gothic architecture there was none more fascinated by it than Horace Walpole, Fourth Earl of Orford. He might criticise Charles Wesley for having preached 'all ugly enthusiasm' but his own extensive correspondence bubbles over with enthusiasm for the building and the stocking of his little Gothick castle at Strawberry Hill.

Horace Walpole, the youngest son of Sir Robert Walpole, the powerful Whig Prime Minister, had lived with Palladian magnificence most of his life, for his father's country house in Norfolk, Houghton Hall, had originally been designed by Colen Campbell, and the furniture and interior was largely the work of William Kent. He made the customary Grand Tour through France and Italy from 1739 to 1741, accompanied by his friend, the poet Thomas Gray.

Strawberry Hill, near Twickenham, the little Gothick country house, was started about 1751 and occupied a great deal of his time for twenty years. There was a somewhat morbid quality in the preoccupation of some Georgian gentlemen with the less desirable aspects of mediaeval life. They liked hermits languishing in cells by the sickly light of the clouded stained glass windows, castles with grim battlements which frowned on the visitor with promise of boiling oil, or horrified him with the sweating walls of their underground dungeons. You will find little of this at Strawberry Hill for Walpole writes . . . 'I do not mean to make my house so Gothic as to exclude conveniences and modern refinements in luxury. It was built to please my own taste and in some degree to realise my own visions.'

His own visions, however, included a Romantic novel, the famous *Castle of Otranto* and this and the later romances of Sir

Walter Scott drew the attention of a wide public to the Middle Ages and paved the way for a spate of Gothic buildings in the next century. From the *Castle of Otranto* too is but a step to *Frankenstein*, a romantic novel by Mary Shelley, published in 1818, and the ancestor of much of our shoddier horror fiction, and our 'X' films. By a strange coincidence, another of his books, printed at Strawberry Hill on his private press (the 'Officina Arbuteana') was *Historic Doubts on Richard III* published in 1768 and destined to be the inspiration of one of our best modern detective stories.*

It is, however, with Walpole's effect on architecture that we must concern ourselves. Crowds flocked to view this unique house, its Holbein chamber, its chapel, its refectory and its picture gallery. They were enchanted with the wallpaper painted to represent gothic carving and the fragments of stained glass, the suit of armour of Francis I, and all the rest of his antiquarian bric-à-brac. (*Plate 32*.)

The house was irregular and rambling in plan – deliberately so, with twenty-three 'lean windows fattened with rich saints in painted glass' which gave him the 'satisfaction of imprinting the gloomth of abbeys and cathedrals on one's house.' It was a continual source of pleasure and expense to its owner and, as he could afford it, he added to it over a period of twenty years.

Much more readily seen, however, is another example of Gothicizing by a Georgian connoisseur, at Arbury Hall, near Nuneaton in Warwickshire, where Sir Roger Newdigate spent half a century converting his house into a Gothick mansion. The dining room with its fan vaulting derived from Henry VII's Chapel and its fireplace from a Perpendicular period tomb, has little classical cupids embracing in Gothic niches, and nude Roman statues with fig leaves oddly at variance with the decorative leaves of the crockets overhead. The South front is battlemented and pinnacled. Its emphatic grid iron windows anticipate the humourless Gothic revival of the Victorians by nearly 100 years, a very different exercise in Gothick from the slightly flippant play acting of Strawberry Hill.

Buildings with a mock mediaeval appearance were, however, something of a rarity in the eighteenth century and most of the building was completely classical in inspiration.

Visitors to country houses of this period are liable to be so overwhelmed by the richness of decoration and the complex beauty of the furniture and fittings that they often fail to realise how practical these buildings were, and how completely they met the needs of the people for whom they were designed. Even the lavish decoration had a function in the widest sense of the words. It proclaimed (if discreetly) the social status of the owner of the house and the decorative

* *Daughter of Time* by Josephine Tey

motifs drawn from the mythology of Greece and Rome implied that
he was conversant with classical learning. Statues brought back from
Italy to adorn his house and garden reinforced the impression already
given of his wealth and education. One function of such a house was
in fact to add to the prestige of its owner. Today a man's status is
more often proclaimed by the car he drives, although his house and
particularly the neighbourhood in which he lives still carry some
weight as well.

Housewives who have to cope single-handed with the cleaning and
dusting of their own homes often criticise these Georgian houses
on the grounds of their being inconvenient – quite ignoring that they
were designed in an age when large numbers of servants were available and indeed essential to the running of such an establishment.
'Look at those chandeliers' they say, used to a smooth plastic
contrivance which can be cleaned with the swish of a mop, 'look at
those chandeliers, nasty dust-hoarding things!' But the chandeliers
with their hundreds of drops of glittering crystal or cut-glass were not
only impressive decorations. They were the most efficient way of
increasing the candlepower of the lights they carried. The shining
surfaces on every drop reflected and re-reflected the candle flames a
thousand times, increasing the illumination very considerably. The
huge mirrors on the walls were not only there as decoration but they,
too, like the mirrors in a modern lighthouse, were designed to increase the light.

Modern architects all too often give the impression that it was not
until the twentieth century that the function of a building has had any
effect on its planning. It is enlightening therefore to read what one
eighteenth-century architect wrote about the difficulty in dealing
with the cooking smells which tend to linger long after a meal. Anyone who has been assailed by the stale smell of brussels sprouts or of
fried fish will applaud Robert Adam, one of the most elegant of
eighteenth-century architects, who wrote

'. . . The eating rooms are considered as apartments of conserva-
tion in which we have to pass a great deal of our time. This renders it
desirable to have them fitted up with elegance and splendour, but in a
style different from that of other apartments. Instead of being hung
with damask, tapestry, etc., they are always finished with stucco, and
adorned with statues and paintings, so that they may not retain the
smell of the victuals.'

Robert Adam, the famous eighteenth-century architect whose
style of interior decoration was to revolutionise the appearance of the
Georgian houses, was very much concerned with the practical aspect
of domestic architecture. Born in Kirkaldy in Scotland, the son of an
able architect named William Adam (a contemporary of James

Gibbs), Robert was educated at Edinburgh University and trained in his father's office. An intelligent and able man, he evolved his own style after having absorbed ideas from a variety of sources. One can see traces of the old Palladian ideas, and of a French influence acquired during his passage through France on his way to Italy in 1750.

In Italy he was not only able to study first hand the ruins of classical Rome, but the newly uncovered domestic architecture of Pompeii and Herculaneum which, until the middle of the eighteenth century, had lain under its coating of lava dust and debris since that dreadful eruption of A.D. 79. He also studied the work of Michelangelo, Raphael and other Renaissance architects, and at great personal danger journeyed to Split (Spalatro) on the Dalmatian coast to investigate the ruins of a mighty palace of the Roman Emperor Diocletian. Here he was arrested as a spy (it is odd how often a perfectly innocent artist excites suspicion because of his interest in old fortifications) but eventually released, and completed his studies before returning.

One of his closest companions in Rome was the architect and archaeologist, Giambattista Piranesi, whose powerfully imaginative engravings of real and fictitious buildings must have been a strong spur to the young Scot's own artistic imagination. Piranesi was also able to demonstrate that, contrary to the Palladian theory, the Romans themselves took considerable liberty with the 'rules' of classical architecture whenever they felt them too restrictive.

One of the first public works undertaken by Robert Adam upon his return was the erection of the Screen in front of the Admiralty building in Whitehall, a charming little work with its decorative sea-horses flanking the main entrance, and an improvement on the building it masks, as Horace Walpole remarks '. . . deservedly veiled by Mr Adam's handsome screen.' Adam established himself with remarkable speed, assisted partly by the powerful influence of his fellow-Scot, the Earl of Bute, and partly by his undoubted ability.

By the time he published the results of his research at Split (or Spalatro as it was then called) he was able to dedicate the book to George III and to style himself 'Robert Adam, Fellow of the Royal Society, Fellow of the Society of Arts, Architect to the King and Queen.' Entitled *Ruins of the Palace of the Emperor Diocletian at Spalatro in Dalmatia* and published in 1764, it was by no means a disinterested piece of architectural research but an astute piece of advertising for the firm of Adam Brothers, and a statement of Robert Adam's own theories on modern architecture. Adam had no intention of following slavishly in the wake of the great Inigo Jones and Andrea Palladio, or of being restricted by the fashionable architects and their patrons who would allow no deviation from the Palladian rules as they interpreted them. He considered that heavy and sumptuous Palladian interiors, such as that at Holkham, however 'correct' they might be archaeologically, were not suited to the ordinary modern house, having been originally designed for Roman temples – an entirely different problem, architecturally. The light, graceful style of interior decoration now known as Adam, took some time to develop, however, and his early works were fairly close to the Palladian ideal in detail, at least, if not in plan.

From 1760 to 1770 the firm of Adam Brothers produced such an impressive volume of work that it would be quite outside the scope of this book to attempt anything approaching a detailed survey of the buildings involved. Many of them were schemes for modernising older houses or for completing those already started by another architect. Kedleston Hall, in Derbyshire, for example had already been started by one architect and was in fact being worked upon by another, James Paine, when Robert Adam started on the interior, and soon assumed control of the whole operation. The imposing Palladian front facing north, with its high portico raised on rusticated arches, is the work of the older man, Paine. The South front, however, is Adam's own design and although it is obviously based upon the pattern of a Roman triumphal arch, already shows his interest in the 'movement' of architectural forms – the kind of flowing relationship of mass and space we have already observed at Blenheim Palace earlier in the century. Much later he was to define his principles of architecture and to lay particular emphasis on his belief that . . . 'Movement is meant to express the rise and fall, the advance and recess with other diversity of form, in the different parts of a building, so as to add greatly to the picturesque of the composition.'

At Kedleston Hall, however, the visitor will see Robert Adam still fairly restricted by the Palladian tradition although he has already abandoned the plan for a central staircase originally in the composition of the house and substituted instead a vast Marble Hall, the top-lit coved ceiling being supported upon great Corinthian columns of richly textured alabaster hewn from local quarries. The expression 'starved' in the North of England usually refers to being perished with cold rather than being hungry, and it would certainly apply in the following extract from Pope's famous lines to Lord Burlington, warning him of unintelligent followers who would be:

'Proud to catch cold at a Venetian door,
Conscious they act a true Venetian part,
And if they starve, they starve by rules of art.'

Certainly to stand by the open door at Kedleston with a brisk March wind whistling in from the golf course and lake beyond, is to realise Pope's worst fears.

It is at Kedleston that we first see how completely Robert Adam dominated the design not only of the house but of everything within. He designed or supervised the design of the fireplaces, the lighting equipment, the furniture. His personal knowledge of Roman interior decoration enabled him to invent fittings necessary to an English house for which no counterpart existed in Italy. The stoves which heat the Saloon at Kedleston, for example, are fashioned in cast iron and made in the form of a Roman altar, to harmonise with the classical appearance of the rest of the room. (It is as flagrant a fake as that carried out today by the manufacturers of electric fires with plastic 'coals' and a revolving fan to simulate the flicker of flame, and the elegance of Adam's altar-stoves is the only defence we can offer.)

Commissions followed in quick succession – his work was original in feeling, and far less ponderously classical than that of his jealous contemporaries. Sir William Chambers was particularly envious and scathing in his comments on Adam's work. Nevertheless, Robert Adam and his carefully picked team of craftsmen were at work during the early sixties at Harewood House and Newby Hall in Yorkshire, Croome Court in Worcestershire, Osterley Park near London, and, perhaps the most splendid of all his houses in the south, Syon House, near Brentford, in Middlesex.

At Syon, Adam was given the task of rebuilding and refurnishing a much older house for the First Duke of Northumberland, and his writings show that he looked forward to it with great enthusiasm, for, as he says, '. . . the idea to me was a favourite one, the subject great, the expense unlimited and the Duke himself a person of extensive knowledge and correct taste in architecture, I endeavoured to render it a noble and elegant habitation, not unworthy of a proprietor who possessed not only wealth to execute a great design, but skill to judge of its merit.'

Although the whole design was never actually carried out – the great domed hall or Pantheon which was to be the central feature being finally omitted, it is still one of the most magnificent examples of Adam's work now open to the public. Adam had an absolutely free hand – and rose to the challenge it offered with a splendidly appointed house. We are so used to seeing Georgian-type banks, town halls and even schools with colour schemes of cream and mahogany that it comes as something of a shock to see how rich and vivid they were in the eighteenth century. The entrance hall at Syon has something of the frozen grandeur which one tends to associate with some stately homes, but the anteroom leading out of it is a blaze of gorgeous colour. This is a truly sumptuous room and certainly Adam thought 'the expense unlimited,' for, at the cost of about £1,000 apiece, he had twelve columns of *verde antique* marble dredged from the River Tiber and brought to Syon. Here they were topped with carved and gilded Ionic capitals, given gilded bases, and set at intervals round the walls of the room to support an entablature on which stood a number of gilded statues in the antique style. The columns have a strangely beautiful bluish-green colour which sets off the gilded panels of carved trophies which form part of the wall decoration.

The floor is of a stained and painted plaster simulating red, blue and yellow marble, known as *scagliola*, made by Italian craftsmen and brought from Italy, and Adam employed the finest plasterer in the country, a certain Joseph Rose, who worked out many of his designs for him, to fashion the ceiling with a pattern which echoes the scagliola design on the floor.

From the splendour of the anteroom we pass to a severely lovely dining-room – the very one which Adam decided should be finished with marble and plaster so that the cooking smells should not linger. The dining-room has a semicircular apse at each end, but these are lightly marked off by a screen of two columns giving the room a rectangular appearance. The ceiling – always such a personal feature in an Adam design – is lightly and shallowly patterned with gilded plaster. (*Plate 30*.)

The red drawing-room leads directly out of the dining-room and here, with no cooking smells to deter him, Adam had the walls hung with deep red Spitalfields silk, and gave his ceiling a deeper coffering than usual, each octagonal shape containing a specially designed painting by an Italian, Cipriani – a sight which gave no pleasure at all to Sir William Chambers who compared the ceiling to 'a myriad skyed dinner plates.'

There could be no greater contrast to the Long Gallery built in the Jacobean period at Syon than the one which is now to be seen there, entirely re-designed by Adam. The room is 44 yards long but only 5 yards wide, with 11 windows looking out upon the lovely water meadows. By the most skilful grouping of flat painted pilasters and by an adroit use of crossed lines on the plaster ceiling, Adam avoided the corridor-like Long Gallery, and contrived an effect more like a series of continuous bays.

His first entirely new house (not normally open to the public today) was Marsham-le-Hatch, in Kent. Its fine furniture, however, is installed in another very lovely Adam interior, at Kenwood House on the edge of Hampstead Heath, now housing the Iveagh Collection.

Kenwood is yet another Georgian house which by its magnificently adorned library, with brilliantly painted and gilded decoration, banishes the 'cream and mahogany' myth. It was built for another Scot, Lord Mansfield, the Lord Chief Justice, and the Adam interiors, the Gainsborough and Reynolds paintings and many of the original fittings designed for the house by Adam give many hundreds of visitors a remarkably truthful idea of the best modern architecture of the middle of the eighteenth century. It is worth noting that engravings of Kenwood House issued by Robert Adam were labelled in both French and English, and that on this occasion at least, French interior decorators were anxious to learn from this side of the Channel.

In 1768, the year in which Kenwood House was completed, the Adam Brothers, who had previously confined their activities almost entirely to country houses, set out to meet the growing demand for town houses in the rapidly expanding area near the Strand, in London. Here they built a group of apartments – elegantly terraced houses of brick and stucco raised above the Thames mud on arches. The scheme was called 'The Adelphi' (from the Greek word for 'The Brothers'). The speculation, for such it proved to be, was not the immediate success they had hoped, despite the backing of the famous Georgian actor, David Garrick. As Fanny Burney, the diarist, observed 'The undertaking was, I believe, too great for them and they have suffered much in their fortunes. I cannot wonder that so noble and elegant a plan should fail of encouragement.' She underestimated the resourcefulness of the firm. Unable to raise a proper mortgage, Robert Adam organised a lottery, issued 4,370 tickets at £50 each and thus made enough money to save the firm from bankruptcy.

Parts of the scheme are still to be found in John Adam Street near Charing Cross station where the flattish, thin design of the front of the Royal Society of Arts building may be taken as typical of the rather shallow, almost colourless façades of this new development of the Adam brothers. The main part of the scheme was destroyed to make way for the huge cubical concrete mass of Shell Mex House, in 1937.

A number of town houses both in London and in Edinburgh survive to show the mastery which the Adam brothers displayed in street architecture as well as in the design of country houses. Railings, balconies, lamp-holders, link-snuffers (metal cones not unlike a modern fire-extinguisher in shape into which torches were thrust to quench the flames before the servant entered the house) and particularly fanlights, all add distinction to the buildings for which Robert Adam designed them. Within, fittings and furniture were designed by the same hand and carried out by such craftsmen as Thomas Chippendale, Josiah Wedgwood, and in the workshops of Matthew Boulton and James Watt in Birmingham.

This method by which the man at the drawing board dominated the man at the work bench had one serious flaw. It drove a wedge between the artist and the craftsman and was to lead to the melancholy state of affairs in the next century from which we are not yet recovered, which debased the craftsman to a mere pair of hands, a human tool with no right to independent creative thought, and exalted the artist to a superior position away from the mess and noise of the workbench, free from the discipline which every craft should exert on the designer. The paper designs which Robert Adam drew so beautifully and which can be seen in their hundreds at the Sir John Soane Museum in London, were lines and patterns skilfully derived from classical details. The same patterns may be carried out in wrought iron, in wood, or in stucco, woven in the carpet or fretted in steel for the grates. At the Geffrye Museum in Shoreditch, you may see the original boxwood moulds from which the details were cast in plaster – the motifs identical with others painted on the walls of the country houses. It ensured a unity of design – the ceiling and the floor at Saltram in Devon are of almost exactly identical pattern – but it left little room for the use of the qualities natural to each material. Wiry linear designs suitable for work in wrought iron were carried out quite unsuitably as mirror frames in wood and freely painted brush designs were converted into plaster patterns so thin that Adam's work was contemptuously referred to as 'filigraine.'

The period from 1770 to 1780 saw the greater part of Adam's time devoted to his town architecture, but later as his popularity in England began to wane, he returned to Scotland to Edinburgh, and built much of his best public work in that beautiful city. There you may see Robert Adam as town planner as well as architect and interior decorator. The last building on which he worked and which was in fact incomplete on his death in 1792 is his monumental Edinburgh University, a building in which he returned to a more solid Roman quality more suited to the nature and temperament of the people for whom it was designed than the frivolous, lighter architecture of the south.

The closing years of the eighteenth century brought a new development in architectural fashion. Because it occurred at about the time that the Prince of Wales had been appointed Prince Regent in the place of his blind and lunatic father, George III, this development is known as Regency architecture, but it is in fact a natural development from the classical influence so evident in Georgian architecture, and one which carried over from the eighteenth century well into the first quarter of the nineteenth century. For this reason we shall close the chapter on the eighteenth century here, and introduce the next chapter which is predominantly that devoted to the nineteenth century, with the Regency period.

Chapter Ten

REGENCY
AND VICTORIAN ARCHITECTURE

THE desire for a picturesque setting and a carefully contrived but apparently natural landscape in which to erect the country house continued long after its original development in the eighteenth century by such men as Capability Brown and his successor, Humphry Repton. It is in fact still with us, in a somewhat debased form, and the love of 'picturesqueness' accounts for much of the average English townsman's sentimental attitude to the country, resulting in continual exasperation to the farmer and to those who work on the land.

It was particularly noticeable during the last war that when they talked of home, men lying under the stars of the Western Desert or in Nissen huts in Italy always dreamed of the country and rarely of the towns in which they lived. Listening to the rich assortment of accents in any barrack room, accents from Birmingham, Oldham, London, Tyneside and Liverpool, a foreigner might have imagined from the conversation that their owners lived in the heart of the country and not in vast industrial cities. That it was a sentimental and rather pathetic illusion was shown all too clearly by their womenfolk who, evacuated with their children to the kindly valleys of Shropshire or the quiet of Devon, flocked back to the shattered cities rather than face the reality of the country of which their husbands talked so wistfully. They preferred the dirt and danger of the Liverpool slums to the safety and quiet of rural homes.

It is true that the cult of the picturesque has been responsible for some of the loveliest aspects of English architecture but its misuse has also produced much which is shoddy and ridiculous. It is not only to be found reflected in the great lakes of Stourhead and Blenheim. It is also mirrored in a thousand little stagnant pools by which dismal little concrete gnomes fish interminably, embedded in the crazy paving and bespattered by the town sparrows.

Nevertheless a romantic attachment to the countryside has been an important factor in the development of our landscape, in town and

191

country, and even in 1838, when the Industrial Revolution was already changing the face of England, the French writer Stendhal noted 'The Picturesque like good stagecoaches and steamboats comes to us from England – a beautiful countryside is as much part and parcel of the religion of the Englishman as his feeling for aristocracy.'

Earlier in the century, Joseph Addison had written: 'Why may not a whole estate be thrown into a kind of garden by frequent plantations that may turn as much to the profit as the pleasure of the owner ... if the walks were a little taken care of a man might make a pretty landscape of his own possessions.'

By 1795 the *Essay on the Picturesque* by Uvedale Price and other similar writings by Richard Payne Knight inspired the owners of many estates to develop their broad acres, and often to enclose common land usually grazed by the few wretched sheep or poultry owned by the peasant or farm worker. In vain the peasants protested:

> 'The law doth punish man or woman
> That steals the goose from off the common,
> But lets the greater felon loose
> Who steals the common from the goose.'

The new owner could perhaps quiet his conscience by pointing out, with some justification, how much more productive the land had become under his hand and by his more intelligent methods of farming, as well as how very picturesque was his mansion in its newly cultivated landscape. One notable example was Coke of Holkham who increased his estate rent rolls from £2,000 to ten times that amount between 1776 and 1816. Between 1780 and 1810 nearly two million acres of waste land were brought under cultivation by his efforts and his persuasion. But for men like him, Napoleon would have succeeded in starving this country into submission. Owners of this kind, however, were all too few, and the prosperity of the new landowner was but poor consolation for the countryman who, deprived of the common and turned off in the slump of 1816, was obliged to seek work for himself and for his children in one of the new factories or mills which were springing up wherever water-power was available.

Shortly after the new lands had been enclosed by robust hedges and absorbed into the estate, the landowner might receive a visit from Humphry Repton, complete with one of his famous red notebooks. Repton would survey the landscape with great care, making a careful watercolour drawing of the house and its surroundings. He would then make another, this time a design which showed the owner how he could improve the appearance of the estate, and lay his second painting on a flap of paper over the first for comparison.

194

Sometimes the suggestions on the flap would entail the destruction of existing buildings or the masking of unsuitable ones with fake Gothick ruins or a plantation of trees. Whole villages might be transferred from one site to another for their pictorial effect. The villages of Milton Abbas and Harewood were transplanted bodily in this way. Valleys might be flooded, rivers dammed or diverted into picturesque serpentine curves, copses planted and woods thinned and reshaped, all for the picturesque effect which would result from this interference with the existing landscape. (*Plates 34, 35.*)

In all this change, the architecture itself could hardly remain unaffected. The Gothic style, hitherto regarded as an amusing and somewhat frivolous relief from the formality of classical buildings was beginning to be regarded as a serious form of architecture.

At Lord Camden's mansion in Kent, Repton ordered that 'the hall and passages should be rather dimly lighted by painted glass to impress a degree of gloom which is essential to grandeur and to render the entrance into the rooms more brilliant and cheerful.'

The same quest for the odd and bizarre as a relief from classical formality gave rise to a number of architectural details somewhat loosely derived from the Far East and even from Egypt.

Exotic plants brought back by explorers from the limits of our growing Empire began to appear in grounds and gardens. Magnolias and monkey-puzzle trees appeared as central features of many a suburban garden – a middle class attempt to compete with the splendour of the foreign plants enriching the great country estates. And with the exotic and alien plants came many odd architectural details to be absorbed into the new architecture of the Regency period. The foreign plants needed some protection if they were to survive the rigours of the English climate – and conservatories were built to 'conserve' them. Repton, for example, designed an orangery from which the frames and glass protecting the plants during the winter might be removed during the summer months and which by a little rearrangement and the addition of an awning could be converted into a summerhouse. Many younger sons who despaired of receiving any part of the family fortune and who had emigrated to India in the middle of the century now returned rich men, settled down to a life of independent ease, and brought new additions to the architectural scene. The verandah came to stay, and craftsmen in wrought iron exercised remarkable ingenuity in translating rattan and bamboo forms into more durable materials, adding slender and beautiful patterns in trellised iron to the fronts of the town houses of Cheltenham and Bath, Buxton and Leamington Spa, and hammering tent-like covers in thin metal to imitate the fabric awnings in use in India.

G

Other men, guided by the splendid series of aquatint etchings of Indian architecture, drawn by the Daniells, nephew and uncle, during their Indian tour in the closing years of the eighteenth century, made good their lack of personal experience of the Far East by copying details from the drawings. Generally, the Oriental style was too alien to make much impact on Regency architecture but there were two notable exceptions. One, a strange country mansion called Sezincote in Gloucestershire, inspired by the Mausoleum of Hyder Ali Khan, was built by Samuel Cockerell for his brother but lately returned from the East, with onion-shaped domes, minarets and all the trappings of an Indian tomb. The second important example was the famous pavilion at Brighton, a strange and exotic 'sport' growing from the main architectural plant which was to have no fruit, but has a fantastic beauty which still gives intense pleasure to the thousands of visitors who visit the famous holiday resort each year.

The early part of the nineteenth century saw the beginnings of a new ritual – a visit to the seaside – which had hitherto played no part in English life. In 1783, George, Prince of Wales, first sought relief in Brighton from the rigours of Court life. His Marine Pavilion in its original classical form was completed there by July 1787. Four or five years later the building was enlivened by the addition of green-painted tent-shaped canopies and iron balconies and Chinese wallpapers with Chinese furnishings made their appearance within. By 1808 Humphry Repton had appeared with his books of 'slides' (as his little paper flaps were called) but he died before sufficient money could be found by the Prince Regent to transform his little holiday house in the classical style into the splendid Oriental fantasy we see in Brighton today. The final building was completed for the new King George IV by January 1821, under the direction of John Nash, his favourite architect, with whom we shall deal at greater length later in the chapter. The whole fantastic building cost about £502,797 and has been the subject of admiration, of derision, pleasure and disgust from the time of its completion to the present day. To visit it is an unforgettable experience, and although no one would wish to imitate its extravagant fantasy, very few of its critics would be capable of such richness of imagination and such decorative invention. The Pavilion is unique. There is nothing of comparable quality in any other country in Europe, and since its restoration and refurnishing during the past few years it would be a poor creature indeed who could walk through its rooms and not be touched by wonder at the sumptuousness of the decoration and the richness of invention displayed there.

The discovery of the seaside gave rise to a type of architecture which is almost worthy of separate study and although most of the

houses on the south coast erected in the early part of the nineteenth
century bear a strong resemblance to those built at the same time at
Cheltenham, at Leamington, at Bath and other similar resorts, there
is a slightly frivolous quality about the tent-like canopies and slender
balcony trellis work which decorates the bow-fronted elevations
facing the beach which makes them still very attractive.

The houses still retain something of the discipline and order of
their Georgian ancestry despite all that 'Sea View' or 'Balmoral
Private Hotel' can do. The crescents, squares and terraces still
demonstrate the need for unity in street design, but the architectural
details, whilst they were still mainly classical in origin, were derived
from a different source. The inspiration was no longer Imperial Rome,
but Ancient Greece. One has only to study the houses on the sea-
front at Hastings, for example, to detect the difference. These houses
were nearly all erected to accommodate the officers of regiments
stationed there in readiness to repel Napoleon's armies should they
attempt to cross the Channel, and they are more readily dated for
that reason. Where columns or pilasters were used they were more
usually of the Doric or Ionic orders, and less frequently of the
Corinthian Order. The creamy stucco which protects the brickwork
from the salt air was moulded with patterns derived from the Greek
honeysuckle pattern, or the Greek fret. The same decorative motifs
appeared on the cast-iron balconies from which the young officers
were wont to use a spy-glass to search for invasion craft, or perhaps
in pursuit of less war-like targets.

It has been stressed how much of the civilised appearance of such
cities as Bath is due to a self-imposed discipline in the arrangement of
houses which form a whole street. The pattern of many continental
cities was determined by military considerations and the star-
shaped defences of such cities as Mannheim in Germany and the
rigid layout of Amsterdam in Holland have left their mark on their
modern counterparts. Berlin in the middle of the eighteenth century
had a population of 90,000 and of that number nearly 21,000 were
soldiers. This vast proportion of the population demanded areas for
drilling and manoeuvres, barracks, stables, arsenals and many other
services which imposed their will on the pattern of the town. No such
pressures were exerted upon the growth of the English town. It is
true that such cities as Plymouth and Portsmouth were bound to be
modified as the demands for the ships for the Navy increased, and a
few others were used as garrison towns, but the whole of the English
army under Wellington's command at Waterloo only numbered
21,000, and whilst they were in this country their numbers could
have had but little effect on the general pattern of the towns through
which they were distributed. Lacking any enforced discipline by

military requirements, the English towns were dependent for their orderly arrangement on the taste of such individual builders as the Woods of Bath.

The first quarter of the nineteenth century, however, saw the beginning of ribbon development and unrestrained private building which pushed the countryside further and further away from the town dweller, overran fine agricultural land, and spread a cancerous growth of mill towns and slag heaps, of ironstone tips and merciless pithead buildings with neither order nor decency, plan or arrangement. It witnessed the disintegration of the town as a unit, and dealt a blow to English architecture from which it is only now just beginning to recover. This did not happen all at once, of course; it was a slow, almost imperceptible, process, and one which took nearly fifty years to reach its final degradation, but it changed the face of England and we shall have to refer to its effects again when we consider the proper relationship of the house to the street and the streets to the town pattern as a whole.

The century opened during the Napoleonic wars, but nevertheless, ambitious schemes were afoot to plan parts of London and to make it a worthy capital city of the most powerful country in Europe apart from France. Its architect was John Nash, born in London in 1752, and trained in the classical tradition as an architect for a short time before launching out on his own account as a speculative builder – a career which ended with his bankruptcy in 1783. After a short stay in Wales where he built Carmarthen Jail in 1789–92, and Cardigan Jail the following year, he crossed the border into England, built Hereford Jail in 1794–6, and established himself very shortly afterwards in London with Humphry Repton, the landscape designer, as his partner. Through the influence of his beautiful wife Nash became acquainted with the Prince Regent, for whom he built the Royal Lodge in Windsor Park. He also carried out extensive alterations to Carlton House which was largely rebuilt by Henry Holland in 1783 in a distinctly French style. Nash modernised the building, making it more suitable as a town house for his royal master, and, as we have said, he worked on the creation of the Royal Pavilion from 1815 to 1823.

His appointment to what appeared to be a very minor post under the Commissioner of Woods and Forests in 1806 was later to give him an opportunity to design Regent's Park (then known as Marylebone Park) and to leave as his memorial one of the most beautifully designed areas in the whole of London. It has been sadly changed since its original creator died, but despite the vandalism of land speculators, the indifference of the public and damage by the Luftwaffe, much of Nash's original scheme still survives. It extends from the Mall, up Lower Regent Street, along Regent Street itself, past Langham Place and Portland Place to the splendour of the stucco landscape of terraces which encloses Regent's Park and forms one of the architectural sights of London. It has been criticised for a number of faults – for coarse details and shoddy workmanship – but it still constitutes one of the major pleasures of London to a visitor who has any feeling for architecture at all. (*Plate 36.*)

The Greek derivation of much of the architectural detail was, like the growing interest in the Gothic, by no means entirely new. As early as 1758, James 'Athenian' Stuart had erected a little Doric temple – a copy of the Theseum at Athens – in the grounds of Lord Lyttleton at Hagley, but it was the book *Antiquities of Athens* which he and another student of Greek archaeology named Nicholas Revett published in several volumes from 1762 onwards, the last volume appearing after Stuart's death, which quickened public interest in this aspect of classical architecture and hastened the adoption of Greek forms as rivals to those of Rome. A fire in 1799 which gutted Wren's Chapel at Greenwich gave Stuart, then Surveyor-General, an opportunity to redesign the building in full-blooded Greek style.

The Radcliffe Observatory, started by Henry Keen, but completed by James Wyatt, was a more or less faithful copy of the Tower of the Winds at Athens, and other examples of antiquarian interest in Greece followed thick and fast. Later, however, Wyatt became a champion of the Gothic revival, and did incalculable harm to many of our cathedrals by his restoring zeal. Fortunately his more ambitious schemes for the re-design of Durham cathedral were thwarted. Meanwhile there was a growing interest in the architecture of ancient Greece.

An architect, Charles Robert Cockerell (not to be confused with the architect who designed the Indian style 'Sezincote') after having spent many years in Greece and Asia Minor, returned in 1817 laden not only with great folios of authentic drawings of ancient Greek architecture and sculpture, but with much of the sculpture itself. This hoard, together with the magnificent frieze from the Parthenon already acquired by Lord Elgin, and now known as the 'Elgin Marbles' became the nucleus of the collection in the British Museum. It was natural that when the British Museum was designed by Robert Smirke from 1825–28 it should be in the Greek style.

This insistence on historic style was not confined to traditional buildings. Even modern ones for which there was no precedent – the railway stations for instance – had to be designed in one historic style or another. Euston Station's huge Doric portico was built at this time and St Pancras followed some time later in a flourish of Gothic.

By the time Queen Victoria came to the throne in 1839 the Battle of the Styles was raging furiously. No matter what the function of the building, what material was to be used, or how it was constructed, it had to mimic, in external detail at least, the style of a past age. The core of all good architectural design – the plan – was of less importance than the external appearance, and the decoration, whether Roman, Greek, Gothic or Egyptian in origin, no longer needed to bear any relation to the construction of the building or the purpose for which it was built. As the reign continued the architectural fancy dress parade became more and more ludicrous.

Few architects and fewer builders who aspired to be known as architects could resist the temptation to loot the heritage of the past for details which could give an illusion of architectural form to their squalid creations, and certainly the mill owners and iron-masters, most of them with little education or taste but anxious to express their new-found wealth and power, were the last people to detect the spurious quality of the houses erected for them. They reasoned that the more decoration the building carried, the greater the cost and the more emphatically it proclaimed the wealth of the man for whom it was built. The clarity of planning and the facts of architectural construction of the true Gothic style were lacking in this Victorian Gothic. However closely he imitated the details of the past, the mock-Gothic architect lacked one essential quality – the spirit of the age of faith which had brought the originals into being. The mediaeval builders who conceived the lantern at Ely, the soaring arches of Wells, and the flying buttresses of York were daring inventors. They, in their own time, were modern architects and engineers expressing the spirit of their own time, not continually looking over their shoulders at a remote past. Their buildings had clarity of purpose and honesty of construction. These were the qualities upon which the Victorian architects might have drawn. Most people will be familiar with the kind of person who 'cannot see the wood for the trees.' The Victorian architect by and large ignored the splendid prospect which the mediaeval wood offered and grubbed away, not only peering away shortsightedly at the trees, but copying their bark without even seeing the trees themselves. The blind architects led their blind patrons on, encouraging an architectural hypocrisy in which every building tried to disguise its true construction and its real purpose. Railway stations masqueraded as cathedrals, town halls as Roman baths, and banks as Greek temples. (It is recorded that a tourist in Greece, familiar with the 'classical' appearance of our banks was heard to remark that he did not realise until he saw the ruins of Ancient Greece how many banks they built in those days!) Very few architects could be found to stand aloof from this architectural charade; and most of them actively encouraged it. It is typical of the Romantic approach that having been awarded a knighthood for remodelling Windsor Castle, grafting a Walt Disney fairy-tale wing on to the mediaeval structure, the architect, Jeffry Wyatt, the nephew of the notorious 'restorer' of cathedrals, changed his name to Sir Jeffry Wyatville.

One of the few architects who refused to be stampeded into the feverish search for novel ways of building and extravagant forms of decoration was Sir John Soane (1753–1837). It is true that he had a mild flirtation with the Gothic revival, but on the whole he remained solidly in favour of the classical feeling for space, proportion and form. His buildings display classical details but these, whether derived from Greece or Rome, are all subordinate to Soane's peculiarly individual planning. There is a monumental quality – one might say an almost aggressive boldness of mass on which the ornament is but a surface refinement. Of all his buildings, the two most readily accessible to the general public are his own houses. His country house, Pitshanger Manor, is now the public library at Ealing, and his town house, or houses (for he combined three to accommodate his remarkable collection of *objets d'art* is now the Sir John Soane Museum in Lincoln's Inn. Here you may see not only a variety of curios – fragments of architectural detail, an early Egyptian tomb, letters from Sir Christopher Wren and a great deal of historic bric-à-brac, including the 'Monk's Parlour,' but can experience the original exciting way in which Soane designed his own house, using a domed ceiling and such devices as carefully placed mirrors to give a feeling of space and air. Much of his most important work at the Bank of England has long since been altered or entirely rebuilt. The Museum which bears his name, besides housing some of the most magnificent paintings of William Hogarth, possesses a superb collection of architectural drawings including many of Soane's own designs. It must be stressed, however, that it would be very foolish to form an opinion of an architect's ability from his drawings alone. There is something so attractive about a well presented drawing that it may not only deceive the layman to whom it is shown, but the very architect who made it. Any artist will tell you that drawings have a knack of getting out of hand, and later in the nineteenth century, Philip Webb, himself an architect, wrote: 'the ability to make picturesque sketches is a fatal gift for an architect.' Much of what passes for architecture today must have looked most attractive on the drawing board with artfully washed-in shadows and a dragged brush texture on the blank walls. It may still have retained something of this persuasive quality in the balsa wood and cardboard model. It is only when the full sized building is erected in the proper materials of concrete and steel, wood and brick, and seen in relation to the scale and appearance of others in the area that its real worth can be assessed.

From Sir John Soane and his contemporary, John Nash, we pass to another generation of architects. Of these, mention must be made of Decimus Burton who was born in 1800, the son of a builder from whom he received most of his training. He was, however, befriended by John Nash and much of his most charming work was but an extension of the Grecian style in brick and stucco so beloved by the older man. Burton, too, built terraced houses in the Regent's Park area, and also a number of buildings for the newly formed Zoological Gardens when the animals were transferred in 1830 from the old menageries at the Tower of London and Windsor Castle. He was, however, a most prolific architect and before he died in 1881 produced so many buildings that it would be quite impossible to mention all in a book of this size. They range from Charing Cross Hospital (1831–4) and the Athenaeum Club in London to Adelaide Crescent in Brighton and estates in Liverpool and Kelvingrove in Glasgow. Perhaps his most original work and one from which many of his contemporaries could have learned much in view of its remarkable construction was the great iron and glass Palm House and Winter Gardens in Kew (1844–66).

Another important architect working at the same time as Burton was Sir Charles Barry. This brilliant and versatile man had spent several years abroad, travelling in Greece, Italy, Egypt and Palestine, before returning to this country and building one of the first of the Gothic Revival churches – St Peter's, Brighton – at no great distance from the Brighton Pavilion, in 1823. Judging by his huge country house, Cliveden in Buckinghamshire, and by his Reform Club in London, Barry's personal preference was for a somewhat florid classical style which owed far more to the splendour of the Renaissance palaces he had seen in Italy than to the more restrained forms of true classical architecture. Nevertheless he is equally at home with Tudor Gothic and it was this style which he employed to build King Edward's School, Birmingham, and with which he won the competition for the new Houses of Parliament in 1836. Actually he had little choice in the competition as the terms stated that the designs had either to be in Tudor Gothic or Elizabethan, and it would seem that as early as 1836 the committee were visualising the future Queen Victoria as the nineteenth-century counterpart of the other young queen under whose guidance England had risen to greatness some three hundred years before. Barry was fortunate in his execution of the Houses of Parliament in having a most remarkable assistant – Augustus Welby Northmore Pugin – of whom we shall hear more later, particularly in connection with the building of churches, and the endowment of the Victorian Gothic style with a high moral purpose which had little to do with its merits architecturally.

Church building, as a whole, had lapsed sadly during the latter half of the eighteenth century and it was not until 1818 that a determined attempt was made to provide facilities for worship for the teeming populations of the new industrial towns. In the first quarter of the nineteenth century, the population of Manchester grew from 94,000 to 160,000 and that of Bolton from 29,000 to 50,000; these increases were typical of all the great industrial centres which had sprung up mushroom-like with the coming of the industrial revolution. Despite such noble men as Wesley and the efforts of other inspired Nonconformists, many thousands of people in this country received less religious instruction than the savages living under the British flag in the new colonies overseas.

The Act of 1818 provided about £1,000,000 to build many new churches and it is significant that of the 214 finally completed, only 40 were classical in design. In the Battle of the Styles this represented a major victory for the Gothic Revivalists.

Naturally, with so many churches to be built not all of them could be well designed, or very well constructed either, at the estimated cost of £8 per head of the congregation. In Arnold Bennett's novel *Riceyman Steps* there is a brilliant description of one of the less impressive examples of this church-building campaign. He is describing an imaginary church called St Andrew's but his words apply equally well to a large number of churches erected in many towns as a result of the 1818 Act. Bennett writes as follows:

'St Andrew's Church of yellow bricks with free-stone dressings, a blue slate roof and a red coping was designed and erected in the brilliant reign of William IV, whose Government, under Lord Grey, had a pious habit, long since lost by governments of building additional churches in populous parishes at its own expense. Unfortunately its taste in architecture was less laudable than its practical interest in the inculcation among the lowly of the Christian doctrine about the wisdom and propriety of turning the other cheek. St Andrew's, of a considerably mixed Gothic character had architecturally nothing whatever to recommend it. Its general proportions, its arched windows, its mullions, its finials, its crosses, its spire and its buttresses, were all and in every detail utterly silly and offensive. The eye could not rest anywhere upon its surface without pain.'

Not all of the churches built at this time were the result of the 1818 Act, and of the others probably the most familiar one to London visitors was built at the expense of the architects in a most emphatically classical style. This is the 'new' Church of St Pancras, built 1819–22, not very far from the station of the same name, and shows the determination of the designers to be Greek in exact detail, despite the Christian services for which it was intended. No doubt the correctness of classical detail (much of it derived from the Erechtheion on the Acropolis at Athens) was due to the knowledge of the younger William Inwood who assisted his father with the design of this church on his return from several months' study in Greece. The Ionic portico and the Caryatid Portico are both direct copies of similar ones on the Erechtheion. The use of such realistically carved figures to bear the weight of the tons of stone forming the porch has always seemed to us one of the less inspired of Greek architectural ideas. The original Caryatid maidens in the serene sunshine of Athens may not look as uncomfortable as their sootbegrimed sisters in the Euston Road but it is difficult when looking at them not to recall the Cockney who remarked . . . 'She's got a weight on 'er mind, aint she?'

A more serious critic and bitter opponent of the classical revival architecture, however, a man who argued his case for Gothic churches as being better fitted for Christian worship with sincerity and to great effect was Augustus Welby Northmore Pugin – often referred to thus to distinguish him from his father, Augustus Charles Pugin. Augustus Charles Pugin was a French refugee who fled to England during the French Revolution and who collaborated with the famous English artist, Thomas Rowlandson, on a remarkably illustrated book called *The Microcosm of London*, published in 1810. He was also an architectural draughtsman for John Nash. His son, A. W. N. Pugin, inherited his father's talent for drawing, and in 1836, when he was 24, published a fiery defence of Gothic architecture, and an equally vehement attack on the classical style. He criticised this country's 'blind admiration for everything Pagan' and declared that 'were it not for the remains of the edifices produced during the Middle Ages, the architectural monuments of this country would be contemptible in the extreme.' (A remarkable change this, since the criticism of Gothic quoted in the last chapter.)

Much of his denunciation of the classical style may be traced to his conversion to the Roman Catholic faith in 1832. It was unthinkable for him to worship a Christian God in a church so blatantly derived from the architectural forms of pagan temples. His delight in mediaeval churches was all part of his longing for a universal catholic faith – the faith which had produced much of England's noblest architecture before the disaster of the Reformation. At times this worship of the Middle Ages conflicted strangely with purely architectural principles which appeared in the books he wrote for the guidance of his contemporaries. In these he stated '. . . the great test of architectural beauty is the fitness of the design for the purpose for which it is intended' and that 'there should be no features about a building which are not necessary for convenience, construction or propriety,' but his own buildings, Scarisbrook Hall in Lancashire and some of his churches contradicted the truth of the principles he laid down for the benefit of others. Neither was he consistent in his use of Gothic details. As we have seen, Gothic architecture embraced a wide variety of styles, from the severity of the lancet windows at York to the riot of fan vaulting of Henry VII's Chapel at Westminster Abbey. When the competition for the Houses of Parliament was in progress, Pugin found himself producing meticulously beautiful detailed drawings for two candidates, Charles Barry, the successful competitor, and James Graham, his rival. At this time Pugin was deriving his inspiration from late Gothic or Tudor work. Some years after, we find him repudiating this period, declaring: 'that moment the flat or four-centred arch was introduced, the spirit of Christian architecture was on the wane.' No one could doubt the sincerity of his writings but mere sincerity is no guarantee of artistic ability. If this were not so, the religious tracts distributed by various sects would be the equal of the poems of Byron, and the artistic efforts which decorate the children's corners in our parish churches rank with the masterpieces of such dangerous free-thinkers as Goya and Toulouse-Lautrec.

Spurred on by his religious convictions, Pugin's personal output of churches was remarkable. They are, in the main, rather 'thin' in design – the clean crisp line-work of the drawings from which they were built made their forms look wiry and unsubstantial when realised in the round. The columns look spidery when compared with the real mediaeval architecture. The churches which suffered least from this weedy quality are probably the church of St Augustine, at Ramsgate, incomplete at his death, and that of St Marie in Derby.

Whilst Pugin continued to write and to pray in the monastic privacy of the Grange at Ramsgate, and other architects, no less sincere, built in whatever style they thought fit, unchecked private enterprise was infiltrating brick and slate buildings deeper and deeper into the surrounding countryside. One of the less desirable legacies of the Victorian period, ribbon development was developing fast. It heralded the collapse of the street as a unit, reducing it to a string of unrelated houses. The crescents of Georgian Bath might be compared to a necklace of carefully graduated pearls, and perhaps the terraces of Regency Cheltenham as well. But the streets of Victorian England had neither order nor decency – each house struggled to be different from its neighbour and to assert itself as an individual. If Mr A built his house in the Greek style, Mr B replied by building his with Elizabethan gables and brickwork nogging. Mr C, not to be outdone, employed an architect known for his partiality for Venetian Gothic, whilst Mr D combined details from all four, with a French château roof to crown all. That 'the Englishman's home is his castle' may be an acceptable cliché but taken literally it makes architectural nonsense – a fact which Charles Dickens was not slow to observe when he poked gentle fun at Mr Wemmick's 'castle' at Walworth with its sunset gun, in *Great Expectations. (Fig. 22.)*

If the hard-faced iron-master could imitate the stately homes of the aristocracy he was replacing by having a sham-Venetian palace or a mock French château in the heart of the Yorkshire countryside, well away from the stark reality of his slag heaps and roaring furnaces, smaller men could mimic him in their own small way. They set down their matchbox mansions in 30-foot frontage 'estates' along the new roads now pushing their macadam limbs into the countryside. The destruction of the street as a civilised unit of town architecture finally took place in the Victorian period. As early as 1829, the caricaturist, George Cruikshank, depicted the haystacks and other inhabitants of the countryside going down before the onslaught of robot-like creatures made of hods and spades firing a volley of bricks from the muzzles of chimney pots, whilst a great arsenal of brick kilns belching black smoke kept them supplied with ammunition. With the disintegration of the street the destruction of the town as a unit was bound to follow.

The appalling conditions of the early industrial centres were the result of this haphazard sprawling growth as, without form or discipline, the tentacles of industry reached out farther and farther. These towns, unexpected and accidental, as they were, had qualities which made them preferable perhaps to later developments in the north. There, they were indeed planned, not with the benevolent discipline of Bath or Buxton, but with a merciless tyranny which overruled every human right and every humane consideration. There were, of course, slums in the Middle Ages, and in the Georgian periods as well, but the slum as we know it in its most debased and squalid form is the legacy of the Victorian town, whether it was the result of accidental development, or whether it was deliberately designed. It is a reproach to our forefathers who created it and to us who still tolerate its hideous presence in our towns and cities. During the past few years much has been written – some in brilliant and persuasive verse – in praise of Victorian architecture. Confronted by the brutal and anonymous face of much of modern building, some writers have sought to enlarge upon the virtues of Victorian architecture, and to turn a blind eye to the hard facts of the towns for which the Victorian architects and their patrons must bear some responsibility. But no rhapsodising over the beauties of the St Pancras skyline or the solemn splendour of the Perpendicular Gothic of the Victorian Public School or Oxford College can hide the grim appearance of the Five Towns, the tenements of Liverpool or the barrack-like monotony of the brick wilderness built to house the drab conscripts of the new industrial army.

The town having lost its old civic form and identity, and the street having ceased to exist except as a straggle of houses or as a mere line in a pattern designed to house as many human industrial units in as small an area as possible, it was to be expected that the individual house would show the same evidence of degeneration.

With vast fortunes accumulating from the toiling men, women and children, the new industrial barons looked at the splendid estates and impressive country houses of the old aristocracy and poured out huge sums of money in an attempt to rival them and to acquire prestige which such buildings carried. They succeeded in imitating almost everything about the stately homes except their taste and refinement. The deliberately rambling plans of their houses which resulted from a pre-occupation with the 'romantic' outside appearance made them often inconvenient to run, ill-lit and atrociously expensive. The servants' quarters, the kitchens and all the other essential parts of the building were often below ground level, particularly in the town houses, for the rising cost of building land demanded a more compact plan and an economy of space. The digging of kitchens and cellars was less expensive than extending the whole area to accommodate them at ground level. It was this kind of house which gave rise to that remarkable opinion expressed so well in *Summer Moonshine* by P. G. Wodehouse, in these words . . . 'Whatever may be said in favour of the Victorians, it is pretty generally admitted that few of them were to be trusted within reach of a trowel and a pile of bricks.' (*Fig. 21.*)

As we descend the social scale, the villas mimic the larger houses as closely as possible. The drawings in Nicholson's *Practical Builder*, a popular handbook of the Victorian period, show that the villa was usually a compact brick box, divided down the middle by the 'hall,' a narrow corridor which stretched the whole depth of the house, and contained the main staircase. Two rooms to one side of the corridor were called 'the library' and the 'dining-room,' the first facing the street, the second to the rear of the house. The whole of the other side of the corridor was occupied by the 'drawing-room.' The kitchens below ground were reached by a dark narrow stair hidden under the staircase in the hall, and received what natural daylight they could from the area in front or the sunken backyard in the rear which normally housed the lavatory and wash-house.

Sometimes the speculative builder found it more economical to join two houses together – the familiar semi-detached pattern, presenting something of the symmetrical appearance of a detached villa at half the cost, and half the convenience. Others abandoned the pretence of a country house which had somehow been subjected to an Alice-in-Wonderland shrinkage and came out frankly with terraced houses joined together, consoling their tenants with a fine display of terracotta or stucco ornament loosely derived from the Doge's Palace in Venice, the cathedrals of Pisa or Siena, the turrets of the Carcassonne in France, or some equally romantic source of historic ornament. That the scale and size of the original buildings was so completely different from those to which it was now applied did not matter in the least. The white-collared workers who lived in these desirable residences – these 'houses of character' as they are now described in modern estate agents' jargon – were indeed fortunate by comparison with the workers with dirty collars, with no collars at all, and with those with scarcely a shirt, in the poorer parts of the expanding towns. The homes in which they lived and died could barely be called buildings, and were certainly remote from anything so exalted as architecture.

It is easy of course to be wise after the event, but no one could have foreseen the development of the industrial towns which overtook England in the early nineteenth century. It is true that William Blake who died in obscurity in 1827 had written of 'those dark Satanic mills,' but these as yet stood in almost open country and much of the industry was still predominantly a cottage industry and not yet of the factory town. The local water supply still served the rural community, and the sewage or night-soil was still spread on the fields. By 1821 the scene was changing rapidly. In 1801 even the population of Liverpool numbered only 77,000 and that of Manchester 95,000, but by 1821 Liverpool had swollen to 118,000 and Manchester nearly 238,000. Every major industrial town showed a similar increase – Leeds, Sheffield, Birmingham – they attracted the dispossessed farm workers, the evicted tenants, and the Irish labourers. As they flocked to the new industrial centres, and scrambled for homes, the price of land rose higher and higher, and the towns spread ever outwards, pushing the true country farther and farther away. In the mad scramble for work and homes little provision had been made for the most elementary needs. The new inhabitants of the towns were still country people, uprooted it is true, but still rural in outlook. Used to piling up his night soil, the countryman persisted in this habit, and even derived some profit

Figs. 21 and 22. The upper part of the page shows the Victorian mansion in Hampstead known as 'The Logs,' drawn from the original perspective made by its architect. It is almost a textbook of historic European architecture in one building. Below – the collapse of the street as an architectural unit from it at first by selling it to the reeking carts who came in from the country daily to collect it. As the towns spread outwards, however, it was scarcely worth while for the carts to make so long a journey and soon the middens remained, a source of dangerous infection. The cholera epidemic of 1832 forced the Government to take action, but the connection of the sewers with the River Thames (for sewers were originally designed to carry off surplus rain water) defiled the main source of drinking water for a large number of Londoners.

The overcrowding and the greed which caused it was almost beyond belief. Land speculators acquired plot after plot, and set to work systematically to cram as many human beings into the space as possible. The more human beings living there, the more rents could be levied and the more profitable the plot. Some areas were originally occupied by a number of houses built round an open court, a stand pipe supplying the water, and a common privy supplied to be shared by the inhabitants of the court. Later, rows of houses were inserted in the court itself, and yet more in the small central yard which remained. Where there was sufficient space the narrow street separating two rows of houses might itself afford building land and the familiar and foul 'back to back' pattern of housing (still with us today) was evolved. (*Fig. 23 and Plate 39.*)

In the sixteenth century, Robert Crowley had written . . .

> 'And this is a city
> In name, but in deed
> It is a pack of people
> That seek after meed*   (* gain)
> For officers and all
> Do seek their own gain
> But for the wealth of the Commons
> Not one taketh pain
> And Hell without order
> I may it well call
> Where every man is for himself
> And no man for all.'

Josiah Wedgwood, when he built Etruria in the last quarter of the eighteenth century, had lived with his work people in the village he and his craftsmen had created. By the middle of the nineteenth century few masters of the coal mine or the iron works, the cotton mill and the other great industrial monsters would have dared to live among their men. When they had built the factory, and then built the houses near by for the factory workers, the houses and the factory were disciplined into an architectural unit, but it was the discipline of the slave-ship, the tyranny of the despot. More recently a negro

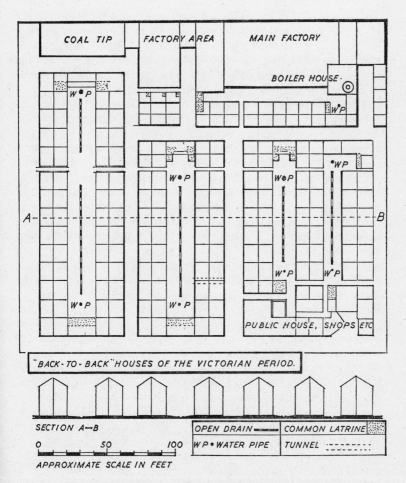

COAL TIP   FACTORY AREA   MAIN FACTORY

BOILER HOUSE·

W • P

W • P

A - B

W • P

°WP

W • P   W • P   W°P   W°P

W • P   W • P

PUBLIC HOUSE, SHOPS ETC

"BACK-TO-BACK" HOUSES OF THE VICTORIAN PERIOD.

SECTION A—B

0   50   100

APPROXIMATE SCALE IN FEET

| OPEN DRAIN | COMMON LATRINE |
| WP • WATER PIPE | TUNNEL |

Fig. 23. Barracks for the conscripts of the Industrial Revolution. Plan of an area of back-to-back housing

spiritual has sung of the plight of the workman who pleads '. . . I sold my soul to the Company Store.' The workman who lost his job in the factory town not only lost his job, but his very home.

At the end of the day the mill-owner left the smoke enshrouded and monotonous desert of brick for his castellated mansion with the French château roof, its crockets and spires, standing in its own grounds far from the town he had created. With his new knighthood, Mr Alfred Muggins could now become Sir Alured Mogyns, and his new mansion, tricked out in all the trappings of the Gothic castle, was a pathetic attempt to stand himself beside the old aristocracy he and his kind were slowly replacing.

In leaving the town behind he was establishing a habit which now seems to be ingrained in every city worker. No one in the last century was capable of imagining that a city could be built in which one could live as well as work. Today, thousands of city workers endure the rush hour and the exhaustion and vexation it entails in order to live and work in two widely separated places. This prejudice against living in cities unfortunately has been the cause of the destruction of much of the real countryside by the creation of vast areas of suburbs which are neither town nor country. As the New Town of our own day evolves it will demonstrate that a town is not necessarily a dirty and uncomfortable place in which to live, but the evil tradition of the Victorian factory town dies hard, and both the architectural and the political scene are still haunted by the ghost of their tyrannical creator.

Not all mill owners or iron masters, of course, were inhuman brutes. One admirable exception was Sir Titus Salt, the mill owner who evolved 'alpaca' cloth. To him we owe one of the best examples of a planned factory town. Saltaire, built near Shipley in Yorkshire, had 800 model dwellings and ample attention was paid to sanitation, light, warmth and ventilation throughout the factory buildings. A Congregational church followed in 1859, factory schools in 1868, almshouses, a club and an institute in 1868/9, and a public park in 1871. By modern standards Saltaire would not be regarded as a model town, but it was incomparably better than anything produced at that time.

In other fields of architecture the Battle of Styles continued. The triumph for the supporters of Gothic was confirmed by the erection of the Tudor/Gothic Houses of Parliament. It must be stressed that much of the discussion over the styles was entirely beside the point, architecturally speaking. Many Victorian architects were obsessed with the outside appearance of the building, and with the accuracy with which it imitated historic details. The function of the building, and the way in which it had to work often received scanty consideration. (The waiting room at St Pancras Station for example, has no windows and its only source of natural light is still the glass panels on the door. This is indeed the 'gloomth of the abbeys.')

The supporters of the classical style gained a temporary victory over their Gothic opponents with the Fitzwilliam Museum at Cambridge, the National Gallery, London, and St George's Hall, Liverpool (built in 1839) and Joseph Hansom's Roman Temple design which won the competition for Birmingham Town Hall in 1831. Its realisation bankrupted its designer, and perhaps it is not surprising that his best known designs – the church at Arundel and the Roman Catholic Cathedral at Plymouth – show his return to Gothic. (He is perhaps best remembered for his invention of the hansom cab.)

Both Oxford and Cambridge came down fairly heavily in favour of Gothic, and certainly one of the most effective and persuasive writers on its behalf, John Ruskin, himself a graduate of Christ Church, Oxford, spared none of its rivals. The classical style, and the Renaissance which stemmed from it were both equally hateful. He poured scorn on 'the foul torrent of the Renaissance' and declared it to be 'base, unnatural, unfruitful, unenjoyable and impious.'

Backed by so influential and important a writer the Gothic style became extremely popular; indeed it was the only style for certain types of building. Some of the architects, sincere admirers of the England of the Middle Ages as they imagined it, copied the outward forms and details of the mediaeval buildings because they thought that these would impart something of the nobility of the originals to their own creations. Others, more commercially inclined, 'went Gothic – or Classic' because it paid them handsomely to do so. They would have built town halls and railway stations shaped like Eskimo igloos if it had been the fashion.

As we have seen, the classical revival in the early years of the century favoured the production of Greek rather than Roman designs. Euston Station, for example, built in 1838 by Philip Hardwick, had an imposing Doric portico. St Pancras Station and Hotel, on the other hand, designed some thirty years later by Sir George Scott is riotously and emphatically Gothic. (*Plate 37.*) So too was his successful design for the Albert Memorial built in 1876.

Only Lewis Cubitt, the designer of King's Cross Station in 1851–52 saw that neither Gothic nor classical styles were suitable for a building so entirely modern in function and in material. No Greek and no mediaeval architect had ever been faced with the problem of designing a railway station, and Cubitt realised that an entirely fresh approach was required. His design, although it has been sadly altered and is half hidden by the pin-table squalor of Euston Road, is still a fine and imposing building. It has a certain dignity and courage, and its creator refused to camouflage its bold silhouette with unsuitable ornament cribbed from a Gothic cathedral or a pagan temple. *The Builder*, an architectural journal founded in 1843 by Joseph Hansom, commented on this lack of historic ornament, remarking that Cubitt had been content with the largeness of some of the features, the fitness of the structures for its purpose, and a characteristic expression of that purpose.'

One of the most imposing buildings of the Victorian period, now no longer standing unfortunately, was designed not by an architect but by a foreman gardener, Joseph Paxton. Born at Milton Bryant in Bedfordshire, in 1801, Paxton served his time as a gardener's apprentice, and by 1826 was foreman gardener at Chatsworth to the Duke of Devonshire. His first 'architectural' attempts were very efficiently designed greenhouses and a conservatory nearly 300 feet long. Accustomed to working in buildings with a light iron framework supporting a glass roof and glass walls, Paxton, a shrewd and intelligent man, who probably knew little about historic ornament and cared less for it, entered his design for a new modern building to house the Great Exhibition of 1851, and carried off the award against 233 other competitors. The building was, in fact, a gigantic greenhouse. The weight of the roof was largely sustained not by the walls, but the tough iron framework, which permitted the spaces between the girders to be filled with glass. Such a construction gave the architect much greater freedom for the walls were no longer so essential for weight bearing and could be used as screens, allowing light and air to penetrate.

A realisation of the possibilities of this girder construction could have revolutionised architecture of the Victorian industrial town, if professional architects had been able to pause for a moment from their frenzied pursuit of a historic style. But with some contempt for the engineer in his sweaty overalls, they continued to fake mills, potteries, warehouses and breweries to look like Gothic churches and Venetian Palaces. (Until recently there used to be a chimneystack opposite the Tate Gallery on Millbank in London which looked uncommonly like a belfry on fire.) The use of iron as an architectural medium, and later of reinforced concrete was regarded by architects as a matter for the engineer and hardly their concern at all.

Iron had been used for architectural details such as hinges and grilles for centuries, but not as a building material, although Sir John Soane had recommended its use in 1818. Nash used iron shafts to support the roof of the kitchens in the Brighton Pavilion and, painted to resemble bamboo, as the main structure of the staircase. It also appears, painted to resemble stone, among the columns of his Carlton House Terrace. Ruskin foresaw that it could be an important factor in architectural design and wrote: 'The time is probably near when a new system of architectural laws will be developed adapted entirely to metallic construction.' A French woodworker named Boileau turned architect and used iron in an entirely unorthodox way in the church of Notre Dame de France, Leicester Place, London. Here, in a Roman Catholic church, fashioned in 1868 from an old Georgian showplace called the Panorama, you may see columns, vaulting ribs and arches, all of iron.

Encouraged by John Ruskin, Sir Thomas Deane and Benjamin Woodward his assistant erected the Oxford Museum in 1856, and used cast iron as the main constructional material. Unfortunately they did not evolve forms peculiar to the qualities of iron, but forced it to assume the character of the Gothic forms and ornamental details which had previously been carried out in stone – a very different material. (We have witnessed the same misunderstanding of a new material in our own time, where the new plastics were fashioned to imitate wood, metal, leather and a host of traditional materials.) Much of the unfortunate appearance of the Oxford Museum may be attributed to the mechanical repetition in cast iron of details which, when they were carried out in stone in the original Gothic buildings, possessed a variety and life entirely absent from the mass produced castings. (*Plate 38.*)

The same monotony is apparent in the application of cast terracotta ornament imitating Gothic stone carving on buildings designed by such architects as Sir George Gilbert Scott, William Butterfield, and Alfred Waterhouse.

Sir George Gilbert Scott had an enormous architectural practice, and only a man of his immense energy could possibly have dealt with all the commissions which poured into his office. He was personally responsible for much of the restoration work carried out in our mediaeval cathedrals and churches, and his handling of Tewkesbury Abbey brought angry protests from the great Socialist craftsman, William Morris (of whom we shall hear more later). Perhaps his most sensitive restoration is to be seen in the Chapter House of Westminster Abbey. As his St Pancras Station shows he was entirely in favour of the Gothic style, although after a very difficult series of interviews with Lord Palmerston, the Prime Minister, he was obliged to redesign the Foreign Office building entirely in an Italianate Renaissance style, very much against his own wishes.

George Street, who had been Scott's assistant for some years, later became an independent architect. Probably his most familiar building is the Law Courts, a vast complex of mongrel Gothic details applied to a difficult and irregularly planned building but with a remarkable grandeur internally, despite the limitations forced upon the architect by the site on which it had to be built.

On the work of William Butterfield little comment is required. He specialised in incorporating alternate bands of highly coloured brick into the fabric of his buildings – a particularly unhappy introduction into the pattern of Oxford Colleges, which are predominantly of stone. Keble College built in 1870–75 is one of his more notorious experiments in this multi-coloured brick and tile. The Gothic flavour of his buildings at Rugby and at other public schools was particularly well suited to the high and almost monastic ideals to which the English Public Schools became dedicated during their overhaul and renewal in the Victorian period.

Another Victorian architect with a considerable output was Alfred Waterhouse. Born in Liverpool in 1830, he was articled to a Manchester architect, and started practice there in 1853. He designed the Manchester Assize Courts in 1859, and the Town Hall in 1868, and these and other buildings brought a so-called Gothic quality to the architecture of a city which, apart from its lovely parish church (now the cathedral) had little enough of architectural merit at that time. His best known and perhaps most admired building in London is the Natural History Museum, in South Kensington and shows his fondness for terracotta ornament and romantic attachment to mediaeval details. Both are also somewhat oddly in evidence in his Prudential Assurance Building in Holborn. His buildings are to be found all over the country – from Brighton, where the Metropole Hotel would be difficult to ignore, to Eaton Hall in Cheshire and the collegiate buildings he designed in Manchester, Liverpool, Leeds, Oxford and Cambridge. Of those he contributed to Cambridge mention must be made of his additions to Caius College. Standing in King's Parade, near the Market Square, and looking towards Trinity, a visitor may see at a glance the real Gothic of St Mary the Great and King's College Chapel, the exquisite proportions and classical serenity of James Gibbs's Senate House, and the spurious Gothic buildings designed by Waterhouse for Caius College which almost seal off the vista down Trinity Street. It is an interesting comparison, for each building is characteristic of the age in which it was designed.

One writer who revolted in particular against the stupidity and ugly ostentation of Victorian architecture was William Morris, the great Socialist writer and artist. He not only wrote articles and books denouncing the vulgarity and dishonesty of much of the contemporary architecture and interior decoration, but by tremendous personal efforts demonstrated how such crafts as weaving, fabric printing, stained glass, metalwork, wallpaper design and book production might be a means of bringing art as a vital and living force into everyday things. We have mentioned how the divorce of art and craft could be traced right back to Robert Adam's paper designs which were carried out by an obedient craftsman in the mid-eighteenth century. By the end of the nineteenth century, the craftsman himself had been degraded to a machine 'hand.' (Note that he was no longer even a 'man' – he was but a 'hand.') Certain that it was only by personal creation that a man might find full happiness in his work, Morris denounced the machine as an evil force, and tried to persuade the public to return to the honest and homely qualities found in hand-made things. He was convinced that until the artist became a craftsman, making the goods he designed, and the craftsman became an artist once more as in the Middle Ages, designing the goods he made, no truly sincere art would emerge in this new industrial age. His ideals were basically sound, and much good came of them, but Morris failed to realise that the machines he despised were in fact complicated tools. They were just as capable of producing a thousand beautiful and well designed things as a thousand ugly and inefficient ones. It was the man who directed the machine who was responsible for the artistic squalor of the Victorian work and not the machine itself.

Morris studied architecture for a year in the studio of G. E. Street. One of his fellow students was a young architect named Philip Webb, and between them they designed Morris's own house – the now famous Red House built in Bexley in Kent, in 1859. This house embodied their ideas on what was desirable in modern architecture. It makes much of the natural qualities of the materials from which it is built. Its plan was evolved to fit the activities and life of its owner, and was not either rigidly symmetrical or just a rambling romantic pattern on paper. The Red House was not without a certain mediaeval flavour, for both Morris and Webb, who later founded the firm of Morris & Co, had great admiration for the high standard of craftsmanship and honesty of construction characteristic of the best work of the Middle Ages. It was in fact the indignation which Morris felt at seeing the damage caused to fine mediaeval architecture by the restoration perpetrated by Sir George Gilbert Scott which caused him to found the Society for the Protection of Ancient Buildings – an organisation which Morris nick-named the 'Anti-Scrape.'

A fellow student of Philip Webb in Street's office was an original young Scotsman named Richard Norman Shaw. After having won a Royal Academy Travelling Scholarship in 1854 he published a book on his visits to the Continent in 1858, and became an independent architect in 1862. Shaw was to bring a new quality into the domestic architecture of the period, and although he had a great respect for the past, he was not addicted to the slavish copying of outworn architectural forms which seems to have bedevilled his contemporaries. Where he drew from the past, his source of inspiration seems to have been largely our own domestic architecture and his sensitive use of brick – unadorned in the main – justifies to some extent the label 'Queen Anne' which has been attached to his work since. His work was rooted in the past, but no sentimental associations or antiquarian pedantry were allowed to affect the originality of the design or the efficiency of the plan. His town houses in Kensington, his offices in the city, and New Scotland Yard in Whitehall, are all essentially the architecture of the city, not country house forms which have been surprised to find themselves alongside other buildings. They belong to the town, just as his huge mansion Bryanston (now a famous school) was designed in the grand style of a country house which constituted a unit in itself. Where he could design buildings which had to 'live together' as at Bedford Park, they belong to a complete scheme, and it is interesting to see this tiny experiment in a planned suburb and to observe how much more civilised it is than the majority of straggling suburbs on the outskirts of any great city at this time. Bedford Park, however, was not designed for the mass of people who still toiled in the factories. They continued to exist in the squalor of the industrial slums, or possibly in the scarcely less grim bye-law wilderness which replaced some of the early industrial estates. The bye-laws controlling the new areas certainly enforced a certain standard of sanitation, and checked the abuse of overcrowding, but their mean spiritless arrangement left much to be desired. They had 'commoditie' of sort, 'firmenes' perhaps, and no 'delight' of any kind.

We have already mentioned the example of Titus Salt who built Saltaire for his work people. Towards the end of the nineteenth century other industrialists bettered his example: such employers as the Cadbury family who moved their employees and works out to a new town near Birmingham called Bournville and a certain soap manufacturer named Lever (later Viscount Leverhulme) who was responsible for Port Sunlight. It is difficult for us to imagine what it must have meant to those few fortunate workers who stood dazzled by the sunshine and fanned by the breeze which rustled the living trees of these newly created towns. Bournville was started in 1879 and Port Sunlight in 1888. By 1898 an obscure shorthand writer in the House of Commons named Ebenezer Howard predicted a revolutionary development in town architecture in a book called *Tomorrow* – a prophecy that one day towns would be evolved 'designed for healthy living and industry, of a size that makes possible a full measure of social life but not larger; surrounded by a rural belt; the whole of the land being held in public ownership or held in trust for the community.' With Ebenezer Howard and his dream of a city which might be a worthy place in which both to live as well as to work, we will turn what Bernard Shaw called 'the most villainous page in history' and prepare to examine English architecture of the twentieth century.

Chapter Eleven

THE TWENTIETH CENTURY

T HERE were two main reasons for the squalor of the nineteenth century town. The first was perhaps social rather than architectural, for the vast industrial slums were the products of an immoral exploitation of people and of land and had little to do with architects as such.

The second was the obsession of the architects with this or that historic style, which concentrated their creative energies on the superficial aspects of individual buildings, when they might have been designing streets and towns fit for human beings to live in.

The tradition of fine townscape by which England led Europe during the eighteenth century was abandoned almost entirely. It disappeared behind a pall of smoke from the kilns and factory chimneys or was submerged by a flood of suburban villas which seeped into the surrounding countryside. Only now are we starting to recover from this nightmare and to re-discover how to build a decent town.

It is easy enough today to see where our forefathers erred, but more difficult to guarantee that we shall not make equally serious mistakes. Perhaps it is because in the past some of the loveliest country mansions have been created in England – buildings which stand in their own grounds or in settings specially created for them, and can be studied and enjoyed in isolation – that our architects have tended to design each building as though it were to live in an architectural vacuum. An inability to distinguish the essential difference between a building standing alone in open country, and one intended for a town is also partly responsible for the higgledy-piggledy muddle of most of our streets today.

At last we are beginning to realise what every Georgian architect took for granted – that town buildings owe a sort of allegiance to each other. Such a town as Blandford in Dorset, rebuilt about 1732 after a disastrous fire, still retains much of the orderly and well-mannered pattern in which the town hall, the shops, the houses and the church were designed to live together as a civic unit.

It is only during the last twenty-odd years that it has been realised that the endearingly haphazard growth which exercises such charm in a village of 500 people has nothing to recommend it when it is applied to a town of ten times that number. And although there are a great many people now who are aware of the incongruity and bad manners of the slick plate-glass neon-sign shop front among the buildings in a quiet Cotswold village, there are not so many who find a pseudo-cottagey villa unsuitable for insertion in a normal town street.

It is because of the importance of looking at buildings not as isolated units but in relation to others that there has been increasing emphasis in this book on the evolution of town planning. Appreciation of the architectural beauties of the stately homes can give a great deal of pleasure, but may have little effect on our towns as they are now and as they must be when building for the future. Indeed a slavish admiration of historical architecture can result all too easily in blind imitation of bygone architectural forms, and produce 'Tudor' garages, 'Georgian' schools, 'Egyptian' factories and 'Elizabethan' multiple stores.

Even the first Garden Cities, nobly conceived as they were, could not escape entirely from the clinging sentimentality of the past. The two most notable examples are Letchworth Garden City, started in 1904, and Welwyn Garden City, planned some fifteen years later shortly after the First World War. Both owed their inception to Ebenezer Howard. Both embodied the principles he set out in his book *Tomorrow – Peaceful Path to Real Reform* and it is significant that his principles were more concerned with setting right social evils than with evolving any new architectural forms. Much as he admired such enlightened employers as the Cadbury family and their town at Bournville, he foresaw that with less scrupulous industrialists such an arrangement might be developed into an instrument of repression. A man whose working conditions were unsatisfactory might be prepared to protest if his action only meant loss of his job, but where the employer owned his house, it might well mean that such a protest would result in his being ejected from his home as well. Howard therefore would have none of the company town. He visualised 'a balanced community which owned and developed its own land and which was partly dependent on local industry and partly on agriculture – that every town should be consciously designed everywhere – even to the humblest cottage – with beauty, space and greenery as basic aims, and that it should be surrounded by a green belt of land permanently used for agriculture and re-creation.'

He did not advocate the nationalisation of land, but he declared the ownership of it by the municipal authorities to be essential to prevent its exploitation for private profit. Land values were to be controlled in the interests of the whole town and the community itself must be self-supporting both industrially and agriculturally. For Howard, it was essential that the inhabitants of his Garden Cities should both live and work in them. They were not merely to be large dormitory suburbs of London or of any other city from which people returned each evening. Finally, seeing the plight of so many unfortunates adrift and unknown, bewildered and rootless, in the vast industrial antheaps of over 100,000 people, Ebenezer Howard fixed the maximum population of his ideal Garden City at approximately 30,000. A town or city any smaller than this would have difficulty in surviving as a financial and social unit, and in a larger one, human beings tended to be overwhelmed by its very size and to lose all sense of 'belonging' – a condition which Howard felt struck at the very roots of human happiness. (Anyone who has lived alone in one of our great industrial cities will appreciate his wisdom.)

It was clear that Howard would encounter opposition to this revolutionary and idealist conception. People were reluctant to live where no work or industry had yet settled, and industrialists were reluctant to build their factories in an area as yet relatively un-populated. He had considerable difficulty in getting financial support, and encountered ridicule and obstruction from politicians Lloyd George and Earl Balfour. Nevertheless, Howard would not be denied: the open competition for the design of the Letchworth Garden City was won by the firm of Unwin and Parker, and work began in 1904. The master plan was largely the work of Raymond Unwin, whilst his young partner, Barry Parker, was mainly respon-sible for the design of the buildings as the city began to evolve.

Ebenezer Howard's own diagram for his ideal Garden City re-sembled a dartboard. The protective wire which encircles the peri-meter of the board corresponds to the position of the railway, for Howard knew the steam locomotive only as a soot-dispersing monster which should not be allowed to bring its grime into the pleasant greenery of his city and banished it to the outer margin. For the same reason he isolated his industrial zone, placing it at the bottom arc of the dartboard, insulating the residential areas from it by woodland. In the early twentieth century nobody visualised the clean, efficient architecture of the modern factory building, and one thought in terms of the 'dark, satanic mills' of the Black Country. A circular park occupied the centre of the dartboard and the main roads, designed for horse-drawn traffic, crossed the city from north to south and diagonally as well. The city occupied 1,000 acres, but was surrounded by a green belt of about 5,000 acres devoted to farming, so that the population of about 30,000 should have fresh fruit, vegetables, dairy produce and eggs, access to the living country-side and all the other benefits of a rural population, even if they worked in the industrial zone. Around the perimeter, and outside the railway appeared convalescent homes, new forests, allotments and so on. To complete the picture this Garden City of 30,000 to 32,000 people was one of a system of five satellites (one of the first occasions on which this word appeared in connection with town-planning) to be grouped some distance from and to be linked by railway and a ring road to a larger central city with a population of 58,000. The city was similarly organised with wedges of green driven into its centre and restricted by a wide agricultural area from spreading into and absorbing its smaller neighbours.

The Garden City ideal was a remarkable one, and its results on balance were admirable. Ebenezer Howard demonstrated that a town could be planned as a place in which one might be glad to live as well as labour. He put grass and flowers, trees and the living country within a few feet of the doorstep and a few hundred yards from the factory, but he could do nothing for the industrial town already in being. This he abandoned as hopeless and sought virgin land for his Garden City. He left the problem of the existing slums, and the bewildering muddle of domestic and industrial buildings to us to disentangle. Convinced of the absolute need for human beings to be continually and intimately in contact with living plants, not shut away from them by a dreary desert of bricks and mortar, he was wasteful in his use of land, and deliberately avoided the compactness of street arrangement, put detached houses apart in huge gardens set back from the road, screened from it and from their neighbours by forest trees. Appalled at concentrations of 800 or more people to the acre in the industrial slum, he planned his city with as few as 20 or 24 to the acre. Haunted by the spectre of the tenements and lodging houses in which these 800 unfortunates lived, he would have no flats which might have economised his use of land and given variety to the architectural skyline. His segregation of industry would have prevented tall factory buildings from relieving the monotony of two-storey architecture, although at that time, with coal-fired ovens and boiler houses (now replaced by electric power) this isolation was not unreasonable.

The houses which constitute the Garden Cities are comely, and well suited in material and planning for their purpose. They belong essentially to rural architecture, based loosely on solid decent village buildings which have been erected all over the country for hundreds of years, but frankly are rather unadventurous, and perhaps a little smug. They were infinitely better than anything a working man either in town or country could find anywhere at that time but they ignored the remarkable discoveries in constructional methods evolving during the latter part of the nineteenth century.

Ebenezer Howard's insistence on detached or semi-detached houses hardened the Englishman's prejudice against the street as an architectural unit, and made the need for the economic use of land by the erection of flats more difficult to accept. Nevertheless, it would be churlish and ungrateful not to acknowledge our debt to the vision and inspiration of this great man and his associates, and if any of our New Towns are to be preferred to his Garden Cities, it will be because we have had the sense and humility to profit by their mistakes. We have learned, for example, that to make a rule such as that which existed early in the history of Bournville, that no house was to occupy more than a quarter of the site on which it was built, in such a small island as this would result in an almost continuous area of Garden City over the whole of England. It is now possible to plan for much higher concentrations of the population than those to be found in the Garden Cities and yet still avoid overcrowding which leads to the creation of slums. But the whole concept that a gracious way of life is possible in an industrial city we owe to Ebenezer Howard, and if we find his cities a little middle-aged now, we must pay humble tribute to the pioneering spirit in which they were conceived. (*Plate 42.*)

To study purely architectural development, as distinct from that of the town, we must retrace our steps a little to the closing decade of the nineteenth century. Whilst many architects were devoting their energies to producing all kinds of buildings in historical fancy dress, a few were much more usefully employed in trying to re-discover the basic principles of good architectural design. Their numbers were small, but their influence has been out of all proportion to the amount of architecture they actually produced. Of this number, mention must be made of Charles Voysey, a young Yorkshire architect born in 1857 who started his own architectural practice about 1890. Although he undoubtedly learned much from the example of William Morris, his interior design has a freshness and originality which owed little to the Middle Ages with which Morris was obsessed.

Voysey's own house at Chorleywood, in Hertfordshire, built in 1900, was freely planned, light, airy, and almost puritanical in its rejection of the over-ornamentation so common in other houses at that time. Its woodwork was painted white, its wallpapers and chintz fabrics gay and fresh, and the furniture, also designed by the archi-tect, is severe and elegant in proportion. Most furniture at this time was made of carved, heavy, dark wood, or had a bogus 'grained' pattern overlaid with treacly varnish. Voysey's furniture relied upon the natural qualities of the woods for its simple appeal. The house he designed in 1891 for Norman Shaw's garden suburb, Bedford Park, was surprisingly original, with wide bare areas of white plastered wall and compactly grouped windows contrasting with the sober red brick of the majority of the other houses on the estate. His influence is wholly confined to domestic architecture, for he built almost no public buildings, not even a church, but his houses were designed with distinction and an understanding of their function as buildings to be lived in and not merely to be looked at. Nevertheless, with his sensitive use of material and siting they are indeed beautiful, and owe nothing to the historical examples of which they occasionally remind us.

If 'Broadleys,' a country mansion on Lake Windermere, has a Regency flavour it is because this, and Regency houses, share a common elegance, and not because Voysey imitated historic forms.

Even more contemptuous of historical ornament and traditional forms of architecture is the work of C. Harrison Townsend, best known perhaps for his brutally non-symmetrical art gallery in Whitechapel, built in 1897–99, and the squat sculptural tower and façade of the Horniman Museum which crowns Forest Hill on the outskirts of London.

The most influential of all the architects who were pursuing their quest for a new contemporary architecture was not an Englishman but a Scot – Charles Rennie Mackintosh. His writings, like his buildings, have an extraordinarily modern quality. In 1894, Mackintosh wrote 'All great and living architecture has been the direct expression of the needs and beliefs of man at the time of its creation, and now if we would have great architecture this should still be so. How absurd it is to see modern churches, theatres, banks, museums, exchanges, municipal buildings, art galleries, etc., made in imitation of Greek temples.' It is a basic architectural truth as valid today as when it was written nearly seventy years ago, but it is one which some architects are still reluctant to admit.

Born in 1868, Mackintosh was articled to an architect in Glasgow, won a travelling scholarship to Italy in 1891, and an open competition for the design of the new School of Art in Glasgow in 1896. It is unfortunate that all the examples of his work are to be found in Scotland, and that strictly they are outside the scope of this book which is confined to English architecture, but so great was his influence that we should be foolish to let a few miles of border country exclude him from our consideration. His architectural career was all too short, for he retired from practice at the age of 45 to become a painter, but his buildings had a profound effect on architectural thinking, and particularly on that of the young modern architects of Austria with whom he came in contact in 1900, when he was invited to show his work and that of his group at their annual exhibition at Vienna.

His almost sculptural way of combining mass with mass, and linking space to space, and the interior decoration which he employed to give emphasis to his carefully placed wall surfaces and light airy supporting members were a revelation to Otto Wagner and his companions and presented to them an entirely different way of architectural creation.

Even today, the exterior of Glasgow School of Art has an individual and almost harsh originality – a modern quality which some people find slightly disturbing, although the building is over sixty years old. The hard, clean masonry, devoid of ornament, the wide functional areas of window and the spidery wrought iron of the palings enclosing the area, have an uncompromising hardness of presentation. The first part of the building was erected from 1896–99, but the library wing, added in 1907–09, rears its craggy form from its sloping site with as much resolution as a Norman keep or a modern power station.

As unlike Mackintosh's buildings as can be imagined are the country houses for which Edwin (later Sir Edwin) Lutyens, a contemporary of Mackintosh, was responsible. Lutyens continued the tradition of Norman Shaw by deriving inspiration from early eighteenth-century English architecture, although his non-symmetrical plans and charming use of traditional materials, brick and tile, slate and native stone, show him to be far more than an imitator. His buildings have a picturesque charm, admirably suited to the country gentleman for whom they were designed, or to take their place in the carefully modulated contours of the new Hampstead Garden Suburb planned at the same time and by the same architects as Letchworth, but they show no desire to investigate new and revolutionary methods of construction already in use in France, Germany and also in the United States. It was as though the English architect, well pleased with his Neo-Georgian architecture, lapsed into a sort of architectural slumber from which he only began to awaken after the end of the First World War. English architecture of the first quarter of the twentieth century is comely, complacent and conservative, and if we would study the origins of the architecture of today, it would be of little use to look round England. It is ironical that the technical skill – the ability to create ships and rolling stock, to span rivers and bays with airy steel bridges, to harness and control mighty waterways for which the British engineer was famous the world over was diverted so little towards his native buildings.

Two very important methods of building evolved during the latter

part of the eighteenth century – the use of steel structure instead of
the traditional weight-bearing walls, and the introduction of reinforced concrete. Before continuing with this survey of English
architecture, we must pause for a while and consider just what these
two new constructional inventions entailed and how they were to
alter the whole aspect of architectural design.

Mention was made in the last chapter of the limited use of iron as
a building material – notably in the construction of the Crystal
Palace in 1851. Although the use of iron supports – some three
thousand cast iron columns were used in this building – and the
accurately pre-fabricated units of iron and glass indicated a new
freedom from the tyranny of the weight-bearing wall, it was not until
technical advances made it possible to replace cast iron by steel
girders that any revolutionary principles could evolve, and even then
it was the engineer and not the architect who was to develop them.

A beam spanning the space between two walls is under two forms
of strain – tension and compression. If you place a long green stick
across the garden from one wall to another you will see that the bark
is wrinkled on the upper surface, and stretched tightly enough to
split it on the lower surface. The wrinkled surface is due to compression and the split surface due to tension. It is not, of course, so
obvious if the timber is stout or if the beam is of metal, but the stress
follows this pattern nevertheless.

Steel girders can therefore be most economically made if they are at
their thickest at the areas of tension and compression and thinnest
between the two where little strain is exerted. This is the reason for
the familiar 'H' shaped section to a girder, or rolled steel joint.
Unlike the variable qualities of types and ages of wooden beams,
which make it difficult to calculate exactly the load which they will
take, the steel joist is capable of standardisation, physically and
chemically, a valuable quality where large quantities are involved in
the framework of buildings. The R.S.J. as the standard joist is
called, is capable of enormous weight-bearing when compared with
the traditional columns of timber, and various kinds of stone.
According to *A Key to Modern Architecture* by F. R. S. Yorke and
Colin Penn – Associates of the Royal Institute of British Architects –
a joist 24 inches deep and $7\frac{1}{2}$ inches wide will carry a load of no less
that 54 tons over a span of 20 feet wide. A beam of pine of the same
dimensions would only be capable of carrying a load of about one
quarter of that weight. It is quite clear that steel is stronger bulk for
bulk than any of the traditional materials. With a compressive
strength of about 4,600 tons per square foot, it is about three times
as strong as the strongest granite, nine times as strong as ordinary
sandstone, and about thirty times as strong as limestone.

H

The massive walls required to sustain the weight of a roof in the Middle Ages therefore are no longer required where the building is constructed with a steel frame, and huge areas of wall, formerly vital to the stability of the building can now be used as windows, or filled with screens of light material. The architect had a new medium at his disposal – a material which enabled him to standardise measurements, to span much larger areas, and moreover to erect much higher buildings than ever before. (The latter is an important consideration when building on expensive sites in city centres.)

There are of course certain disadvantages in the extensive use of steel framework. It is vulnerable to weather and must be clad or painted to protect it from rust and corrosion. The ceaseless painting operation on the Forth Bridge is an obvious example of this disadvantage. Steel is also liable to buckle, warp and collapse if the building it supports should catch fire, as the tangled ruins of blitzed factories and warehouses showed during the last war.

It is not a cheap material to make or to transport, but its quick and dry assembly saves a great deal of time on the building site. The standard lengths and sizes of steel joints can be welded or riveted together in a variety of ways, and the strains on whole buildings calculated accurately.

We have already mentioned the jetting of upper floors by mediaeval architects, the wooden timbers of the second and third storeys being allowed to project some distance in front of the lower one. This elementary form of cantilever in wood pointed the way to far more daring experiments with steel joists. (Perhaps the most familiar form of cantilever is a springboard at the swimming bath which, secured to the side projects far out over the water.) Steel joists were capable of projecting much further and of staying more rigid over far greater areas than their wooden prototypes.

When these and other qualities – its lightness combined with great strength – began to be realised and exploited, more and more buildings were evolved to take advantage of them. By 1899 French engineer/architects had succeeded in spanning a 375-foot exhibition hall without internal supports, and the superb latticework of the Eiffel Tower was a new feature of the Parisian skyline. Five years later, its English counterpart, the famous Tower at Blackpool, about half the height of the Eiffel Tower, was opened to the public. It was regarded by most English architects as an exhibition freak scarcely worthy of their serious contemplation and certainly few of them realised at that time the vast constructional possibilities its erection implied.

Across the Atlantic, however, the first steel-framed skyscrapers were rearing their gaunt skeletons, and a new progressive school of architecture, of which Louis Sullivan (1856–1924) was one of the outstanding members, was evolving strange and exciting architectural forms in Chicago.

The second method of construction which has entirely altered the course of architectural design during this century is the use of reinforced concrete.

Concrete is basically an artificial stone made from sand, shingle, cement and water. It is not a new material, for as we have seen, it was used in Early Roman architecture, but its modern use may be said to date from the discovery of Portland cement in 1824.

Reinforced concrete, however, was largely the invention of a young French architect named François Hennebique, towards the end of the nineteenth century. As we have shown, any beam suspended on supports at regular intervals is subject to tensile stresses at certain points on its length. The reinforcing of a concrete beam entails bending steel rods to meet the extra stress at those points, and then putting the rods in position so that they are embedded in the semi-liquid concrete as it is poured into its mould. Not only do the reinforcing rods strengthen the beam but the concrete itself protects them from weather corrosion and from fire. The reinforcing is not, of course, confined to beam construction. It is possible to cast concrete in almost any form and although its very adaptability may leave it open to abuse, the sensitive artist (and a man *must* be sensitive if he is to be a good architect) will always evolve forms which are particularly suitable to this new medium.

This principle of reinforcing concrete had been patented by an American named Thaddeus Hyatt as early as 1878, but it was Hennebique who erected the first reinforced concrete-framed building and incorporated reinforced slabs into his beam construction.

Early in the twentieth century, two brothers, Auguste and Gustave Perret, after studying architecture at the Ecole des Beaux Arts in Paris, started an architectural practice there, and produced some of the first truly modern buildings in this new medium. Unlike some of their contemporaries, both in Europe and in America, they made no attempt to imitate the forms of more traditional materials, but evolved for themselves designs which grew quite naturally out of the new methods of construction and the new material which they were handling. Of their many buildings mention must be made of the Champs Elysées Theatre, built in Paris in 1911, the church of Notre Dame at Raincy (1922–23) and the Marignane Airport built shortly after the last war in 1947.

With the Perret brothers, we have crossed the threshold of a new architectural era, for working in their office was a young Swiss named Charles Edouard Jeanneret, later to be known all over the world as

'Le Corbusier,' and destined to become one of the most powerful influences on the development of modern architecture. We shall be dealing at greater length with Le Corbusier, with his German contemporary, Walter Gropius, with Frank Lloyd Wright and with others who have made their impact on our architecture, later. For the present, we must return to the story of English architecture where we left it, with C. F. A. Voysey still producing charming detached houses, Edwin Lutyens gracing the English countryside with his sensitive manors, and a pedestrian safe style of a new 'Georgian' architecture permeating our municipal life.

Even the First World War with the emphasis it laid on the new methods of mass-production (directed at this time to mass destruction) produced little alteration in our ways of thinking about architectural methods and the architectural forms evolving from them. Work continued on the last great Gothic cathedral in Liverpool, designed in 1903 by Giles (later Sir Giles) Gilbert Scott, the brilliant grandson of the architect of St Pancras Station and the Albert Memorial, but on the whole the country seemed to experience an architectural inertia. It can of course be attributed to exhaustion after the war, although the defeated countries, Germany and Austria, no less weary, flung themselves into a programme of daring and experimental building. Certainly our own government offered no comparable backing to that which the Weimar Republic gave to the few young architects who survived the slaughter of Passchendale, Vimy Ridge, Ypres and the Somme. It is true that Ebenezer Howard's idealism was recognised by the award of an O.B.E. in 1924 and a knighthood in 1927. His standard of a maximum of twelve houses to the acre was even adopted by municipal authorities engaged on creating 'homes for heroes' but in the main this country seemed content to reproduce both in private and in public buildings the sedate and unadventurous forms loosely resembling Georgian buildings.

The period between the end of the First World War and the outbreak of the Second means very different things to different people. To some it represents the coming of Jazz, the Charleston and a form of entertainment which is enjoying a nostalgic revival. To others it recalls bitter memories of hunger-marchers from Jarrow and of Welsh miners dragging reluctant feet through the streets of London, the rich throaty harmonies of their singing punctuated by the rattle of stray coppers in collecting boxes. It means the black greasy lines they made low down on little whitewashed bridges overlooking the Rhondda and Amman valleys, as they squatted on their hunkers, day after day, waiting for the tell-tale wisp of smoke from the boiler houses which would tell them that the pit was at work again. Some

36. Chester Terrace, London, from the south, *c.* 1825. The architecture of the street – truly urban in design – by John Nash, the architect of the Prince Regent. No vulgar self-assertion here

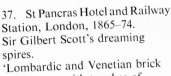

37. St Pancras Hotel and Railway Station, London, 1865–74. Sir Gilbert Scott's dreaming spires.
'Lombardic and Venetian brick Gothic . . . with touches of Milan and other Italian terra-cotta buildings, interlaced with good reproductions of details from Winchester and Salisbury cathedrals, Westminster Abbey, etc'

38. Oxford, The University Museum, 1860. Ruskin's theories carried out by Deane and Woodward in castriron 'Veronese Gothic'

39. Back-to-back houses of the mid-Victorian industrial slum. After the dreaming spires, the ugly nightmare still with us

40.   The Palm House, Kew Gardens, 1844–48, showing the frank acceptance by Decimus Burton of the function of the building and of the new techniques of construction now developing

41.   The Red House, Bexley Heath, Kent, 1859. Designed by Philip Webb and William Morris for the latter, who was a great craftsman and social reformer. A simplification of materials and forms

42. Early Garden City architecture at Letchworth, *c.* 1904. Sir Barry Parker's realisation in bricks and mortar of Ebenezer Howard's dream of a city as a place in which to live as well as to work, with living trees and grass at hand

43. Brutal destruction of comely Adam façade durir the thirties. Vandalism in 1 town only equalled by the desecration of the countryside which accompanied it. The offen took place almost opposit the headquarters of the Royal Institute of British Architects

44 and 45. Arnos Grove Underground Station, 1932. Underground stations represent some of the best architecture executed during the period between the wars. The exterior (above); (left) the interior of the entrance hall showing the reinforced concrete mushroom which carries the roof, and leaves the walls to act as a non-weightbearing screen. (compare this structure with the Chapter House, Lincoln.) Architects, Adams, Holden and Pearson

46. Research Laboratories for I.C.I., Welwyn, designed by E. Jefferiss Mathews. Research buildings must have constantly changing room sizes and it is therefore essential that no internal walls should be a permanent part of the structure. The building and its components were designed on a 4 foot module – a unit which controls the shape and proportion of walls, windows, floors and ceilings

47. The Mark Hall County Secondary School, Harlow, designed by Richard Sheppard and Partners, and built in 1955. Walls and screens virtually suspended from beams cantilevered from within

48.   The Market Square, Harlow, Essex, 1960. The segregation of the shopping centre from the main traffic in one of the first of the New Towns. The shopping centre is on two levels (note staircase)

49.   B.B.C. Television Centre, completed 1962. Architects Messrs Norman and Dawbarn. The first complete building in this country specifically designed for the whole complex business of television

50.   Coventry Cathedral, 1962 (incomplete). Architect, Sir Basil Spence, R.A. A contemporary building for Christian worship

51.   Model of new building for the Commonwealth Institute, 1962. Architects, Messrs Robert Matthew and Johnson-Marshall. The light copper-sheathed roof frees about 33,000 square feet of floor space for exhibitions

will remember derelict farms, and farm hands adding to the long queues outside the Labour Exchanges.

To us, concerned with architectural development, this period represents the hey-day of the speculative builder. It means the dismemberment and disappearance of some of the most beautiful English estates and the buildings on them, and their replacement by a bungaloid growth which smothered parkland and downs alike under a scrabble of mean brick boxes. The period between the wars saw the strangulation of our great arterial roads by unashamed ribbon development which despoiled the countryside and made the true country less and less accessible to the townsman, in the pretence of bringing it to his doorstep. It was the period of Suburbia rampant.

D. H. Lawrence, appalled and outraged by what he saw, not only around his own city, but in every part of England, wrote 'The English are town birds through and through. Yet they don't know how to build a city, how to think of one, or how to live in one. They are all suburban, pseudo-cottagey, and not one of them knows how to be truly urban . . .'

We may not agree with Lawrence, but looking at the face of England after the speculative builder had done his work, it is difficult to find much to contradict his bitter denunciation.

Speculative building is not in itself necessarily an evil thing, any more than any other kind of commercial activity. There were speculative builders whose houses were properly designed by architects, not drawn up by the plasterer's son who had done a little technical drawing at night-school. There were a few who sited their buildings so that they gave no offence to others already in the area, and who preserved the great trees which the old estate had nurtured for five hundred years. But that kind of builder was a rarity. Most were jobbing carpenters or foremen bricklayers who, having raised a little capital, bought up, piece-meal, a few plots of farming land, or a few unproductive fields on the outskirts of the town or along the fringe of the main arterial roads, and then 'developed' the area to their own benefit. With the profits in hand, they decamped to another part of the country to repeat the process. They left roads which went nowhere, and a litter of jerry-built houses in whose insecure walls fungoid growths rapidly spread as the winter came, and through whose warped timbers the rain seeped. Some copied the externals of the comely little Voysey houses, mimicking the white-plastered walls, and gabled ends. Others replaced the Elizabethan mansions whose grounds they had usurped by brick houses to which they nailed a plywood mockery of a timber-framed house, complete with dummy pegs, inserting little latticed windows of artfully leaded glass. After a few hot days the 'timber-framing' curled from the wall surface like burnt toast, and rain produced dismal red streaks of rust marking the positions of the six-inch nails by which it was fastened to the wall. Some builders 'went modern' by producing travesties of the somewhat bald cubical house architecture appearing on the Continent. This particular brand of modernity showed itself by 'stream-lining' surfaces of objects never intended to move, and by dividing door panels, garden gates and even windows in as eccentric and as unsymmetrical a manner as possible. Even if the houses them-selves were well constructed and properly designed, and if some thought had been given to siting, layout and appearance of the roads, the new estates were still only a conglomeration of houses, stretching octopus-like in every direction, sprawling into the countryside with neither plan nor coherence. Occasionally two or more estates would meet, leaving an irregular no-man's land between them of torn scrub and builders' rubble. At this point one could see houses as bogus-Elizabethan and as flimsy as the settings for 'Merrie England' side by side with chalet-type villas with dummy shutters and modernistic blocks from whose fronts projected two concrete 'gun turrets' in place of the more traditional bay windows.

After some time the tenants of these desirable residences discovered that the few shops in the neighbourhood were on the other side of a roaring main road. They found no church, no school, no clinic, no library, no cinema, not even a corrugated iron scout hut, closer than the nearest town, and the intermittent bus service hardly ever coincided with a fast train for the City. They were trapped in a two-storey desert of bricks and mortar as far as ever from the country they had hoped to find, and even farther from the city in which the adult members of the family had to work, and the younger members of the family went to school. In the squalid heart of the cities from which they had come, these people on the estate had had at least some sense of community. In their new surroundings they had none and the speculative builder had made no provision for buildings which might have engendered it. They had not even the sense of direction and purpose which had held the early tenants of the Garden Cities together when difficulties had seemed overwhelming.

Those whose homes lined the arterial roads were soon besieging the local authorities, begging them to put a stop to the rising tide of road deaths as their children on the way to school, their wives on their way to the shops and their returning husbands fell victims to the heavy traffic which roared ceaselessly past their front doors. In desperation the authorities tried to remedy the tragic situation by erecting Belisha beacons at specially sited pedestrian crossings, appointed wardens to guide school-children across the busy roads, and put traffic lights at intervals along all the arterial roads within the town boundaries. The traffic for which the roads had originally been designed slowed to a crawl of frustration.

This is what we mean by the Thirties – a heritage of greed and mismanagement, of architectural futility and waste, which inflicted almost as much damage on our country as the brutality of the century before. The nineteenth-century Englishman had the reputation of saying '. . . There's a rare bird – shoot it!' The Thirties replied with 'There's a lovely bit of country – let's build on it!'

It would be unfair and untrue to suggest that the spoliation of the countryside and the low architectural standards of many of the buildings erected during the Thirties went un-noticed, or in fact that no fine architecture was built at all. No period is wholly bad, or wholly good, and a great many able and intelligent people not only deplored the vandalism which was so apparent all over the country, but took vigorous steps to make their protests effective. Of the many books, articles, broadcasts and lectures, we can mention but one example – that entitled *England and the Octopus* written in 1928 by Clough Williams-Ellis. It was a well-documented and scathing denunciation of bad architecture, badly-sited advertisements, and all the other evils associated with private profit at public expense, which did much to stir a reluctant public opinion before it was too late.

Side by side with the speculative rubbish, honest and intelligently designed buildings were being erected in which full advantage was taken of the technical advances which had been made during the first quarter of the century to solve architectural problems for which there had been no previous precedent. Some of the best of these new buildings were to be found among factories, hospitals, airports, Underground railway stations, pithead baths, and other buildings where the architects were able to tackle problems at the purely functional level, without being affected by a sentiment for the past or bullied by historic examples in the immediate neighbourhood. It was largely through these functional buildings that the public gradually learned to accept the new appearance which came with the new methods of construction.

One of the most beautiful of these early buildings was a great exhibition hall of reinforced concrete erected in London in 1926. This is the Horticultural Hall, Westminster, designed by an Aberdonian, John Easton and his partner Howard (now Sir Howard) Robertson. The lofty and graceful curves of the parabolic arcs which sustain the weight of the roof could hardly have been designed or carried out in any other material.

Some five years later a new factory at Beeston, in Nottingham, was to exploit reinforced concrete construction in an entirely unfamiliar and delightful way. Sir Owen Williams, the engineer who designed this new factory for Boots, the Chemists, needed clear areas of floor space, and large sheltered bays for the loading and unloading of materials. He therefore erected a number of reinforced concrete pillars at selected points, but flared out the upper part of each into a mushroom shape, and incorporated them into the slabs which formed the ceiling, and, of course, the floor above. By this means he was able to produce cantilevered floors which project for 30 feet without any additional support. The walls of this mighty building are substantially glass screens, bearing none of the weight of the roof.

This remarkable construction, and others like it on the Continent and elsewhere, was one of the reasons for the formation of a most valuable group of architects and engineers known as MARS – the Modern Architectural Research Group – which included young men both British and Continental who are now recognised to have been pioneers of the Modern Movement in England.

Unfamiliar forms of architecture are not immediately acceptable to any but the most enlightened patrons, and it is to them that we must be grateful when we see the Shakespeare Memorial Theatre at Stratford-on-Avon today. It was designed in 1932 and was produced by an architectural team – Scott, Chesterton and Shepherd, and it says much for the judges of this particular competition, that resisting the bogus Elizabethan rubbish which bedevils many a historic town, they accepted a modern design.

At about the same time, the London Underground were singularly fortunate in being directed by the remarkable Frank Pick, who, seeing the muddle and mess of the average railway station, set to work to create a team of architects and designers who, under his direction, produced some of the most beautifully planned and most admirably decorated buildings in Europe. One has only to compare the interior arrangements, the lettering and directional signs of the 'Metro' in Paris, with those in the London Underground to see how superior are those of our own country. The clean, dignified lines of such stations as Arnos Grove, or Cockfosters, were not only echoed in the design of ticket booths and other station furniture, but in the legible and well-designed lettering evolved by the great Edward Johnston. (*Plates 44, 45.*)

Other industrial buildings which showed the possibilities of new materials applied to the solution of new problems were the pithead baths now being built in various mining districts, new hospitals and new clinics. Methods by which roofs and balconies could be cantilevered out with no pillars to interrupt the view were to prove a great advantage in the design of such buildings as theatres and football stands where a clear view of the play was essential to the patrons.

Canopies extending over the pavement also provided shelter in

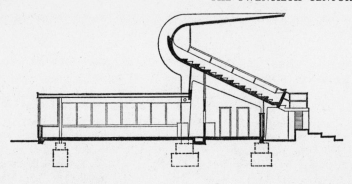

SECTION

Fig. 24. A sectional drawing of the grandstand designed for the Richmond Athletic Association by the firm of Manning and Clamp, architects. It demonstrates the cantilevering of the reinforced concrete cover, which projects over 25 feet, and requires no supporting columns
(*Reproduced by courtesy of the Cement and Concrete Association*)

streets for the shoppers and the large areas of clear glass made possible by the non-weightbearing walls gave admirable opportunities for commercial display in shop windows. One of the most impressive stores in London is that of Peter Jones in Sloane Square, built about 1936. The consultant architect was the great Professor C. H. Reilly whose inspired direction of the School of Architecture at Liverpool University has had very considerable influence in the formation of an English style in this century. The open plan which the new methods of construction made possible by abolishing the internal walls and opening up large areas of floor space could only be completely free if the flat roof was to replace the traditional pitched roof. The latter produced all kinds of complications and awkward intersections of gable and slope but the flat roof could take the most complicated open plan in its stride, and once the teething troubles of sound waterproofing were over was little more difficult to build than a concrete lid.

One of the first open plan houses to be erected successfully in this country was designed by E. Maxwell Fry – the Sun House in Frognal Way, Hampstead, where the freedom and space within is apparent from the lightness of structure and huge window areas seen from outside.

The following year (1936) in Ladbroke Grove, London the same architect evolved Kensal House, one of the most beautiful of the many schemes of flats which were slowly replacing the old tenements and the worn-out slums of many of our cities, and utilising the site of an old gasholder, allied the reinforced concrete blocks of flats to a charming little steel-framed nursery school which served them.

I

English people have been slow to accept flats as a logical method of building dwellings on valuable sites in the heart of the city, and yet there is much to recommend them, as an essential part of a planned townscape. Horror of the huge concrete and steel monsters which have transformed much of New York and other cities into a jungle of reverberating walls and deep sunless canyons has prejudiced the public against high buildings and against flats as such, but so long as they are properly controlled and are not sited so that they condemn the inhabitants of small houses near by to perpetual sunlessness, they have a great deal to offer to the city dweller, particularly to certain sections of the population to whom a whole house and garden is an embarrassment rather than an advantage. The bachelor, whether male or female, the young married couple who both go out to work, the elderly folk no longer able to cope with a full house or to tend a large garden: these are some of the folk to whom the flat has much to offer.

The main advantage to the town itself is, of course, the much more economical use of land and the concentration of such services as lighting, heating, telephone and so on. The use of land can best perhaps be demonstrated by imagining an ordinary baize-covered card table to represent an area in the centre of a town. Deal out the fifty-two cards as for a game of patience, and each card might be equal to an ordinary house and garden. Very little green space is left over. Deal out the cards in four piles as for bridge, and there is a surprising amount of green space available. Put the whole pack of cards wherever you like on the table top and it will show how much more readily the open space now free can be organised to provide facilities – swimming baths, tennis courts, garages, and so on, which would be quite impossible in any other distribution of space.

The standardisation of equipment – of baths, sinks, fitted cup-boards, the control and ease of handling of heating and lighting, and the provision, in the same building, of laundry facilities, and of shops, all contribute to the attractiveness of flat life for those sections of the population we have mentioned. It is not so desirable where families of young children are involved. Concrete floors require very careful sound insulation if the thunder of little feet overhead is not to turn mere bachelors into confirmed bachelors, and young people with a child to bring up are much happier in a house and garden of their own.

Nevertheless, the more enlightened city councils, in London, in Leeds, Manchester, Liverpool and other towns with a desperate housing shortage and a long history of slums turned their attention to the erection of blocks of flats, and many admirable schemes evolved. Not all were as well designed as the Quarry Hill Scheme in

Leeds, the work of R. Livett, the City Architect. Many, in fact, bore the mark of uninspired officialdom, but they were a vast improvement on what had stood in their place, and considerably better for the country as a whole than the unchecked sprawl of which we have written.

A great many of the best examples of architectural design at this time were the result of the co-operation of our own native architects with foreigners from countries where the political régime had proved too restrictive for them, or where they had suffered from racial discrimination.

One of the most important of these foreign architects and one whose collaboration with our own men was to have such fortunate results was the German, Walter Gropius. The son of a Berlin architect, Gropius worked for some time under Peter Behrens whose co-operation with W. J. Bassett-Lowke in England in 1926 produced one of the first of our obviously modern houses. Gropius was appointed director of a school of applied art and building at Weimar, known as the Bauhaus, and when it transferred to Dessau was personally responsible for the design of some of its main workshops – airy, spaciously contrived buildings fitting the functions for which they were evolved beautifully and economically. Under Gropius, the Bauhaus, a combined school and workshop in which master craftsmen, artists, and architects worked side by side, was to become one of the most dynamic sources in Europe in the formation of a recognisably industrial art. His visit to this country from 1934–36 was to give considerable encouragement to the less conservative of our architects. His collaboration with E. Maxwell Fry was to result in the group of County Colleges – schools by day, and adult education centres by night for which Cambridgeshire is famous. The first – still very much a dynamo of educational activity after nearly thirty years – is at Impington, and its low serene single-storey class room blocks were to point the way to an entirely new way of designing school buildings.

Meanwhile, other foreign architects – notably Erich Mendelsohn, Serge Chermayeff and Marcel Breuer, were enriching the English architectural vocabulary, and Berthold Lubetkin, with a group of five promising young English architects, had formed the famous 'Tecton' – a firm which was to contribute much to our architecture during these valuable experimental years.

The best known example of the work of Mendelsohn and Chermayeff is the De la Warr Pavilion at Bexhill, in Sussex. This is a steel and concrete structure which provides many different kinds of entertainment which one associates with a seaside holiday, and although there has been no conscious attempt to impart a nautical flavour to the building by draping it with netting or hanging lifebelts on its walls, it is nevertheless a particularly happy example of seaside architecture.

Marcel Breuer, a Hungarian, is better known for his work in the U.N.E.S.C.O. building in Paris than for the house he designed in collaboration with our own F.R.S. Yorke at Angmering at about the same time – that is, the early thirties.

Berthold Lubetkin, the Russian founder of the firm of 'Tecton,' studied in Moscow, Warsaw, Vienna and later joined Auguste Perret in Paris, before moving to London about 1930.

The first public buildings to be seen of this remarkable team were the new buildings at the London Zoo – the gorilla house, which quite apart from its unusual flexibility of construction, housed these delicate creatures with considerably more understanding than that normally extended to the human animal in 1933.

Another charming and frivolous Zoo building, designed with a sense of fun and excitement of shape was the Penguin Pool at Dudley Zoo, where delightfully curved ramps and flowing concrete shapes of platforms at different levels were strongly reminiscent of similar experiments in modern sculpture. It was a building which could hardly have been evolved before the end of the thirties and it was suggested that, starkly functional as Tecton's 'High Point' flats appeared, the firm had a lighter side, too, when the occasion demanded. The first block of the High Point flats, built in 1934, had weight-bearing external walls of reinforced concrete, but the firm evidently found that this type of construction imposed too rigid a discipline on the elevation, and left them too little freedom to give variety of pattern to the wall surfaces, so that the second wing, built in 1938, was constructed on a different principle. Here the weight-bearing walls are on the inside of the building, running across the width of the building so that the outer walls are but screens and can be as light and as varied as the different parts of the building or the nature of the panels forming them demands. Their most beautiful pre-war building, however, was the Finsbury Health Centre, a charming, symmetrically planned building with an exterior of glazed tile and glass bricks which is easily cleaned, and a logically planned layout to cater for the many types of activity with which such a building has to deal.

At about the same time, E. Maxwell Fry, working independently of Gropius produced an exciting showroom for the Central London Electricity Authority, in Regent Street. The most striking feature of this design was a lightly framed steel staircase contained in a clear glass drum – and imparting an air of lightness and grace to the whole building.

All too soon however, architects, like their patrons were to find themselves more concerned with buildings which were being blown apart than those which were being put together, and the England which was to emerge finally from the Second World War was to offer a challenge to their ingenuity and an opportunity for them to display their skill unrivalled in the history of English architecture.

Chapter Twelve

ARCHITECTURE
SINCE THE SECOND WORLD WAR

IN every period of our history our native architects have derived information and inspiration from those of other countries, and have in their turn sent architectural ideas abroad. Never has there been such a free interchange of architectural ideas, however, as we have at present. It is not only among architects that these ideas are circulating. Architecture is now news, and scarcely a day passes without allusion being made in newspapers, on the radio and television or in popular magazines, to buildings which have been erected or are under construction, not only in this country, but in more remote parts of the world. This has resulted in a certain 'international' appearance to many buildings erected after the war, and before we go on to consider our own architecture, it would be as well perhaps to study the work of a number of foreign architects whose writings and whose buildings have had a profound effect on our own architectural thought in the last few years.

Walter Gropius, Erich Mendelsohn, and Lubetkin are all foreign architects whose work can be seen here, but one man whose writings and whose buildings have made a revolutionary impact on our architecture has no examples of his work in this country. This is the Swiss architect, Charles-Edouard Jeanneret, better known as Le Corbusier, the name by which we shall refer to him from now on. He was born at Chaux-de-Fonds in Switzerland in 1887, studied architecture in Vienna, then in Berlin under Peter Behrens, and later in Paris with Auguste Perret – an exhilarating and valuable experience for a young man of 22. It was with Perret that he learned the unsuspected possibilities of reinforced concrete and similar constructions, and by 1922, when his first important book *Vers une Architecture* was published he had already investigated and defined his principles of architectural design. His definition 'a house is a machine for living in' has been widely misquoted and misapplied, and has given rise to a cold inhuman conception of architecture quite the contrary of what Le Corbusier intended. It is quite clear from his writings that he meant that a house should fit the complex activities of the family life, bringing as much intelligent planning to the problem of a home as one would use in the design of a factory, an airport, or any other building with needs peculiar to itself.

Many of his own houses bear the hallmarks of construction which we now associate with 'modern architecture.' Using a light framework which leaves his plan unencumbered by solid weight-bearing walls, he erects his living-room on stilts, and uses the space below to bring the garden into a more intimate contact with the house. The flat roof which such a free plan requires he uses for roof gardens and sun-lounges, although many English architects have serious misgivings about this type of roof in districts where several inches of snow may be expected during the winter months. (We should add, however, that one large department store in London has a permanent roof garden of some 1½ acres.)

His imaginative plans for new towns, although condemned as impracticable by a number of architects were nevertheless most valuable and stimulating documents in the early twenties, and much of what Le Corbusier and his predecessor Tony Garnier predicted has now come to pass.

In 1927 his competition design for the Palace of the League of Nations at Geneva gave him his first real opportunity to design on a large scale, and this was followed by the huge stilted Pavillon Suisse – the hostel for Swiss students at the University City on the outskirts of Paris, in 1930–32. 1927 saw also the erection of a villa at Garches – a building in which Corbusier carried out a most elaborate series of experiments with 'the Golden Mean' with which, like Andrea Palladio, he sought not only to design a functional building but one based on the mathematical perfection of proportion, a geometrical relation of space to space and space to mass which should approach the perfection of classical buildings.

The result of his search for a mathematical basis of beauty was the evolution of a measure known as 'The Modulor'. The foundation of these mathematical proportions is a six-foot male figure. But although there is plenty of historical evidence of architects using one mathematical system or another, it is hotly contested by some that such a system can never be any substitute for creative ability, although it may help the artist from time to time. Professor Nikolaus Pevsner has attacked the Modulor in an open debate held in September 1957 at the Royal Institute of British Architects, dismissing it as 'a quack panacea.' Nevertheless, Le Corbusier uses his Modulor extensively. It is to be found at work in the huge block of flats he designed at Marseilles in 1947–52, the famous Unité d'Habitation, where two-storey flats, shops, etc., cater for 1600 people. He has used it for the designs he worked out in conjunction with our own E. Maxwell Fry and Jane Drew for Chandigarh, the new capital of the Punjab, now under course of construction, and his theories have been largely responsible for the appearance of some of the capital cities now arising in South America. Perhaps his most striking building of recent years has been the chapel of Notre-Dame-du-Haut at Ronchamp in France, completed about 1955, a church which seems to be more closely related to carving from the solid mass than to a building erected on a frame.

Le Corbusier is not the only architect and writer whose work has had a decisive impact on the course of English architectural history. Of the European architects certainly the original work in Finland by Alvar Aalto, and particularly his treatment and use of laminated wood in the construction and decoration of buildings has attracted a great deal of attention in this country. In Italy Pier Nervi has made a remarkable contribution in the exploitation of reinforced concrete forms. Nervi trained as an engineer before becoming an architect, and his expressive forms have a great deal in common with the clean efficient surfaces and shapes of a jet aircraft or a modern car. He evolved for himself a method of pre-cast units in concrete which eliminated the discipline imposed by the more normal use of wooden shutterings. The great Stadium in Rome at which the 1960 Olympic Games were held is characteristic of the lightness of Nervi's structure and the rapidity with which his units can be assembled, for the domed building was erected in forty days. The Italian architects as a whole are adept at creating fine shell-like forms in reinforced concrete, and to us, used in this country to the more lumpish treatment of this medium, their buildings look almost dangerously adventurous.

The work of another foreign architect which has had a profound effect on our own architectural design is that of Ludwig Mies van der Rohe. Although there is no building in this country by Van der Rohe, his influence on some of our English architecture has been so strong that he was awarded the Gold Medal of the Royal Institute of British Architects in 1959.

Born in Aachen in 1886, Van der Rohe, like Gropius, studied under Peter Behrens, and he, too, became a Director of the Bauhaus at Dessau in 1930. Blocks of municipal flats erected in Berlin after the First World War showed something of his ability to handle large masses with great ease and, despite their size, with a feeling of astonishing lightness, and this airy quality attracted a great deal of attention from the architects who saw his German Pavilion at the International Exhibition at Barcelona in 1929. He left Europe for America in 1937, and unfortunately few of us will have any opportunity of seeing his work there, notably in Chicago. Nevertheless,

from the photographs and drawings of Van der Roh
and from the admiring comments made by a num
architects, it is clear that he has a remarkable ability to
glass as the main constructional elements in his build
give an entirely personal quality to these materials. Expr
as 'elegant crystalline structures,' 'space and structure ha
absolute truth' were among the tributes paid to him at the
tion ceremony at the Royal Institute of British Architects   59,
and there is no doubt that his work has inspired the airy appearance
of some of the most recent of our own buildings of steel and glass.

The only other architect of comparable status to influence English
architecture was the American, Frank Lloyd Wright, whose writings
always advocated the need for a free and flexible plan in the architecture of the home.

Born in Wisconsin in 1869 he worked for some time in the office
of Louis Sullivan, but his spacious treatment and uninterrupted flow
of area from room to room may well be due to his study of Japanese
architecture. Personal investigation of his work for the purpose of
this book has not been possible, but on paper and in photographs,
his work shows a romantic and almost theatrical quality, with an
emphatic statement of the relationship between the building and the
site in which it is placed. One of his most provocative buildings is
the Guggenheim Museum in New York, still under construction
when he died in 1959.

With this very brief survey of foreign architectural ideas which
have modified our own we must turn to the problems which faced
our architects and town-planners when the Second World War came
to an end. Plans had been evolving, even whilst the bombs were
shattering our cities, for their rebuilding, and for righting the most
obvious evils with which they had been beset before 1939.

The shortage of men and materials, and the methods of mass production by which aircraft and other precision machines had been
made in enormous quantities had emphasised the need for architects
to revise our own architectural and building methods. The pre-
fabricated houses, admittedly only intended to be a temporary
measure, were more intelligently and economically planned than
many other houses built in the traditional way. It was clear that if
we were to provide houses for those rendered homeless by bombing
and for the men who were returning, and at the same time to replace our industrial slums with something more worthy of our
architectural heritage, some hard thinking and careful planning
would be needed.

The most urgent task was to survey the great cities – Coventry,
Plymouth, London, Manchester, Liverpool, and all the other

,ictims of Nazi attack to decide what was to be preserved, and what was to be destroyed, and then to develop a plan which might proceed by stages so that the industrial life of the country might not be unduly disrupted. The dispersal of the population and the decentralisation of industry which the war had made necessary was found to have certain advantages and it was decided that it was a process that might be continued, in many overcrowded cities at least.

It says much for the high courage and unquestioning belief in ultimate victory of the British people, that, in April 1943, when as yet no major Allied force had succeeded in landing and maintaining a foothold on the mainland of Europe, the *Architectural Review* for that month should have devoted most of its pages to a brilliant survey of the problems of town-planning and the task which lay ahead when the war was over. After a brief historical sketch it proceeded to show the method by which modern town-planners were already at work, and although, for various social and economic reasons, the method has had to be modified, in principle it is the same which has been responsible for the success of the New Towns now in course of construction. It can almost be reduced to the sort of table by which we learnt arithmetic when we were very young, only instead of chanting 'twice one are two, twice two are four, twice three are six' and so on, the infant town-planner would be saying . . .

'Two hundred families is one Residential Unit'
'Five Residential Units is one Neighbourhood'
'Eight Neighbourhood Units is one Borough.'

The numbers involved in this table are much the same as ones which have been used in all the planning which has taken place since that optimistic April in 1943, with very little change. As you can see, the basis of all planning, very properly, is the family, and the average family is the father and mother, and two children. Planning has to start at the Residential Unit of two hundred families, that is, for about seven to eight hundred people, the sort of population to be found in the usual group of flats to be found in most industrial cities. The important difference between the pre-war ideas in which accommodation and no more would be offered, was the provision for extending the planning beyond the mere dwellings to certain basic needs which a community of this size must have available. It envisaged that in addition to the flats, or the homes in which the two hundred families would live, they should have a communal laundry, a community hall, a club-room, a nursery school and space made available for young children to play in freely. Such a community would naturally require certain shops within immediate reach, not several hundred yards away across a main road. These shops would naturally include a butcher, baker, grocer and a shoe-repairer. Other amenities suggested for this unit included a public house but the planners could hardly have anticipated the impact that the coming of widespread television would have on the drinking habits of this country.

The next unit – the Neighbourhood Unit – of about 1,000 families is quite a large one – about 3,000 to 4,000 people is nearly the size of a small country town, and a great deal more preparation must be made for their welfare. Some primary education will certainly be required, a clinic for the young children and mothers, a larger and more extensive area of shops, a larger hall for theatricals, for dances, a restaurant and possibly a cinema – although here again, television has modified the original plan. Some forms of church will certainly be needed and perhaps a small hotel for commercial travellers and for visitors, and at least one branch library.

With the Borough Unit – about 8,000 families, or 30,000 people – we are reaching a town of respectable proportions, the limit in fact which Ebenezer Howard had visualised for his Garden Cities. A hospital must certainly be added at this stage, with accommodation estimated at about five beds per thousand of the population, school accommodation increased to provide senior education – a grammar or modern school – buildings for transport – coach station, railway station, extensive car park – and a main shopping centre, closely related to the need for some sort of civic buildings – town hall, municipal library – as a focal point for the new town.

From the borough unit the planners move towards the concept of a city – a very much larger unit, but still carefully planned and controlled, and built up in just the same way, from family to residential units, from residential units to neighbourhood units, and so on.

When war finally ended, every great city which had suffered severe damage from air attack had its plans under way and as men and machines turned from war to peace, the plans began to take effect. The Town and Country Planning Act of 1947 was an official attempt to ensure that the 'thirties should not be repeated in the 'forties, and although there have been bitter disappointments with the architectural standards of some of the new buildings, those of us who can remember what some of the town areas were like before the bombs fell, know what improvements have been made despite all sorts of obstacles and interference.

The plans for the rebuilding of Coventry, of Plymouth, Exeter and other blitzed cities are no longer paper drawings – vague aspirations – they are to be seen in actuality, in bricks and mortar, concrete and steel. There have been injustices and misunderstandings, perhaps some disillusionment, but by and large the cities compare favourably with those from whose ashes they have arisen.

The County of London Plan, the work of the late Professor Sir Patrick Abercrombie and J. H. Forshaw, published in 1943, has had to be modified considerably owing to our economic difficulties, but a visit to West Ham, or to Poplar, to the Tecton flats at Finsbury, or to Pimlico, Paddington or the borders of Richmond Park, will show that a great deal of well-designed, beautifully proportioned and well sited architecture has resulted from those 1943 ideals. Travel into London by train after dark, and see how the lights of the tall towers of concrete and glass twinkle and glow like permanent beacons over the shattered remnants of the wrecks of Industrial Revolution buildings from which they have sprung. Walk slowly past the new L.C.C. schools with their gay interiors and well designed classrooms and workshops, and then pity the school teachers and the children who are still condemned to work in the grim Board School buildings awaiting demolition.

Some of the most exciting architectural developments during recent years have taken place in school design. Certainly our English schools, particularly those built under the direction of C. H. Aslin, the Chief Architect to the Hertfordshire County Council, have attracted a great deal of favourable comment from the foreign architects confronted with similar problems of providing good schools flexibly and intelligently designed not only for present day needs but for expansion in the future.

The re-design of our schools was long overdue. Approximately eighty per cent of our schools are still out of date when checked with the standards laid down by the 1944 Act, but such pre-fabricated schools as that at Cheshunt anticipate a rapid and efficient method of assembly which has much to recommend it in view of the pressing need for school accommodation.

Ever since the Cambridge County Colleges of pre-war days, school buildings have assumed a new role – that of providing facilities as well for adult education in the widest sense, and this complicated function is bound to affect the overall design of the school buildings. At Stevenage, one of the New Towns, the architects of the secondary school, F. R. S. Yorke, E. Rosenberg, and C. S. Mardall succeeded in designing the whole complex in such a way that more than one half of the school buildings in use by the children by day are available for adult use after school hours.

One of the major experiments in architectural form and in town planning is in fact the New Towns of Britain. They came into being on paper at least with the New Towns Act of 1946, and at present fifteen of them are living, growing entities. Harlow, Stevenage,

Hatfield, Hemel Hempstead, Basildon, Bracknell and Crawley are designed primarily to deal with London's human and industrial congestion, together with an addition to Welwyn Garden City to whose founder they owe so much.

In Scotland, the new towns at East Kilbride and Cumbernauld offer similar relief to Glasgow, whilst Glenrothes is being built to meet the needs of Fife. Over the border of Wales, the New Town of Cwmbran in Monmouthshire, is designed to accommodate the work-people who run the newly introduced light industries which have been started there to ensure that the district shall never again endure the agony of the coal mining slump.

The other New Towns are Corby, near Leicester, and Birming-ham, and Peterlee and Newton Aycliffe near Durham.

Harlow is probably the most advanced of the English New Towns, for work actually started under the direction of Frederick Gibberd in 1947 and planning, which had been organised very much on the basis of the figures predicted in the *Architectural Review* in 1943, is already showing astonishing results. Visitors to the town will prob-ably find an excessive use of open space and an abnormally high proportion of small houses with gardens, but it must be remembered that Harlow, at present, is a town which still lacks a municipal centre and that it has a numerically unbalanced type of population – a far higher proportion of young people and children than one would find in a more mature town, and as we have said, young couples must have a garden for their babies and young children.

One development which is common to all the New Towns is the provision of shopping precincts from which all traffic is excluded. It is an experiment which has proved extremely successful, and to-gether with shops on two levels, overlooking the town centre, is likely to be developed further.

Some of the housing in the New Towns is a little undistinguished, and it is a pity that the same quality of fine proportion, sensitive use of site and materials and generally pleasant appearance with which shops, schools and particularly factories, have been endowed is not so apparent in domestic architecture. (*Plate 48.*)

There is a certain similarity in New Town architecture no matter in what part of the country it is to be found. This is not surprising, neither is it as opposed to the English architectural tradition as the critics would have us believe. We have been independent of purely local materials for a very long time, and a common method of construction is bound to result in a similarity of appearance. It would be a bold man who could distinguish a photograph of a timber-framed house in Herefordshire from that of one in Kent, or who could without some hesitation say whether the Georgian building

at which he was looking came from Buxton or Bath, from Cheltenham or Chelsea. That the architecture has a 'Continental' look may
well be true – a nation which has long admired Canterbury Cathedral
(built largely by foreign labour and with foreign materials) the Queen's
House at Greenwich, St Paul's Cathedral and the Palladian fronts of
many a country house, to say nothing of the Royal Pavilion at
Brighton, can hardly be said to be unreceptive to ideas from across
the Channel, and it must be stressed that the influence is not one way
only. Many of our architectural ideas have found root in foreign soil
– some, naturally in the British Commonwealth, but others in
countries with whom we have no such ties. The interest and admiration shown by foreign visitors to the Festival of Britain on the South
Bank in 1951, and particularly their excitement at the remarkable
Dome of Discovery by Ralph Tubbs and the more permanent
pleasure of the Royal Festival Hall suggest that even if we learn from
abroad, we have also much to offer to other countries as well. It was
reported that Italian architects, for example, confronted by the
complete primary school from England erected at the Milan Trien-
nale Exhibition in 1960 found it difficult to believe that it represented
a standard product of English architects and was not a special
'exhibition' school designed for show.

We have mentioned the successful collaboration of E. Maxwell
Fry and other British architects with Le Corbusier in the planning
and building of Chandigarh, the new capital of the Punjab, in 1951–
56, but this is by no means an isolated instance of our contribution to
the architectural scene abroad. At Ibadan University in Nigeria may
be seen work by E. Maxwell Fry, Jane Drew and their associates,
whilst James Cubitt and Partners have recently completed the
College of Technology at Kumasi in Ghana.

The *Sunday Telegraph* of August 13, 1961, devoted a good deal of
one page to the announcement that L. Hugh Wilson, the architect
largely responsible for Cumbernauld New Town in Scotland, has
been invited to submit designs for the first of Germany's 'New
Towns' near Essen. These examples and many others show that
foreign countries are by no means unaware of what English architecture has to offer, even if we are all too prone to ignore it ourselves.

The exhibition of 'Architecture Today' – a joint exhibition staged
by the Arts Council of Great Britain and the Royal Institute of
British Architects in 1961, demonstrated beyond any doubt the
vitality of our architecture when sympathetic and sensitive patrons
were available. The Theatre Workshops for the 'Old Vic,' British
Railways' new station at Harlow, Princess Margaret Hospital
at Swindon, Gatwick Airport, and educational buildings from
primary school to university level, showed that there was no aspect

of English life in which the modern English architect was not actively and progressively concerned. The designs for Coventry Cathedral, and some of the remarkable churches in the New Towns show that the English architect of today has much to offer to the Church. Experimental and exciting forms of architecture appear daily in our capital cities, as for example the new Commonwealth building in course of construction in Kensington. A number of lively young men such as Eric Lyons have turned their attention to speculative building and have demonstrated that it need not mean badly designed houses, shoddy workmanship and pseudo-historic styles. It is not, in fact, from the 'modern' architect that our architectural tradition is in danger, but from the 'Merrie England'-er and mock-Georgian who, looking over their shoulders at our historic past, are yet blind to the lessons it has to offer.

Architecture is not merely an affair of this style or that, or of historic ornament. It is a living and a developing art, and its health is vital to our civilisation. It is just possible that we could make shift without painting or sculpture, music or literature, although life would hardly be worth living if we did, but we cannot do without a living architecture – it is truly the 'indispensable art.' But the patrons of the past who encouraged great architecture – the Church and the nobility – have lost much of their influence and their wealth. The new patrons of architecture are now the directors of vast industrial combines, City companies, the elected representatives on town and county councils, and the ordinary men and women of a 'property-owning democracy.' The architectural development in this country is largely in their hands. If they accept their responsibilities, encouraging the creative architect by showing an intelligent interest in what he is trying to do, they will not only prove themselves worthy of the great patrons of architecture of the past, but will ensure the continuation of the best of our architectural tradition into the future.

ABACUS. A slab of stone forming the top part of a capital. (*ill.*) That of the Greek, Roman and Norman capitals is rectangular in plan. That of the Gothic period, normally round or octagonal.

ADULTERINE CASTLES. An unlicensed castle – many destroyed by Henry II because the Royal consent to their construction had not been obtained.

AMBULATORY. Normally the processional aisle or 'walk' round the east end of a large church, behind the high altar.

AMPHITHEATRE. An oval or elliptical building with seats arranged in tiers for the display of sports, gladiatorial contests, etc.

APSE. The semi-circular or polygonal end to the presbytery or aisle of a church. It is often roofed with a dome.

ARCADE. A row of arches. If attached to the solid wall – a 'blind' arcade.

ARCHITRAVE. The lowest member of the entablature or superstructure in Classical architecture, i.e., that actually in contact with the capital. (See Fig. 1.)

BALL-FLOWER MOULDING. An enrichment of the mouldings of the late 13th and most of the 14th centuries. (*ill.*)

BALL-FLOWER MOULDING

BALUSTER. A small shaft which may be round or square in section, but with a variable diameter.

BASILICA. A large hall which in Roman times served as a law-court and exchange. Early Christian churches adopted the plan.

BULL'S EYE WINDOW. A circular window, often found in Norman architecture.

BOSS. A decoratively carved stone which marks the central junction of the ribs of a vault, or the termination of other architectural features.

BRASSES, MEMORIAL. Sheets of metal cut and engraved with the representation of a deceased person, and inset in the lid of their tomb. The metal resembles brass, but was usually 'latten' – a similar alloy.

BROACH. The half pyramid which enables an octagonal spire to be added to a square tower. (See Fig. 10.)

CANTILEVER. A beam which, projecting from a wall is so secured by the weight of the building along part of its length that it is able to carry weight for the remainder of its projection without supporting columns. Mediaeval jetting of timbers is an early use of the cantilever but modern techniques have made it a more familiar constructive device. (Fig. 4.)

CAPITAL. A fashioned stone topping a column and forming a wider bearing for the superstructure or entablature. The illustrations show that inspection of the capital can often provide a valuable guide to the recognition of the period of architecture to which the building belongs. (*ill.*)

CARTOON. A full-sized working drawing for a mural decoration, tapestry, stained glass window, etc.

CARYATID. A sculptured figure used as a column, as in the Erechtheion at Athens.

CARRELL. A small room in a cloister to form a private study for a monk.

CELLA. The central part of a Greek or Roman temple enclosed by a wall.

CHANTRY CHAPEL. A chapel specially erected or set aside for the singing of masses for the dead. It is frequently within the main church building.

CHEVET. The apsidal end of a church from which a number of chapels radiate, e.g., Henry VI's Chapel at Westminster Abbey.

CHOIR—*see* Quire.

CLEARSTOREY (clere-storey). The windows above the nave which give light to the body of the church. In a cathedral they are normally above the triforium.

COFFERED CEILING. A ceiling in which the timbers or other construction leave a series of deeply sunk panels or coffers.

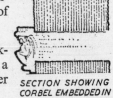

CORBEL. A stone which, embedded in the thickness of a wall, projects sufficiently to provide a strong bracket for supporting a roof timber or some other weight. (*ill.*)

SECTION SHOWING
CORBEL EMBEDDED IN
WALL

CORNICE. The top member of the entablature.

CRUCK. Curved or shaped timbers forming the main support of the ends of a primitive dwelling. (Fig. 3.)

CRYPT. That part of a church which is partly or wholly underground.

CUPOLA. A curved or dome-like roof, over a square, round or polygonal area.

CURTAIN WALL. In castles the length of wall spanning the space between two towers. In modern architecture it refers normally to a thin non-weight-bearing wall. (Fig. 4 for mediaeval use. Plates 45, 46 and 47 for modern examples.)

CUSP. A projection carved on the inner side of a Gothic arch and forming a decorative interruption in the area forming its sides. It has no functional purpose. (*ill.*)

CUSP

DIAPER. A repeating pattern, usually of rectangular units painted and carved on a mediaeval building. Westminster Abbey has areas of diapered wall, carved during the 13th century.

DOG-TOOTH MOULDING

DOG-TOOTH (OR NAIL-HEAD) MOULDING. A decorative moulding almost entirely confined to the Early English period. (*ill.*)

DOOM PAINTING. A representation of the Last Judgement painted over the chancel arch. (A well preserved one is still to be seen at the church of St Thomas of Canterbury, in Salisbury.)

DORMER WINDOW. A window projecting vertically from the sloping roof of a house.

EASTER SEPULCHRE. A recess, usually on the north side of the chancel which, because of the representation of the Resurrection carved on its front, used to form a focal point of the Easter celebrations. It is usually a tomb made of stone and in position permanently.

ECHINUS. In classical architecture the convex moulding directly under the abacus on a Doric capital. (*ill.*)

ENTABLATURE. The whole of the horizontal superstructure supported by columns in a classical building. It normally consists of the architrave, frieze and cornice. (See Fig. 1.)

ENTASIS. A slight thickening about one third up the shaft of a classical column. It is skilfully graduated to correct the optical illusion that the sides of a column curve inwards. (See Fig. 1.)

EYE-CATCHER. An architectural motif built as part of a landscape for the sole purpose of visual delight. The terms cover mock Gothic 'ruins,' 'Temples of Virtue' and other pieces of architectural scenery erected as part of a picturesque landscape.

FAN VAULTING. The final phase of the Gothic vault. (See Plate 14.

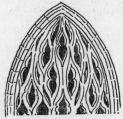

FLAMBOYANT TRACERY. Richly curving window tracery, more commonly encountered on the Continent than in English churches. Generally regarded as a manifestation of the later phase of the Decorated period of English architecture. (*ill.*)

FLAMBOYANT TRACERY

FLINT FLUSHWORK. Panels of flint embedded into walls made from Kentish ragstone, limestone and other local materials, used in both secular and ecclesiastical buildings during the Middle Ages.

GARDE-ROBE. A water-closet built in the thickness of the wall of a mediaeval castle.

GRISAILLE PAINTING. Painted decoration executed in a series of grey tones. (See Plate 20.)

GROIN. The sharp edge produced by the intersection of two vaulting surfaces. (Fig. 5.)

JETTED TIMBERS. Balks of timber, normally floor joists, which project beyond the normal floor area and not only therefore enlarge the area of the room beyond the supporting walls, but provide an overhang for the street below. (See Fig. 15.)

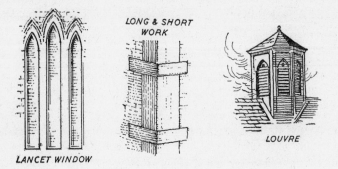

LONG & SHORT WORK

LOUVRE

LANCET WINDOW

LANCET WINDOW. The long narrow window characteristic of the Early English period. (*ill.*)

LIERNE RIB. A short rib in a late Gothic vault which connects two main ribs. (See Fig. 9 and Fig. 13.)

LOGGIA. A covered gallery, usually open on one side, sometimes on both.

LONG AND SHORT WORK. A Saxon method of building the angles of stone wall. (*ill.*) (Plate 4.)

LOUVRE (OR LOUVER). A small tower-like structure on mediaeval roofs for ventilation. The sides are slatted to prevent down-draught. (*ill.*)

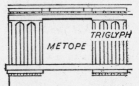

METOPE. The square depression between the triglyphs on a Doric frieze. (*ill.*)

MISERERE (OR MISERICORD). A hinged seat with a bracket beneath which afforded some support when the seat was tipped up. (See Fig. 14.)

MODULE. A unit of proportion upon which a whole order of architecture is based. In contemporary architecture it is an agreed unit which controls the dimensions of a building and all its details (e.g., the module for the I.C.I. Laboratory in Plate 46 is four feet).

MOSAIC. A decoration composed of many tiny cubes of stone, pottery, etc., embedded in cement or plaster.

MULLION. The vertical member of a window, generally of stone or wood.

NEWEL POST. At first the central post or pillar of a spiral staircase, the term is now used to define the angle posts or terminals of an ordinary staircase. (For carved newel posts see Plate 20.)

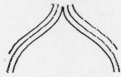

OGEE OR OGYVAL ARCH. An arch in which the curve is partly convex and partly concave which makes its appearance during the 14th century. (*ill.*) (An excellent example may be seen in Plate 10.)

OGEE OR OGYVAL ARCH   ORIEL WINDOW. A bow window in a Gothic or Tudor building which may be supported on corbels, or stand on the ground. (See a number on Oxburgh, Plate 15.)

PEDIMENT. The gable, usually triangular, which surmounts a Classical or Renaissance building or details such as windows or doors in those buildings. (See Plates 1, 27, 29 and 30.)

PENDANT. An elongated boss hanging down from a fan vault.

PIANO NOBILE (Italian 'noble floor'). The main suite of rooms in a Palladian building, one storey above ground level. (See Plates 22, 23 and 31.)

PILASTER. A flat rectangular column fastened to a wall. It may be plain or fluted.

PINNACLE. A small tower of solid stone usually surmounted by a spire or by gables, placed on top of a buttress, or decorating a wall. (*ill.*)

PINNACLE

PISCINA. A shallow stone bowl in a niche usually found by an altar and used for washing the sacred vessels. (*ill.*)

PISCINA

PLATE TRACERY (AND BAR-TRACERY). Where a number of small windows were grouped under one head, the space left above was pierced or fretted with a simple geometric device – i.e., a trefoil or quatrefoil. The area of window so pierced formed plate-tracery. Later instead of piercing the geometrical forms they are built from separate pieces of stone, and become bar-tracery.

PULPITUM. A stone gallery supported in a stone screen separating the chancel from the nave in a cathedral or abbey church. It carried the crucifix or rood with its attendant sculpture.

QUADRIPARTITE VAULT. A simple vault divided into four compartments by its groins or ribs. (Figs. 5 and 6.)

QUIRE. The early spelling of 'choir.' Today it is more usual to regard 'Quire' as the area occupied by the choristers, and the 'choir' as the singers.

QUOIN. A corner stone.

REINFORCED CONCRETE (OR FERRO-CONCRETE). Concrete of which the tensile strength is considerably increased by the embedding of steel rods or steel mesh into it before it is set.

REREDOS. The screen of wood or stone to the rear of the altar. It is usually enriched with sculpture.

RUSTICATION. (Rusticated stone.) A treatment accorded usually to the lower courses of stonework on a large Renaissance building. Although the stones are cut square, the surface is left rough or even artificially roughened to impart an appearance of rugged strength. (*ill.*)

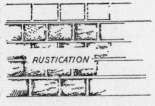

RUSTICATION

SCAGLIOLA. Plaster stained with different colours to resemble marble inlay. Much favoured by Georgian gentlemen for floors, table tops, etc.

SEDILIA. Seats for the clergy usually set in the south wall of the chancel. (*ill.*)

SOLAR. An upper chamber in medieval houses or castles, to which the noble and his wife could retire for privacy from the general melee of the Great Hall.

SEDILIA

SPANDREL. A triangular space included by an arch, or arches, and the mouldings above it, or the rectangular corner of a door. (See Plate 9.)

SQUINCH (OR SQUINCH ARCH). A series of arch forms by which the corners of an octagonal spire can be supported upon a square tower. (See Fig. 10.)

SQUINT (OR HAGIOSCOPE). An opening through the wall of a church in an oblique direction to enable worshippers in the transepts or aisles to see the high altar. It can also be a narrow window in the wall of the solar which gives a view of the Hall below.

STUCCO. Smooth hard plaster, much favoured by the architects of the 17th and 18th centuries for the surfaces of both inside and outside walls, in imitation of masonry.

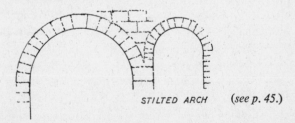

STILTED ARCH   (see p. 45.)

TIERCERON RIBS. See Fig. 9.

TRANSEPT. This is any part of the church which is as high as the nave or the quire and which projects at right angles to them.

TRANSOM. The horizontal crossbar to a window. It appears early in domestic architecture as a means of attachment for casements or shutters, but somewhat later in ecclesiastical buildings. It is one of the most marked features in the window tracery of the Perpendicular period.

TRIFORIUM (OR BLIND STOREY). The gallery in a cathedral or large parish church immediately above the arches of the nave. It is immediately below the clearstorey.

TRIGLYPH. An ornamental panel in a Doric frieze consisting of three vertical channels separated by narrow flat spaces. (*ill. p. 254.*)

TROMPE L'OEIL PAINTING (*Fr.*, deceive the eye). The use of perspective, foreshortening and light and shade to create the illusion of architectural features on blank spaces. The houses at Pompeii show examples of trompe l'oeil, but it reaches its height in certain 18th century buildings where it is so skilfully done that it is almost impossible to detect where the actual architecture ends and the illusionist painting begins, e.g., the Saloon at Blenheim.

UNDERCROFT. The bottom storey in a mediaeval building, partly or wholly underground.

VENETIAN WINDOW. A composite window consisting of a central round-headed window, flanked by two square headed ones. The first in this country appears to be that in Marlborough House Chapel, built by Inigo Jones between 1623–27.

VOLUTE. The spiral scroll of the Ionic capital. (*ill.*)

VOUSSOIR. One of the slightly wedge-shaped stones or bricks forming an arch. The central one is called a keystone.

VENETIAN WINDOW

VOLUTE

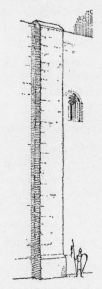

NORMAN BUTTRESS

FLYING BUTTRESS

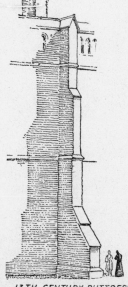

13TH CENTURY BUTTRESS

Evolution of the Buttress

INDEX

Abbeys:
  Bath, 96
  Buckland, 99
  Lacock, 99
  Selby, 58
  Sherborne, 96
  Tewkesbury, 38, 81, 213
  Westminster: see London
Ambulatory, 41 (Glossary)
Amphitheatre, 15, 16, 24
Apse, 41 (Glossary)
Aqueduct, 16, 17
Architects, practising and literary:
  Aalto, Alvar, 240
  Abercrombie, Sir Patrick, 244
  Adam Bros and Robert Adam, 183 *et seq.*
  Adams, Holden and Pearson (Plate 44)
  Alberti, Leone Battista, 135, 144
  Aslin, C. H., 294
  Barry, Sir Charles, 220, *et seq.*
  Bastard, John and William, 176
  Behrens, Peter, 235, 238, 240
  Bernini, Gianlorenzo, 147, 148, 176
  Bell, Henry, 161
  Boyle, Richard, Third Earl of Burlington, 168 *et seq.*
  Bramante, Donato, 136
  Breuer, Marcel, 235
  Brown, Lancelot (Capability), 172 *et seq.*
  Burton, Decimus, 200
  Butterfield, William, 214
  Campbell, Colen (Colin), 169
  Chambers, Sir William, 179 *et seq*, 186, 187
  Chermayeff, Serge, 235
  Cockerell, Charles Robert, 197
  Cockerell, Samuel, 194
  Cubitt, Lewis, 211
  Deane, Sir Thomas, 213
  De l'Orme, Philibert, 117, 123, 137
  De Staunton, Adam, 80
  De Vries, Vredeman, 118
  Dietterlin, Wendel, 118
  Drew, Jane, 240, 246
  Du Cerceau, Jacques, 118
  Easton, John, 231
  Ellis, Clough-Williams, 231
  Forshaw, J. H., 244
  Fry, E. Maxwell, 233, 235, 240, 246
  Garnier, Tony, 239
  Gibberd, Fredk., 245
  Gibbs, James, 168, 176 *et seq.*
  Gropius, Walter, 228, 235, 238, 240
  Hansom, Joseph Aloysius, 211
  Hardwick, Phillip, R. A., 211

Hawksmoor, Nicholas, 159, 164, 167
Hennebique, Francois, 227
Holland, Henry, 196
Honnecourt, Villard de, 72
Howard, Ebenezer, 216, 219 *et seq*, 228
Hyatt, Thaddeus, 227
Inwood, H. W., 202
Jeanneret: see Le Corbusier
Jones, Inigo, 136 *et seq*, 154, 168, 170, 184
Kent, William, 169 *et seq.*
Le Corbusier, 227–8, 238 *et seq*, 246
Leoni, Giacomo, 169
Livett, R., 235
Lubetkin, Berthold, 238
Lutyens, Sir Edwin, O. M., R.A., 224, 228
Lyming(e), Robert, 146
Lyons, Eric, 247
Mackintosh, Charles Rennie, 223 *et seq.*
Mardell, G. S., 244
M.A.R.S., 232
May, Hugh, 149
Mendelsohn, Erich, 235, 238
Michelangelo, 156
Mills, Peter, 146
Morris, William, 213, 222
Nash, John, 194, 196 *et seq*, 200, 212
Nervi, Pier Luigi, 240
Orme, Philibert de L': see de L'Orme
Paine, James
Palladio, Andrea, 136, 137, 142, 168, 169, 170, 239
Parker, Barry, 220
Paxton, Joseph, 212
Penn, Colin, 225
Perret, Auguste and Gustave, 227, 238
Pevsner, Prof. Nikolaus, 69, 239
Pratt, Roger, 149
Pugin, Augustus Charles, 202
Pugin, A.W.N., 200, 202 *et seq.*
Reilly, Sir Charles Herbert, 233
Repton, Humphry, 191 *et seq.*
Robertson, Sir H. M., R.A., 231
Rohe, Ludwig Mies van der, 240
Rosenberg, E., 244
Ruskin, John, 211 *et seq.*
Salt, Sir Titus, 210
Sansovino, Jacopo, 129
Scamozzi, Vincenzo, 137
Scott, Chesterton and Shepherd, 232
Scott, Sir George Gilbert R.A., 211, 213, 215
Scott, Sir Giles Gilbert, O. M., R.A., 228

258

BIBLIOGRAPHY

GENERAL SURVEYS OF ARCHITECTURE

BRETT, L. *The Things We See. Houses.* (Penguin, 1947)
BRIGGS, M. S. *Everyman's Concise Encyclopaedia of Architecture.* (Dent, 1959)
BRIGGS, M. S. *The Architect in History.* (Oxford, 1927)
DINHAM ATKINSON, T. *Local Style in English Architecture.* (Batsford, 1947)
FLETCHER, SIR BANISTER F. *A History of Architecture.* (Batsford, 1956)
FRY, MAXWELL. *Fine Building.* (Faber & Faber, 1944)
GIBBERD, F. *The Architecture of England.* (The Architectural Press, 1938)
GODFREY, W. H. *Our Building Inheritance.* (Readers Union and Faber, 1944)
PEVSNER, N. *An Outline of European Architecture.* (John Murray, 1948)
SITWELL, S. *British Architects and Craftsmen.* (Batsford, 1945)
TUBBS, R. *The Englishman Builds.* (Penguin, 1945)

SPECIAL ASPECTS

1 Ecclesiastical Architecture

BATSFORD, H. AND FRY, C. *The Cathedrals of England.* (Batsford, 1934)
COBB, G. *The Old Churches of London.* (Batsford, 1942)
COX, J. C. *The Parish Churches of England.* (Batsford, 1938)

2 Domestic Architecture

BRAUN, H. *The Story of the English House.* (Batsford, 1940)
DUTTON, R. *The English Interior.* (Batsford, 1948)
DUTTON, R. *The English Country House.* (Batsford, 1935)
GLOAG, J. *The Englishman's Castle.* (Eyre & Spottiswoode, 1944)
HOLE, C. *English Home Life.* (Batsford, 1947)

3 Studies of Selected Periods

HARVEY, J. *Gothic England.* (Batsford, 1947)
SUMMERSON, J. *The Pelican History of Art, Architecture in Britain* 1530 *to* 1830. (Penguin, 1953)
LEES-MILNE, J. *Tudor Renaissance.* (Batsford, 1951)
LEES-MILNE, J. *The Age of Adam.* (Batsford, 1947)
RICHARDSON, A. E. *Georgian England.* (Batsford, 1931)
SUMMERSON, J. *Georgian London.* (Pleiades Books, 1947)
WHIFFEN, M. *Stuart and Georgian Churches.* (Batsford, 1947)

*   *

PILCHER, D. *The Regency Style.* (Batsford, 1947)
GOODHART-RENDEL. *English Architecture Since the Regency.* (Constable, 1953)
TURNOR, R. *Nineteenth Century Architecture in Britain.* (Batsford, 1950)

*   *

CONDER, N. *An Introduction to Modern Architecture.* (London: Art and Technics, 1949)
JOEDICKE, J. *A History of Modern Architecture.* (The Architectural Press, 1959)
RICHARDS, J. M. *An Introduction to Modern Architecture.* (Penguin, 1940)
YORKE, F. R. S. AND PENN, C. *A Key to Modern Architecture.* (Blackie, 1939)

Town Planning

HIORNS, F. R. *Townbuilding in History.* (Harrap, 1956)
SHARP, T. *English Panorama.* (The Architectural Press, 1936)
MUMFORD, Lewis. *The Culture of Cities.* (Secker & Warburg, 1938)